Practical Threat Detection Engineering

A hands-on guide to planning, developing, and validating detection capabilities

Megan Roddie

Jason Deyalsingh

Gary J. Katz

BIRMINGHAM—MUMBAI

Practical Threat Detection Engineering

Group Product Manager: Pavan Ramchandani
Publishing Product Manager: Neha Sharma
Senior Content Development Editor: Adrija Mitra
Technical Editor: Rajat Sharma
Copy Editor: Safis Editing
Project Coordinator: Sean Lobo
Proofreader: Safis Editing
Indexer: Tejal Soni
Production Designer: Ponraj Dhandapani
Marketing Coordinator: Marylou De Mello

First published: July 2023

Production reference: 1230623

Published by Packt Publishing Ltd.
Livery Place
35 Livery Street
Birmingham
B3 2PB, UK.

ISBN 978-1-80107-671-5

www.packtpub.com

First, thank you to my parents, Geraldine and Michael Roddie, who have consistently pushed me toward success, for supporting me in all aspects of life, no matter how many times I drive them crazy. To my fiancé, Kelvin Clay Fonseca, who unexpectedly came into my life and constantly reminds me of my capabilities, giving me the confidence to face challenges head-on. Finally, thank you to all my present and previous employers and colleagues who gave me amazing opportunities and put me on a path that led me to write this book.

– Megan Roddie

Thank you first to my dad, Sheldon Katz, who taught me to be an inquiring engineer, never complicating technical explanations unnecessarily, and by teaching science wherever it was needed, whether on a food court napkin or late-night studying. To my mom, Ruth Katz, whose positive impact on students, and me, will continue to be relevant in our lives long after the technology in this book becomes dated. Most importantly, I want to thank my amazing wife, Heather, who supported me as I filled each weekend morning at the coffee shop writing this book. To the OneDo coffee shop in Baltimore, which provides a place for so many people to work on their pet projects, study, and get a great cup of coffee. To my coffee shop companion and friend, Katie Walsh, whose encouragement while writing this book was greatly appreciated. To my… okay, I should probably stop.

– Gary Katz

I'd like to express my sincere appreciation to everyone who contributed to this effort. Thanks for the work, thanks for your help, thanks for your guidance, thanks for listening, thanks for the motivation, and thanks for the lulz. Finally, thanks to my family and friends for being patient with me…you might need to continue being patient with me for the foreseeable future! :-/

– Jason Deyalsingh

Contributors

About the authors

Megan Roddie is an experienced information security professional with a diverse background ranging from incident response to threat intelligence to her current role as a detection engineer. Additionally, Megan is a course author and instructor with the SANS Institute where she regularly publishes research on cloud incident response and forensics. Outside of the cyber security industry, Megan trains and competes as a high-level amateur Muay Thai fighter in Austin, TX.

I would like to thank my parents, Geraldine and Mike, for a lifetime of love and support and for always pushing me toward greatness. I would also like to thank my fiancé, Kelvin, for being my biggest cheerleader throughout this process. Finally, thank you to everyone who has played a role in my career thus far, ultimately leading me to write this book.

Jason Deyalsingh is an experienced consultant with over nine years of experience in the cyber security space. He has spent the last 5 years focused on **digital forensics and incident response** (**DFIR**). His current hobbies include playing with data and failing to learn Rust.

To the cyber security community and everyone I ever worked with directly or indirectly. Keep crushing it!

Gary J. Katz is still trying to figure out what to do with his life while contemplating what its purpose really is. While not spiraling into this metaphysical black hole compounded by the plagues and insanity of this world, he sometimes thinks about cyber security problems and writes them down. These ruminations are, on occasion, captured in articles and books.

To those who read a technical book from cover to cover, I admire you, even if I could never be one of you.

About the reviewers

Dr. Chelsea Hicks (she/they) has worked in cyber security for more than 10 years, with the last 5 years being focused on threat hunting and incident response. Dr Hicks also has previous experience with machine learning, scripting, and infrastructure building. Dr Hicks received their BSc in computer science, MSc in information technology, and PhD in information technology from the University of Texas at San Antonio. You can find Dr Hicks as the social media coordinator for BSidesSATX, and presenting at events such as SANS Blue Team Summit, Blue Team Village, and Texas Cyber Summit.

Obligatory remark: Nothing I reviewed or provided feedback on in this book represents my employers; it is 100% based on my opinion and thoughts outside of work.

I'd like to thank my family and friends – especially my spouse and mom, who always encourage me and understand the time and commitment it takes to try to stay sharp in this field. I'd also like to thank them for keeping me grounded and making sure I maintain my work-life balance. Thank you to the amazing DFIR and threat-hunting fields for your supportiveness in helping these fields grow – especially folks like hacks4pancakes and shortxstack!

Terrence Williams has worked in the cyber security space for nearly 10 years, with 4 years focused on cloud forensics, incident response, and detection engineering. He began his career in the US Marine Corps, developing skills in hunting advanced persistent threats. Terrence received his BSc in computer science from Saint Leo University and is currently pursuing an MSc in computer science from Vanderbilt University. He has honed his cyber security skills through his roles at Amazon Web Services, Meta Platforms, and Google. Additionally, he serves as a SANS Instructor for the FOR509 course, which focuses on enterprise forensics and incident response.

Rod Soto is a security researcher and co-founder of HackMiami and Pacific Hackers. He was the winner of the 2012 BlackHat Las Vegas CTF competition and Red Alert ICS CTF at DEFCON 2022 contest. He is the founder and lead developer of the Kommand && KonTroll/NOQRTR CTF competitive hacking tournament series.

Table of Contents

Part 1: Introduction to Detection Engineering

1

2

3

Building a Detection Engineering Test Lab   41

Part 2: Detection Creation

4

Detection Data Sources   73

Part 4: Metrics and Management   249

11

Performance Management   251

Part 5: Detection Engineering as a Career   281

12

Career Guidance for Detection Engineers   283

Preface

Over the past several years, the field of detection engineering has become more and more at the forefront of cyber security defense discussions. While the number of conference talks, blog posts, and webcasts surrounding detection engineering has increased, a dedicated book on the topic has not yet appeared on the market. We hope that we can fill the gap with the release of this book. While learning resources for related fields such as threat hunting, threat intelligence, and red teaming are plentiful, detection engineering has a long way to go in providing the training necessary to develop detection engineers.

Our goal is to not only provide a discussion on the topic but to provide you with practical skills using hands-on exercises throughout the book. Furthermore, we hope that these exercises, in combination with the creation of the detection engineering test lab, lead you to continue your education and training by practicing the skills you've learned for your own use cases.

The authors of this book have worked in various areas of security, with a current focus on detection engineering, and derived this content from real-life experiences throughout their careers. This, combined with research taken from some of the top minds in this field, provides you with a comprehensive overview of the topics necessary to understand detection engineering. With topics including the detection engineering life cycle, creating and validating detections, careers guidance for detection engineers, and everything in between, you should walk away feeling confident in your understanding of what detection engineering is and what it means to the cyber security industry.

We hope this book inspires continued content creation and community contributions in detection engineering.

Who this book is for

This book provides insights into detection engineering via a hands-on methodology for those with an interest in the field. It is primarily focused on security engineers who have some experience in the area. Mid- to senior-level security analysts can also learn from this book. To fully understand the content and follow the labs, you should understand foundational security concepts. Additionally, you should have the technical ability to work with technologies such as virtual machines and containers, which are leveraged in hands-on exercises throughout the book.

What this book covers

Chapter 1, Fundamentals of Detection Engineering, provides an introduction to the foundational concepts that will be referenced throughout the book. It also defines detection engineering to help you understand what exactly detection engineering is.

Chapter 2, The Detection Engineering Life Cycle, introduces the phases of the detection engineering life cycle and different types of continuous monitoring. Each phase of the life cycle will be discussed in depth in later chapters.

Chapter 3, Building a Detection Engineering Test Lab, introduces the technologies that will be used to build a detection engineering test lab. The subsequent hands-on exercises will teach you how to deploy the detection engineering lab that will be leveraged for future labs throughout the book, and how to create a simple detection.

Chapter 4, Detection Data Sources, discusses what detection data sources are, their importance, and the potential challenges faced when leveraging data sources. It will then provide a hands-on exercise to connect a new data source to the detection engineering test lab.

Chapter 5, Investigating Detection Requirements, looks at the first two phases of the detection engineering life cycle. It discusses how to identify and triage detection requirements from a variety of sources and the related methods and processes to be implemented.

Chapter 6, Developing Detections Using Indicators of Compromise, discusses the use of indicators of compromise for the purpose of detection engineering. The concept is demonstrated through an example scenario based on a real-life threat. As part of the exercise, Sysmon will also be introduced and installed in the detection engineering lab.

Chapter 7, Developing Detections Using Behavioral Indicators, builds on *Chapter 6* by moving on to developing detections at the behavioral indicator level. Two scenarios and associated exercises are leveraged to introduce the concept: one focused on detecting adversary tools and one focused on detecting **tactics, techniques, and procedures (TTPs)**.

Chapter 8, Documentation and Detection Pipelines, provides an overview of how detections should be documented in order to effectively manage a detection engineering program. It then introduces concepts related to deployment processes and automation, such as CI/CD, along with a lab to demonstrate creating a detection pipeline.

Chapter 9, Detection Validation, provides an overview of validating detections using various methodologies. It will introduce two tools, Atomic Red Team and CALDERA, that can be used for performing validation. An associated hands-on exercise will allow you to work with these tools in your detection engineering test lab.

Chapter 10, Leveraging Threat Intelligence, provides an introduction to cyber threat intelligence with a focus on how it relates to detection engineering. A series of examples is used to demonstrate the use of open source intelligence for detection engineering. Additionally, the chapter will discuss the use of threat assessments to develop detection requirements.

Chapter 11, Performance Management, provides an overview of how to evaluate a detection engineering program as a whole. It includes methodologies for calculating the effectiveness and efficiency of the detections in an organization. Then, it discusses how such data can be used to improve the detection engineering program.

Chapter 12, Career Guidance for Detection Engineers, closes off the book with a discussion on careers in detection engineering. This includes finding jobs, improving your skill sets, and associated training. It then provides insights into the future of detection engineering as a field. Finally, it looks at ways in which detection engineers can contribute to the community.

To get the most out of this book

The primary software used in this book is Docker and virtualization software. All other software and operating systems are run within these technologies. Due to the use of virtualization software, these labs cannot be run on ARM-based systems, such as M1 Macs. For the labs, we provide setup instructions for both Linux and Windows systems.

Software/hardware covered in the book	Operating system requirements
Docker	Windows or Linux
VirtualBox	Windows or Linux

While the book uses steps and screenshots specific to VirtualBox in the exercises, users who have an understanding of virtualization software may use VMware or other solutions of their choice.

If you are using the digital version of this book, we advise you to type the code yourself or access the code from the book's GitHub repository (a link is available in the next section). Doing so will help you avoid any potential errors related to the copying and pasting of code.

Download the example code files

You can download the example code files for this book from GitHub at `https://github.com/PacktPublishing/Practical-Threat-Detection-Engineering`. If there's an update to the code, it will be updated in the GitHub repository.

We also have other code bundles from our rich catalog of books and videos available at `https://github.com/PacktPublishing/`. Check them out!

Download the color images

We also provide a PDF file that has color images of the screenshots and diagrams used in this book. You can download it here: `https://packt.link/qt1nr`.

Conventions used

There are a number of text conventions used throughout this book.

`Code in text`: Indicates code words in text, database table names, folder names, filenames, file extensions, pathnames, dummy URLs, user input, and Twitter handles. Here is an example: "The process described on Elastic's site involves the use of `docker-compose.yaml` and a `.env` file, which `docker-compose` then interprets to build the Elastic and Kibana nodes."

A block of code is set as follows:

```
ES1_DATA=/path/to/large/disk/elasticdata/es01
ES2_DATA=/path/to/large/disk/elasticdata/es02
KIBANA_DATA=/path/to/large/disk/elasticdata/kibana_data
```

Any command-line input or output is written as follows:

```
$ docker --version
Docker version v20.10.12, build 20.10.12-0ubuntu4
```

Bold: Indicates a new term, an important word, or words that you see onscreen. For instance, words in menus or dialog boxes appear in **bold**. Here is an example: "At this point, you are probably wondering what type of data is being sent back to the Elasticsearch backend. You can view this data by navigating to the **Discover** page, under **Analytics** in the hamburger menu."

> **Tips or important notes**
> Appear like this.

Get in touch

Feedback from our readers is always welcome.

General feedback: If you have questions about any aspect of this book, email us at `customercare@packtpub.com` and mention the book title in the subject of your message.

Errata: Although we have taken every care to ensure the accuracy of our content, mistakes do happen. If you have found a mistake in this book, we would be grateful if you would report this to us. Please visit `www.packtpub.com/support/errata` and fill in the form.

Piracy: If you come across any illegal copies of our works in any form on the internet, we would be grateful if you would provide us with the location address or website name. Please contact us at copyright@packt.com with a link to the material.

If you are interested in becoming an author: If there is a topic that you have expertise in and you are interested in either writing or contributing to a book, please visit authors.packtpub.com.

Share Your Thoughts

Once you've read *Practical Threat Detection Engineering*, we'd love to hear your thoughts! Scan the QR code below to go straight to the Amazon review page for this book and share your feedback.

https://packt.link/r/1801076715

Your review is important to us and the tech community and will help us make sure we're delivering excellent quality content.

Download a free PDF copy of this book

Thanks for purchasing this book!

Do you like to read on the go but are unable to carry your print books everywhere?

Is your eBook purchase not compatible with the device of your choice?

Don't worry, now with every Packt book you get a DRM-free PDF version of that book at no cost.

Read anywhere, any place, on any device. Search, copy, and paste code from your favorite technical books directly into your application.

The perks don't stop there, you can get exclusive access to discounts, newsletters, and great free content in your inbox daily

Follow these simple steps to get the benefits:

1. Scan the QR code or visit the link below

https://packt.link/free-ebook/9781801076715

2. Submit your proof of purchase

3. That's it! We'll send your free PDF and other benefits to your email directly

Part 1: Introduction to Detection Engineering

In this part, you will learn about some foundational concepts related to detection engineering. After establishing this baseline knowledge, you'll be introduced to the detection engineering life cycle, which will be followed throughout the book. To wrap up this part, we'll guide you through deploying a detection engineering lab, which will support the labs throughout the book.

This section has the following chapters:

- *Chapter 1, Fundamentals of Detection Engineering*
- *Chapter 2, The Detection Engineering Life Cycle*
- *Chapter 3, Building a Detection Engineering Test Lab*

1
Fundamentals of Detection Engineering

Across nearly every industry, a top concern for executives and board members is the security of their digital assets. It's an understandable concern, given that companies are now more interconnected and reliant on technology than ever before. Digital assets and their supporting infrastructure comprise ever-increasing portions of a typical organization's inventory. Additionally, more processes are becoming reliant on robust communication technologies. In most cases, these technologies enable companies to operate more effectively. The management and defense of this new digital landscape, however, can be challenging for organizations of any size.

Additionally, where sophisticated attacks used to be limited to nation-state adversaries, the increased interconnectedness of technology, coupled with the emergence of cryptocurrencies, creates a near-perfect environment for cyber criminals to operate in. The addition of sophisticated threat actors motivated by financial gain rather than those limited to nation-state motivations has dramatically broadened the number of organizations that must be able to identify and respond to such threats. Stopping these attacks requires increased agility by an organization to combat the adversary. A detection engineering program provides that agility, improving an organization's ops tempo to operationalize intelligence about new threats. The primary goal of detection engineering is to develop the rules or algorithmic models to automatically identify the presence of threat actors, or malicious activity in general, promptly so that the relevant teams can take mitigative action.

In this chapter, we will discuss several topics that will provide you with knowledge that will be relevant throughout this book:

- Foundational concepts, such as attack frameworks, common attack types, and the definition of detection engineering
- The value of a detection engineering program
- An overview of this book

Foundational concepts

The foundation of how we can track and categorize an adversary's actions allows us to prioritize and understand the scope or coverage of our detections. The following subsection covers common frameworks and models that will be referenced throughout this book. They provide a starting model for framing cyberattacks, their granular sub-components, and how to defend against them.

The Unified Kill Chain

Cyberattacks tend to follow a predictable pattern that should be understood by defenders. This pattern was initially documented as the now famous Lockheed Martin Cyber Kill Chain. This model has been adapted and modernized over time by multiple vendors. The **Unified Kill Chain** is a notable modernization of the model. This model defines 18 broad tactics across three generalized goals, which provides defenders with a reasonable framework for designing appropriate defenses according to attackers' objectives. Let's look at these goals:

- **In**: The attacker's goal at this phase is to research the potential victim, discover possible attack vectors, and gain and maintain reliable access to a target environment.

- **Through**: Having gained access to a target environment, the threat actor needs to orient themselves and gather supplemental resources required for the remainder of the attack, such as privileged credentials.

- **Out**: These tactics are focused on completing the objective of the cyberattack. In the case of double extortion ransomware, this would include staging files for exfiltration, copying those files to attacker infrastructure, and, finally, the large-scale deployment of ransomware.

Figure 1.1, based on the *Unified Kill Chain* whitepaper by *Paul Pols*, shows the individual tactics in each phase of the kill chain:

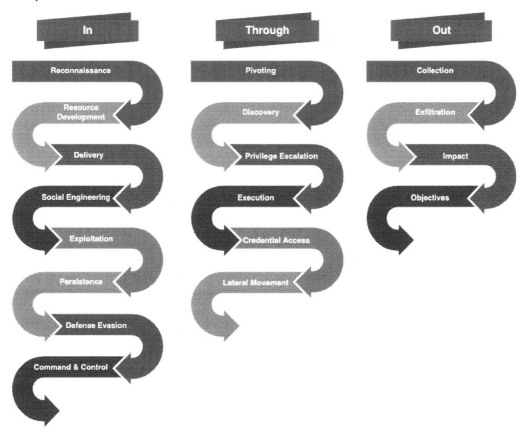

Figure 1.1 – The Unified Kill Chain

To better understand how the Unified Kill Chain applies to cyberattacks, let's look at how it maps to a well-known attack. We are specifically going to look at an Emotet attack campaign. Emotet is a malicious payload often distributed via email and used to deliver additional payloads that will carry out the attacker's final objectives. The specific campaign we will analyze is one reported on by *The DFIR Report* in November 2022: `https://thedfirreport.com/2022/11/28/emotet-strikes-again-lnk-file-leads-to-domain-wide-ransomware/`.

Table 1.1 lists the stages of the attack, as reported in the article, and how they map to the Unified Kill Chain:

Attack Event	Unified Kill Chain Phase Group	Unified Kill Chain Phase
Emotet executed via LNK malspam attachment	In	Delivery
Emotet sends outbound SMTP spam email	Network propagation	Pivoting
Domain enumeration via Cobalt Strike	Through	Discovery
Lateral movement to user workstation	Through	Pivoting
SMB share enumeration	Through	Discovery
Zerologon exploit attempt	In	Exploitation
Remote Management Agent installed	In	Command and control/persistence
Exfiltration via Rclone to Mega	Out	Exfiltration
Ransomware execution	Out	Impact

Table 1.1 – Unified Kill Chain mapping for Emotet attack chain

As can be seen from *Table 1.1*, not all phases will take place in every attack and may not occur in a linear order.

To read the full *Unified Kill Chain* whitepaper, visit this link: `https://www.unifiedkillchain.com/assets/The-Unified-Kill-Chain.pdf`.

While this follows the progression of a typical cyberattack, as the paper outlines and as our example shots show, it is not uncommon for the attacker to execute some tactics outside this expected order. While the Unified Kill Chain provides a model for how threat actors carry out attacks, it does not dive into the detailed techniques that can be used to achieve the goals of each phase in the kill chain. The MITRE ATT&CK framework provides more granular insight into the tactics, techniques, and procedures leveraged by threat actors.

The MITRE ATT&CK framework

The **MITRE ATT&CK framework** is a knowledge base developed by the MITRE Corporation. The framework classifies threat actor objectives and catalogs the granular tools and activities related to achieving those objectives.

ATT&CK stands for **Adversarial Tactics**, **Techniques**, and **Common Knowledge**. The MITRE ATT&CK framework groups adversarial techniques into high-level categories called tactics. Each tactic represents a smaller immediate goal within the overall cyberattack. This framework will be referenced frequently throughout this book, providing an effective model for designing and validating detections. The following points detail the high-level tactics included as part of the Enterprise ATT&CK framework:

- **Reconnaissance**: This tactic falls within the *initial foothold* phase of the Unified Kill Chain. Here, the threat actor gathers information about their target. At this stage, the attacker may use tools to passively collect technical details about the target, such as any publicly accessible infrastructure, emails, vulnerable associate businesses, and the like. In ideal cases, the threat actor may identify publicly accessible and vulnerable interfaces, but reconnaissance can also include gathering information about employees of an organization to identify possible targets for social engineering and understand how various internal business processes work.

- **Resource development**: This tactic falls within the *initial foothold* phase of the Unified Kill Chain. Having identified a plausible attack vector, threat actors design an appropriate attack and develop technical resources to facilitate the attack. This phase includes creating, purchasing, or stealing credentials, infrastructure, or capabilities specifically to support the operation against the target.

- **Initial access**: This tactic falls within the *initial foothold* phase of the Unified Kill Chain. The threat actor attempts to gain access to an asset in the victim-controlled environment. A variety of tools can be leveraged in combination at this point, ranging from cleverly designed phishing campaigns to deploying code that weaponizes yet-undisclosed vulnerabilities in exposed software interfaces (also known as zero-day attacks).

- **Execution**: Tactics in this category fall within the *initial foothold* and *network propagation* phases of the Unified Kill Chain. The attacker aims to execute their code on a target asset. Code used in this phase typically attempts to collect additional details about the target network, understand the security context the code is executing under, or collect data and return it to infrastructure controlled by the threat actor.

- **Persistence**: This tactic falls within the *initial foothold* category of the Unified Kill Chain. Initial access to a foreign environment can be volatile. Threat actors prefer robust and survivable access to target systems. Persistence techniques focus on maintaining access despite system restarts or modifications to identities and infrastructure.

- **Privilege escalation**: This tactic falls within the *network propagation* category of the Unified Kill Chain. Having gained access to the victim control environment, the threat actor typically attempts to attain the highest level of privileges possible. Privileged access provides a means for executing nearly every option available to the administrators of the victim, removing many roadblocks that may prevent them from taking action on the attacker's objectives. Having privileged access can also make threat actor activities more challenging to detect.

- **Defense evasion**: This tactic falls within the *initial foothold* category of the Unified Kill Chain. Threat actors must understand the victim's defense systems to design appropriate methods for avoiding them. Successful evasion of defense increases the likelihood of a successful operation. These tactics focus specifically on finding ways to subvert or otherwise avoid the target's defensive controls.

- **Credential access**: This tactic falls within the *initial foothold* and *action on objectives* categories of the Unified Kill Chain. Identities control access to systems. Harvesting credentials or credential material is essential for completely dominating a victim's environment. Access to multiple systems and credentials makes navigating environments easier and lets attackers pivot if the event credentials are modified.

- **Discovery**: This tactic falls within the *network propagation* category of the Unified Kill Chain. These techniques focus on understanding the victim's internal environment. The internal network layout, infrastructure configuration, identity information, and defense systems must be understood to plan for the remaining phases of the attack.

- **Lateral movement**: This tactic falls within the *action on objectives* category of the Unified Kill Chain. Systems that are accessed for the first time often do not have the information or resources (tools, credential material, direct connectivity, or visibility) required to complete objectives. Following the discovery of connected systems, and with the proper credentials, the adversary can, and often needs to, move from the current system to other connected systems. These techniques are all focused on traversing the victim's environment.

- **Collection**: This tactic falls within the *action on objectives* category of the Unified Kill Chain. These techniques focus on performing internal reconnaissance. Access to new environments provides new visibility, and understanding the technical environment is essential for planning the subsequent phases of the attack.

- **Command and control**: This tactic falls within the *initial access* category of the Unified Kill Chain. It allows us to implement systems so that we can remotely control the victim's environment.

- **Exfiltration**: This tactic falls within the *action on objectives* category of the Unified Kill Chain. Not all attacks involve exfiltration activities, but tactics in this category have become more popular with the rise of ransomware double extortion attacks. You can find a more detailed description of double extortion ransomware attacks at `https://www.zscaler.com/resources/security-terms-glossary/what-is-double-extortion-ransomware`. These tactics aim to copy data out of the victim's environment to an attacker-controlled infrastructure.

- **Impact**: This tactic falls within the *action on objectives* category of the Unified Kill Chain. At this point, the threat actor can take steps to complete their attack. For example, in the case of a ransomware attack, the large-scale encryption of data would fall into this phase.

We encourage you to explore the MITRE ATT&CK framework in full at `https://attack.mitre.org/`. In this book, we are specifically going to focus on the Enterprise ATT&CK framework, but MITRE also provides frameworks for ICS and mobile-based attacks as well. The ATT&CK Navigator, located at `https://mitre-attack.github.io/attack-navigator/`, is also extremely useful for defenders to quickly search for and qualify tactics.

Most publications documenting incident response observations typically provide kill chain and MITRE ATT&CK tactics, which help defenders understand how to design detections and other preventative controls.

The Pyramid of Pain

Another helpful model for defenders to understand is the **Pyramid of Pain**. This model, developed by **David Bianco**, visualizes the relationship between the categories of indicators and the impact of defending each. This impact is expressed as the effort required by the threat actor to modify their attack once an effective defense is implemented for a given indicator category. *Figure 1.2* shows the concept of the Pyramid of Pain:

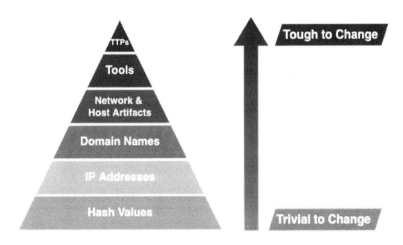

Figure 1.2 – David Bianco's Pyramid of Pain

As we can see, controls designed to operate on static indicators such as domain names, IP addresses, and hash values are trivial for adversaries to evade. For example, modifying the hash of a binary simply involves changing a single bit. It is far more difficult for an adversary to modify their **tools, tactics, and procedures** (**TTPs**), which are essentially the foundation of their attack playbook. The gold standard for defensive controls is those that target TTPs. However, these are usually more difficult to implement and require reliable data from protected assets, as well as a deep understanding of the adversary's tactics and capabilities. Defensive controls designed for static indicators are effective for short-term, tactical defense. You can read David Bianco's full blog post here: `https://detect-respond.blogspot.com/2013/03/the-pyramid-of-pain.html`.

Throughout the remainder of this book, we will frequently reference these concepts. In later chapters, we will illustrate how these models can be used to understand cyberattacks, translate high-level business objectives for defense into detections, and measure coverage against known attacks.

Now that we have gained an understanding of the model for framing cyberattacks, let's look into the most common types of cyberattacks.

Types of cyberattacks

To detect cyberattacks, detection engineers need to have a base understanding of the attacks that they will face. Some of the most prevalent attacks at the time of writing are summarized here to provide some introductory insight into the attacks we are trying to defend against.

Business Email Compromise (BEC)

The FBI reported receiving a total of 19,954 complaints related to **Business Email Compromise** (**BEC**) incidents in 2021. They estimate these complaints represent a cumulative loss of 2.4 billion dollars (USD). The full report can be accessed at `https://www.ic3.gov/Media/PDF/AnnualReport/2021_IC3Report.pdf`.

BEC attacks target users of the most popular and accessible user collaboration tool available – email. The electronic transfer of funds is a normal part of business operations for many organizations. Threat actors research organizations and identify personnel likely to be involved in correspondence related to the exchange of funds. Having identified a target, the threat actor leverages several techniques to gain access to the target's mailbox (or someone adjacent from a business process perspective). With this access, the threat actor's objective pivots to observing email exchanges to understand internal processes. During this time, the threat actor needs to understand the communication flows and key players. In ideal cases, they will identify a third-party contractor whom the organization conducts routine business with, the people who typically send correspondence for payments, and the person who approves these payments on behalf of the organization. Once the right opportunity arises, the threat actor can intercept and alter email conversations about payment, changing destination account numbers. If this goes unnoticed, funds may be deposited into the attacker's account instead of the intended recipient.

Denial of service (DoS)

Denial of service (**DoS**) attacks attempt to make services unavailable to legitimate users by overwhelming the service or otherwise impairing the infrastructure the service depends on. There are three main types of DoS attacks: volumetric, protocol, and application attacks.

Volumetric attacks are executed by sending an inordinate volume of traffic to a target system. If the attack persists, it can degrade the service or disrupt it entirely. Protocol attacks focus on the network and transport layer and attempt to deplete the available resources of the networking devices, making the target service available. Application attacks send large volumes of requests to a target service. The service attempts to process each request, which consumes processing power on the underlying systems. Eventually, the available resources are exhausted, and service response times increase to the point where the service becomes unavailable. These types of attacks can be further categorized by their degree of automation and the techniques used.

Increasing the number of systems executing the attack can significantly increase the impact. By making use of compromised systems, threat actors can conduct synchronized DoS attacks against a single target, known as **distributed denial of service (DDoS)** attacks.

Malware outbreak

When malicious software, or malware, manages to evade defensive controls, the impact can range broadly, depending on the specific malware family. In low-impact cases, an end user may be bombarded with unsolicited pop-up ads, and in more extreme scenarios, malware can give full control of a system to a remote threat actor. The presence of malware in an enterprise environment usually indicates a possible deficiency in security controls. Seemingly low-impact malware infections can lead to more significant incidents, including full-blown ransomware attacks.

Insider threats

Employees of an organization who perform malicious activity against that organization are known as insider threats. Insider threats can exist at any level of the organization and have various motivations. Malicious insiders can be difficult to defend against since the organization has granted them a degree of trust.

Phishing

Phishing attacks fall under the category of social engineering, where threat actors design attacks around communication and collaboration tools, such as email, instant messaging apps, SMS text messages, and even regular phone calls. The underlying objective in all cases is to entice users to reveal sensitive information, such as credentials or banking information. BEC attacks typically leverage phishing techniques.

Ransomware

While the threat landscape is full of countless actors, with diverse goals ranging from stealthy cyber espionage to tech-support scams, the most prolific and impactful of these is the modern ransomware attack.

The goal of a ransomware attack is to interrupt critical business operations by taking critical systems offline and demanding payment, or a ransom, from the organization. In exchange for a successful payment, the threat actors claim they will return systems to a normal operating state.

Recently, some ransomware operators have added a separate extortion component to their playbook. During their ransomware attack, they exfiltrate sensitive data from the organization's environment to attacker-controlled systems. Ransomware operators then threaten to publicize this data unless the ransom is paid. This attack is commonly referred to as the double-extortion ransomware attack.

Successful ransomware operations put businesses in a frightening predicament. Apart from untangling the deep complexities of determining whether to pay the ransom, recovering from a successful cyberattack can take months or sometimes years.

These malicious operations have become increasingly sophisticated and successful over time. According to CrowdStrike, the first instance of modern ransomware was recorded in 2005. Between then and now, the frequency, scale, and sophistication of ransomware attacks have only increased. CrowdStrike's *History of Ransomware* article provides a summary of the evolution of ransomware. You can read the full article here: `https://www.crowdstrike.com/cybersecurity-101/ransomware/history-of-ransomware/`.

The motivation for detection engineering

Successful breaches can have expensive impacts, requiring thousands of man-hours to remediate. IBM's 2022 *Cost of a Data Breach* report found that the average total cost of a data breach amounted to 4.35 million USD. Typically, the earlier a threat is detected, the lower the cost of remediation. For every phase that an attacker advances through the kill chain, the cost of remediation goes up. While a threat hunt allows an organization to search for an adversary already inside its environment, the identification occurs when and if a search is performed. This detection, though, allows an organization to identify malicious behavior when the activity is performed, reducing the mean time to detect. Given that the same IBM *Cost of a Data Breach* report determined that the average time to identify and contain a breach was 277 days, there is much work to be done in attempting to reduce the time to detection.

To understand how the time to detect an attack greatly determines the impact on the business, let's consider a scenario where a threat actor can gain initial access to an internet-connected workstation via a successful phishing campaign. This unauthorized access was immediately detected by the organization's security team. They quickly isolated this workstation and performed a full re-imaging of its contents to a known-good state. They also performed a full reset of the user's credentials, along with any other user who interacted with that workstation. Administrators identified the phishing email in their enterprise email solution, and all recipients had their workstations re-imaged and their credentials reset.

In this scenario, the steps that were taken by the security team were relatively simple to execute and would likely be sufficient to remove the threat from the environment. In contrast, if the threat actors were able to gain privileged access, exfiltrate data, and then deploy ransomware across all systems, the task becomes significantly more onerous. The security team would be faced with the dual task of understanding what happened while simultaneously advising on the best way to restore the business's ability to operate safely. The following table summarizes how the number of assets impacted, the investigative requirements, and typical remediation efforts change across the Unified Kill Chain goals:

	Initial Foothold	Network Propagation	Action on Objectives
Assets impacted	Low value. Typically, this involves edge devices, public-facing servers, or user workstations. Because of their position in modern architectures, these devices are typically untrusted by default.	Medium value. Some internal systems. Typically at this phase, the threat actor has access to some member servers within the environment and has a reliable C2 channel established.	High value. Critical servers such as Active Directory domain controllers, backup servers, or file servers.
Threat actor's degree of control	Low. The threat actor has unreliable access to a system or is attempting to obtain access to a system, typically through phishing or attacking publicly facing services. Typically, this phase is the best opportunity for defenders to remove a threat.	Medium. The threat actor has enough control to traverse the network, but not enough control to execute objectives. At this point, threat actors typically have some credentials and have a reliable C2 channel established.	High. The threat actor is fully comfortable operating in the environment. They found all the resources needed to execute their objectives. At this point, they likely have the highest level of privileges available in the environment.
Data requirement for investigation	Relatively low. Typically, impact at this phase is limited to a small number of assets. Once identified at this phase, the data required for fully scoping the event is limited to a single host.	Significant. The capability to traverse the internal network typically indicates the presence of a reliable C2 channel. A higher volume of historic and real-time data is required to identify impacted assets. At this point, incident responders will need to have visibility of all connected assets to fully track lateral movement.	High. Investigators will require access to historical and real-time data from all connected assets. Additionally, in cases where data exfiltration is an objective, telemetry for the access and movement of data will also be required. This data is difficult to collect and is not typically tracked.
Effort required to remediate	Low. Activities at this phase typically occur on edge devices or public-facing assets. The typical posture is to treat these assets as untrusted, so it is common for environments to have capabilities for rapidly isolating these assets.	Medium. Traversing the network requires more investigative work to identify the individual assets that were accessed, the degree to which they were utilized, and the requirements for remediating.	High. In nearly every case, this requires rebuilding critical infrastructure. Often, this needs to occur with the added pressure of returning the business to a minimally operational state, to minimize losses.

Table 1.2 – Generalized asset impact and effort versus kill chain goals

It's plain to see the importance of finding out about cyberattacks in your environment and, more so, the importance of finding out as early as possible. The right person needs to get the relevant information about cyberattacks in a timely fashion. This is the primary objective of detection engineering.

Defining detection engineering

Quickly identifying, qualifying, and mitigating potential security incidents is a top priority for security teams. Identifying potential security incidents quickly is a fairly complicated problem to solve. In general terms, security personnel need to be able to do the following:

1. Collect events from assets that require protection, as well as assets that can indirectly impact them.

2. Identify events that may indicate a security incident, ideally as soon as they happen.

3. Understand the impact of the potential incident.

4. Communicate the high-value details of the event to all relevant teams for investigation and mitigation.

5. Receive feedback from investigative teams to determine how the whole process can be improved.

Each of these steps can be difficult to execute within small environments. The complexity increases radically for any increase in the size of a managed environment.

> **Detection engineering definition**
>
> Detection engineering can be defined as a set of processes that enable potential threats to be detected within an environment. These processes encompass the end-to-end life cycle, from collecting detection requirements, aggregating system telemetry, and implementing and maintaining detection logic to validating program effectiveness.

To accomplish these goals, a good detection engineering program typically needs to implement four main processes:

- **Discovery**: This involves collecting detection requirements. Here, you must determine whether the requirements are met with existing detections. You must also determine the criticality of the detection, as well as the audiences and timeframes for alerting.

- **Design, development, and testing**: The detection requirement is interpreted, and a plan for implementing the detection is formulated. The designed detection is implemented first in a test environment and tested to ensure it produces the expected results.

- **Implementation and post-implementation monitoring**: Detection is implemented in the production detection environment. Here, the performance of the detection and the detection systems is monitored.

- **Validation**: Routine testing to determine the effectiveness of the detection engineering program as a whole:

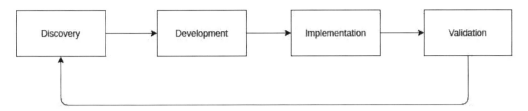

Figure 1.3 – The detection engineering processes

Chapter 2, *The Detection Engineering Life Cycle*, takes a deeper dive into each of these processes.

Important distinctions

Detection engineering can be misunderstood, partly because some processes overlap with other functions within a security organization. We can clarify detection engineering's position with the following distinctions:

- **Threat hunting**: The threat hunting process proactively develops investigative analyses based on a hypothesis that assumes a successful, undetected breach. The threat hunting process can identify active threats in the environment that managed to evade current security controls. This process provides input to the detection engineering program as it can identify deficiencies in detections. The data that's available to detection engineering is typically the same data that threat hunters utilize. Therefore, threat hunting can also identify deficiencies in the existing data collection infrastructure that will need to be solved and integrated with the detection infrastructure.

- **Security operations center (SOC) operations**: SOC teams typically focus on monitoring the security environment, whereas detection engineering provides inputs to SOC teams. While the SOC consumes the products of the detection engineering functions, they typically work very closely with them to provide feedback for detection or collection improvements.

- **Data engineering**: Data engineers design, implement, and maintain systems to collect, transform, and distribute data, typically to satisfy data analytics and business intelligence requirements. This aligns with several goals of detection engineering; however, the detection engineering program is heavily security-focused and relies on data engineering to produce the data it needs to build detections.

In this section, we examined some basic cyber security concepts that will be useful throughout this book as we dive into the detection engineering process. Furthermore, we established a definition for detection engineering. With this definition in mind, the following section will examine the value that a detection engineering program brings to an organization.

The value of a detection engineering program

Before a detection engineering program can be established, it must be justified to stakeholders in the organization so that funding can be received. This section will discuss the importance of detection engineering. Specifically, we will look at the increasing need for good detections, how we define the quality of a detection, and how a detection engineering program fills this need.

The need for better detection

Advancements in software development such as open source, cloud computing, **infrastructure as Code (IaC)**, and **continuous integrations/continuous deployment (CI/CD)** pipelines have reaped benefits for organizations. These advancements allow organizations to easily build upon the technology of others, frequently deploy new versions of their software, quickly stand up and break down infrastructure, and adapt quickly to changes in their landscape.

Unfortunately, these same advancements have aided threat actors as well. Open source repositories provide a plethora of offensive tools. Cloud computing and IaC allow adversaries to quickly deploy and break down their C2 infrastructure, while advances in software processes and automation have increased their ops tempo in updating and creating new capabilities. These changes have further deteriorated the value of static indicators and necessitate the need for better, more sophisticated detections. As such, the field of detection engineering is beginning to evolve to support efforts for more sophisticated detections. With an effective detection engineering program, organizations can go beyond detecting static indicators and instead detect malicious activity at a technique level.

The qualities of good detection

There is no one definition for *good* detection. Individual cyber security organizations will have varying thresholds for false positive rates – that is, the rate of detections triggering when they shouldn't. Additionally, the adversaries they face will differ in sophistication, and the visibility and tools at their disposal will vary. As a detection engineer, you must identify metrics and evaluation criteria that align with your organization's needs. In *Chapter 9*, we will review processes and approaches that will help guide those decisions. These evaluation criteria can be broken into three areas:

- The ability to detect the adversary
- The cost of that ability to the cyber security organization
- The cost to the adversary to evade that detection

The ability to detect the adversary can be broken into a detection's **coverage**, or the scope of the activity that the detection identifies. This can most easily be understood in terms of MITRE ATT&CK. As mentioned earlier, the framework provides definitions at varying levels of specificity, starting with tactics as the most general grouping, broken into techniques, and then procedures as the most fine-grained classification. Most behavioral detections focus on detecting one or more procedures taken by an adversary to implement a technique. Increasing a detection's coverage by detecting multiple procedures associated with a technique or creating a detection that works across multiple techniques often increases the complexity of the detection but can also improve a detection's **durability**.

Where a detection's coverage can be thought of as the surface area across the MITRE ATT&CK TTPs, the durability of the detection identifies how long the detection is expected to be effective. Understanding the volatility of an adversary's infrastructure, tools, and procedures and the relative cost to change them can help predict the durability of a detection.

These two evaluation criteria define what portion of attacks we can detect and for how long we expect those detections to be effective. Unfortunately, quantifying these evaluation criteria into metrics requires complete knowledge of an adversary's capabilities and their ops tempo to change those capabilities. Despite this, we can use these criteria to rank the effectiveness and quality of our detections as we strive to improve our ability to detect the adversary.

However, we can calculate an organization's historical effectiveness by calculating our mean time to detection as the time from the start of the attack on the organization to the time it took to detect the adversary.

Our ability to detect the adversary does not come without **costs to the cyber security organization**. These costs can be realized in the creation, running, and maintenance of detections, the resources spent reviewing associated alerts, and the actions taken based on those alerts. Later in this chapter, we will review the workflow of detection engineering. The **creation time** to perform that workflow defines the costs for creating that detection. For example, researching approaches to a technique is necessary to improve the coverage and durability of a detection but also increase the cost of creation. As a detection engineer, understanding the **complexity** of the detection affects future analysts' abilities to understand and maintain the detection. It also affects the efficiency of running the detection (both positively and negatively). Maintaining the detections within an organization is an ongoing process. **Staleness** can be used to define the continued effectiveness or value of a detection. Is that technique or tool still being actively used? Is the detection used to detect something that is fully patched or protect infrastructure/software that is no longer on your network?

Each alert that an analyst must review comes at a cost. The **confidence** of a detection measures the probability that the alert is a true positive – that is, the alert is triggered under the expected conditions. However, tuning a detection to reduce the false positive rate can decrease the detection's coverage and result in not identifying the attack. In contrast, the noisiness of a detection identifies how often a detection creates an alert that does not result in remediation. The **noisiness** of a detection might result from low confidence – that is, a high false positive rate – but it could also be related to the **impact** of the detection. Understanding the potential impact allows us to measure the importance or severity of what has been detected.

For example, a detection might identify reconnaissance scanning of the network. The lack of actionability on this activity, despite the confidence in the detection, might result in the noisiness of the detection being unacceptable. Each organization must identify its tolerance for false positives when tuning its detections. However, confidence in detection and the associated potential impact can be used to prioritize an organization's alerts. In *Chapter 5*, we will review how low-fidelity detections can be valuable without significantly affecting analyst productivity.

The **actionability** of a detection defines how easy it is for a SOC analyst to leverage the detection to either further analyze the threat or remediate it. This does not mean that every detection must have an immediate action or response. A detection may have such significantly low confidence that it is ineffective to immediately investigate or respond to. Instead, the action associated with the alert is to increase confidence in other related identified activities or support potential root cause analysis. Unactionable intelligence, however, has limited value. The **specificity** of a detection supports this actionability by explaining what was detected. As an example, a machine learning model may provide increased coverage in detection with a high confidence level but may be unable to explain specifically why the alert was created. This lack of specificity, such as identifying the malware family, could reduce the actionability by not identifying the capabilities, persistence mechanisms, or other details about the malware required to properly triage or remediate the threat.

Lastly, when evaluating a detection, we must look at the **cost to the adversary**. While we will not, in most cases, have an inside look at the detailed costs associated with implementing an attack, we can look at indirect evidence in determining adversary cost. Inherent knowledge of how easily an adversary can evade detection, such as referencing the Pyramid of Pain, can provide guidance for ranking the cost to the adversary. As an example, the cost of changing a malware hash is significantly less than the cost of changing the malware's C2 protocol. The volatility of an attacker's infrastructure, tools, and procedures measures how often the attacker changes their attack in a way that would mitigate the detection. Identifying parts of an attack with lower volatility allows the defender to increase the durability of their detection.

The benefits of a detection engineering program

When selling the concept of a detection engineering program to executives, there's only one justification that matters: a detection engineering program dramatically reduces the risk that a sophisticated adversary can penetrate their network and wreak havoc on their company. While this should be true about every aspect of your cyber security organization, each organization achieves this differently. A detection engineering program differs from other aspects of a cyber security program by allowing organizations to respond to new attacks quickly. It can leverage internal intelligence about adversaries targeting their industry and specifics about their company's network to customize detections.

While detection solutions from any given vendor are typically bundled with vendor-provided detections, these detections are created based on a customer-agnostic approach to detection. They are written in such a way that they can be mass-distributed to client devices without impacting business. As such, vendor detections focus on rules and signatures that can apply to any environment. However, this does not catch the edge cases; that is where detection engineering within your organization comes in. By establishing a detection engineering program, you have control over the focus of your detections and can plan them in such a way that they cover the use cases specific to your environment. For example, the vendors cannot block all logins from foreign countries as that would impact their client base negatively. However, an internal detection engineering team can determine that there should not be any foreign logins and write the detection accordingly. We'll dive deeper into designing detections tailored to your environment in *Chapter 2* and *Chapter 5*.

In addition to this core benefit, there are additional secondary benefits that cyber security organizations can expect from a well-established detection engineering program. Specifically, we will dive into the following key advantages:

- Standardized and version-controlled detection code
- Automated testing
- Cost and time savings

Let's take a look.

Standardized and version-controlled detection code

As part of building a detection engineering program, you will set the standards for how detections are written. This allows the code to be easily understood and compatible with detection solutions, regardless of the author of the detection. Without such standardization, the author will write rules at their discretion, potentially confusing peers trying to interpret the rule.

Furthermore, a detection repository will be leveraged so that all code is version-controlled and peer-reviewed and tested before it's implemented in production. Maintaining a centralized repository of detection code reduces the chance of untested changes or rules being introduced into production environments and makes it easier to track any problematic code. We'll discuss maintaining a repository of detections in *Chapter 5*.

Automated testing

By automating detection testing, we reduce the risk of new or modified detection code introducing errors into production environments. Furthermore, the more automation that is integrated into the environment, the less time detection engineers must spend manually testing code. The detection validation process will be thoroughly discussed in *Part 3*.

Cost and time savings

The cost and time savings of detection engineering are major selling points to stakeholders. For any funding provided to the program, stakeholders and management will look for a **return on investment** (**ROI**) as soon as possible. This ROI comes in the form of cost and time savings resulting from numerous factors. For example, automated testing will improve the quality of detections. This will reduce the time spent on testing detections and it will reduce the time the analysts spend responding to bad detections.

The largest cost and time savings deduction results from reducing the probability of a network breach. Reducing the risk of a breach by implementing well-developed detections reduces the risk of the cost associated with breaches.

In this section, we demonstrated the value of a detection engineering program and the benefits this has for an organization that implements such a program. The next section will close out this chapter by outlining the material you can expect to see throughout this book.

A guide to using this book

The previous sections in this chapter provided the foundational knowledge you will need to fully grasp the contents of this book. In this final section, we'll provide a brief overview of the rest of this book and the topics covered in each chapter.

The book's structure

This book aims to provide you with a thorough walk-through of building a detection engineering program. Along with in-depth knowledge of various aspects of the detection engineering life cycle, this book provides hands-on labs to allow you to learn the tools and skills discussed throughout this book practically. This book is broken into four parts, each providing insight into a different aspect of detection engineering.

Part 1 establishes the foundational knowledge required for the rest of this book. The previous sections of this chapter provided key concepts and terminology that will be referenced throughout this book. We also covered the justification for establishing a detection engineering program and the benefits it brings an organization. In *Chapter 2*, we will dive into each phase of the detection engineering life cycle and provide a high-level overview of the actions that occur at each phase. Finally, *Chapter 3* will guide you through building a detection engineering lab. This lab will be used throughout the rest of this book for hands-on exercises.

Part 2 focuses on the creation side of the detection engineering life cycle. It starts with *Chapter 4*, which focuses on identifying and evaluating the data sources available to detection engineers. This chapter includes a lab that will show you how to add detection sources to the lab you will have built in *Chapter 3*. *Chapter 5* will help you understand your detection requirements and establish the procedure and method for storing detection code. *Part 2* ends with *Chapter 6*, where you will be provided with a hands-on walk-through of turning the detection requirements you established previously into detection code that can be tested within the lab.

Part 3 moves on to the concept of testing and validating detections. First, *Chapter 7* provides practical guidance on validating detection by using existing data and generating simulated data. Additionally, it provides an introduction to proving TTP coverage via the results of the validation. *Chapter 8* introduces the idea of leveraging threat intelligence in your detection engineering program, as a detection source, detection requirement, and method of understanding coverage. *Chapter 9* closes off *Part 3* with a discussion on performance management. This includes methods of measuring the effectiveness of your detections, as well as your detection engineering program as a whole. Furthermore, you will learn how to implement continuous improvement into your detection engineering program.

Part 4 ends this book with *Chapter 10*. This chapter is for those who want to learn more about detection engineering as a career. It will dive into the skill sets that will be required for a career in detection engineering and the day-to-day role of a detection engineer. Here, you will see where the future of detection engineering is going and how you can get involved in the detection engineering community.

Practical exercises

One of the authors' goals with this book is to provide not just text-based knowledge but also practical hands-on exercises that will allow you to experience the detection engineering process. These labs begin in *Chapter 3*, where we'll build out a test environment that will contain all the infrastructure and tooling required for the rest of the labs in this book.

With this test environment in place, most chapters will include exercises that will allow you to write and evaluate detections. These labs will include both those that relate to specific detection technologies and those that look at the environment's coverage as a whole.

All code related to these labs is hosted publicly on GitHub at `https://github.com/PacktPublishing/Practical-Threat-Detection-Engineering`.

The hope is that the practical knowledge provided by this book will enable detection engineers to take actionable lessons learned and implement such strategies and techniques in their environments.

Summary

In this chapter, we provided a high-level introduction to some of the foundational cyber security concepts that will be referenced throughout this book. With this knowledge established, we justified a detection engineering program – specifically, the benefits and value provided to organizations implementing such a program. Finally, we closed out this chapter by providing an overview of what you can expect from the rest of this book.

In the next chapter, we'll begin to look at how organizations can identify and plan out their specific detection requirements. We'll also dive further into the detection engineering life cycle steps that were introduced in this chapter.

2

The Detection Engineering Life Cycle

In *Chapter 1*, we introduced the foundational concepts that will be referenced throughout this book. With this baseline knowledge, we can begin diving further into **detection engineering** (**DE**) and its practical implementation. This chapter will cover the DE life cycle to help you understand the purpose of each phase. We will also consider the inputs and outputs of each phase to see how the different phases interact with each other for a holistic approach to DE.

To begin, we'll introduce the DE life cycle and its subcomponents. *Figure 2.1* shows the life cycle as a flow chart to help you understand the order of operations:

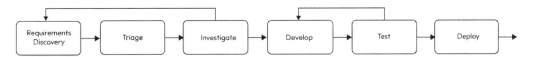

Figure 2.1 – DE life cycle

The top section shows the six primary phases, each of which we will dive into at a high level in the following sections of this chapter. The phases operate in sequence, aligning with the order shown in *Figure 2.1*, with the Test and Investigate phases potentially feeding back into previous phases. We will review these phases in the order that they occur within the subsections of this chapter:

1. Requirements Discovery
2. Triage
3. Investigate
4. Develop
5. Test
6. Deploy

Future chapters will go into each phase in more depth but this chapter will give you the insight needed to know how each phase feeds into the next and the functioning of the life cycle as a whole.

Along with these phases, four key continuous activities are involved in DE that focus on the DE program as a whole, based on developed content, and can help identify areas of improvement:

- Monitoring
- Maintenance
- Metrics
- Comprehensive validation

Despite laying outside the DE life cycle, these activities may lead to the creation of new detection requirements. We'll discuss these activities briefly in this chapter, and then in more depth in *Chapter 10*.

The majority of this chapter will focus on introducing each phase at a high level so that when future chapters begin to reference these phases, you are prepared with the baseline knowledge. Where information is expanded on in future chapters, we will provide a reference, but we recommend that you continue progressing through this book in order rather than skipping ahead as many of the chapters build on the previous ones. Knowledge of the DE life cycle will help you understand how the various topics discussed in future chapters fit into the DE process as a whole.

Phase 1 – Requirements Discovery

The first task in the DE life cycle is to collect detection requirements. The Requirements Discovery phase can be initiated from multiple sources, as described here, and results in detection requirements, which will be passed onto the Triage phase for further evaluation. At a high level, we can analyze inputs and outputs for each phase. In this case, we have the following:

- **Input**: Findings from detection requirement sources
- **Output**: Detection requirement(s) with the details specified in the *Characteristics of a complete detection requirement* section

This section will outline various aspects of the Requirements Discovery phase, such as what a detection requirement should include and where those requirements come from. To start, we'll examine the characteristics of a complete detection and provide a template so that you can gather such information in your organization. Then, we'll dive into the sources that detection requirements can come from and how to identify which are most relevant to your organization.

Characteristics of a complete detection requirement

The result of the Requirements Discovery process should be well-defined detection requirements. The detection engineers need to work with the stakeholders who will be submitting detection requirements, to ensure these requirements are written clearly. At a minimum, the following details should be collected:

- **Requesting organization**: The organization that requested the requirement. This should also include the individual, if applicable, that issued the request, allowing the detection engineer to reach out for additional details if necessary. It is also important to inform the requester once the detection has been created. This provides feedback to the requestor and assures them that their inputs are being acted upon.

- **Description**: What needs to be detected? Descriptions can be phrased in technical terms, such as *detect when new files are written to a web server code directory*, or in broader, less technical terms, such as *notify line managers and the security team if an end user uses unauthorized remote administration software*. Any links to open source material, analysis performed by the requesting team, or other information would be provided by the requestor.

- **Reason**: In many cases, the reason may be self-evident from the description. As an example, the detection requirement was based on a forensic analysis of an attempted attack against the company network. In other cases, the reason can be used to help triage the importance of implementing the detection. Was the ticket placed by an analyst reading a blog about a new attack or was it created based on the **tactics, techniques, and procedures** (**TTPs**) of the adversaries targeting other companies within your industry?

- **Exceptions**: Under what conditions should an alert not be triggered? An example of this is if the event is an authorized developer modification.

- **Scope**: The scope describes where the detection should be applied. Similar to exceptions, the scope can be used to limit the false-positive rate of the detection. The scope can also inform the detection engineer of the purpose of the detection, types of telemetry available, or limitations of the detection.

- **Evidence**: Links to malware, logs, PCAP, or other data collected that can be used to create or test the detection. Any detection request created by the **security operations center** (**SOC**), IR, or hunt team should contain the associated network or endpoint artifacts that were acquired during their investigation.

Next, we will take a look at where these detection requirements can be sourced from within your organization.

Detection requirement sources

Detection requirement sources refer to where the information used to create the requirement originated. These sources can be internal to the DE team or external teams. Furthermore, the detection requirement sources may involve ad hoc requests or can result from findings during the DE process.

In this subsection, we are going to look at the most common requirement sources, including examples of how these sources can be leveraged. Future chapters will go into more depth on some of the most significant sources. The following sources will be covered in this subsection:

- Threat intelligence:

  - Internal threat intelligence

  - Open source threat intelligence

- Business security requirements

- Red Team exercises

- SOC requests

- Continuous activities

Each of these sources plays a unique role in guiding the DE team's work and providing complete detection coverage.

Threat intelligence

Threat intelligence plays a major role in detection development. When developing detections, it is important to prioritize your efforts toward threats that you are likely to face in your environment. Otherwise, your efforts may be wasted on irrelevant detections.

For example, **Transparent Tribe** is a threat group that targets diplomatic, defense, and research organizations in India and Afghanistan. If your organization is a retail organization in the US, writing detections for Transparent Tribe is likely not to have a major impact on your defenses. However, writing detections for **FIN7**, a threat actor that targets organizations in the US retail, restaurant, and hospitality industries, typically through point-of-sale malware, would provide much more value as they are more likely to target your organization.

The following are some questions you can ask to start identifying specific threats of importance to your organization:

- What are the most common threats against your organization's technologies?

- What types of attacks does your organization most often observe (based on historical incident tracking)?

- Which active threat groups are targeting your industry?

- What types of attacks are most impactful to your organization (ransomware, DoS, IP loss, and so on)?

With the context gained from asking these questions, organizations can begin to identify which detections will have the biggest impact on their defenses. Threat intelligence reporting will help you identify the TTPs used by the threat actors likely to target your organization. These TTPs, in turn, can be used to design and develop detections.

As another brief note on threat intelligence: we can further distinguish threat intelligence into two categories: *open source* and *internal*. **Open source intelligence** (**OSINT**), as the name implies, is publicly available. This can be in the form of blog posts, tweets, whitepapers, or online security tools, such as VirusTotal. Internal threat intelligence is sourced from previous incidents targeting your organization. This knowledge can be used to identify common attacks and trends. For example, based on an analysis of previous incidents reported by the SOC, phishing is the most common attack vector seen by organizations. In this case, we would want to discuss how we could better detect such attacks. Bigger organizations may have a dedicated threat intelligence team producing reports for the rest of their security teams, sourced from both OSINT and internal data. Smaller organizations, however, may not have dedicated analysts to provide this information and the detection engineers will be responsible for identifying relevant intelligence.

In *Chapter 8*, we'll dive further into the role threat intelligence plays in a DE program and provide further guidance on evaluating which threat intelligence sources will provide the most value to your organization.

Business security requirements

Organizations often have acceptable use policies that define how their devices should be used. This often reduces the risk of users visiting illegitimate websites that could present a security risk. For example, an organization may choose to prohibit the use of BitTorrent. An alternative to blocking traffic using a firewall would be to leverage detection systems instead and alert others to such a policy violation. This assists in detecting both malicious actors using such services and users attempting to violate corporate policy without causing any disruptions for potentially legitimate but unknown use cases. Questions to ask yourself that will assist you in identifying these business security requirements are as follows:

- What software is prohibited by company security policies?

- What system administrative tools may be used legitimately and by who?

- What network technologies are not common to the organization (RDP, SSH, and so on)?

Security operations center requests

SOC analysts are on the front lines when it comes to observing malicious activity. They may start observing new threats before the DE team has identified the need for new detection. Alternatively, if a detection is performing poorly and needs to be fine-tuned, it is going to be the SOC that is flooded with false positive alerts. As such, it is important to have a constant feedback loop between SOC analysts and detection engineers. If there is an issue with an existing detection or if a detection gap is identified, the SOC should ensure the DE team is aware. The DE team should, in turn, leverage the observability the SOC has and use its feedback as a source for detection requirements.

For this detection requirement source, it is especially important to define the process by which this feedback loop occurs. The methods of communication between the SOC and DE teams, as well as the information required by the DE team from the SOC, are both key procedures to document. Assuming a ticketing system is in place for tracking work when the SOC or any other requirement stakeholder identifies a detection requirement, it should be submitted to the DE team via the ticketing system. The templates for any requests that are to be submitted should include all the information discussed in the previous section, *Characteristics of a complete detection requirement*.

Red Team exercises

Red Team exercises are designed to help identify an organization's security weaknesses. One of the security controls that is tested is the ability to detect the Red Team's activity in the environment. If their activity is not successfully detected, it indicates the need for improvements to detection systems. Like with the SOC requests requirement source, a process must be in place for communicating the requirements between the Red Team and the DE team.

One unique differentiation from SOC requests is that since SOC observations are based on real, corporate activity, it is not as easy to simulate the exact circumstances that led to the need for that detection. Forensic analysis can help identify related samples or logs but is limited to the organization's visibility and data retention policies. Red Teams, however, can replay the attack under the same conditions to identify whether the detection is successful.

Continuous activities

As part of continuous activities, such as monitoring and validation, the DE program will identify where their existing detections fall short as it pertains to their validation criteria. This information can then be used to direct the design of new detections.

In the introduction to this chapter, we covered the different continuous activities involved in a DE program. Specifically, this includes the following:

- Monitoring
- Maintenance
- Metrics
- Comprehensive validation

This subsection will briefly describe each of these activities and how they act as detection requirement sources.

Monitoring

Monitoring is the process of continuously assessing detections that have been implemented in production. Regardless of how much testing is performed during the DE life cycles, there will always be unexpected results when implemented in production. During development, you will test for certain expected false positives and make sure that the detection fires under specially crafted circumstances. So, here, monitoring allows you to capture how the rule performs in "real-world" deployments.

These unexpected results are the output from the monitoring phase and act as input for the detection requirements. For example, let's say you deploy a rule that checks for the presence of nc in a command line (to detect Netcat activity). During testing, you ensure executing an nc command results in the detection firing. You also use a sample set of random data to check for false positives but nothing triggers, so you deploy it to production.

Given the limited nature of your sample dataset, you can't guarantee there won't be false positives on a more wide-scale deployment. That's where the monitoring phase comes in. As per our previous example, let's say there's a command line with the sync string present. Since the rule is triggering in the presence of "nc," this command line will result in a detection for Netcat, despite it being unrelated. This information should be used to create a detection requirement to tune the existing detection and reduce false positives. This process may continue multiple times for some detections if edge cases that aren't expected during testing arise. Monitoring will be discussed in more detail in *Chapter 9*.

Maintenance

The idea of maintaining detections results from the fact that the cyber security landscape is constantly evolving. As threats evolve, so must our detections; otherwise, we won't be able to keep up with threat actors. Some detections will remain relevant and consistent throughout their lifetime, while others will need updating as part of the maintenance phase.

An example of this would be if you write a detection for a specific campaign you've observed targeting your organization. Let's say that this campaign involves a threat actor sending a malicious executable in a ZIP archive via email. With this knowledge, the DE team develops a rule for ZIP attachments that spawns an executable. But what if the threat actor changes their tactics and decides to put the executable in a TAR archive instead? If this occurs, the original detection will no longer work. Therefore, the detection logic for this campaign needs to be updated to now look for TARs. The output of the maintenance phase is a detection requirement for updating an existing detection. Maintenance will be discussed further in *Chapter 10*.

Metrics

Metrics are essentially a statistical analysis of the performance of your rules. They can be used from a variety of perspectives to increase the effectiveness of your ruleset by identifying unexpected results.

First, we can look at metrics that simply indicate how many times a detection has been triggered. This allows us to identify rules that need to be tuned. For example, if metrics highlight a detection that is triggering an excessive number of alerts compared to other detections, it may indicate the detection is causing a high number of false positives. From the other perspective, if there is a detection that has never resulted in an alert, we should review whether the rule is functioning as expected. Some rules may be looking for such niche activity that we don't expect them to trigger, but that should be verified.

Next, we can look at metrics regarding the final determination of triggered detection. This requires your organization to have some method of tracking the outcomes of incident response – for example, a case management system that analysts provide a reason for closing after completion. From there, you'd be able to retrieve statistics regarding which detections result in false positives based on a manual analyst review.

The final metric to be discussed here is performance metrics. Due to the technical limitations of detection technologies, it is important to ensure that your rule is not only resulting in accurate detections but also efficient detections. If detections are not built for efficient performance, you risk impacting production systems. During detection development, you will implement best practices to avoid deploying resource-intensive resources. As your detection repository grows, however, performance may be affected in the scope of the entire detection deployment. We'll discuss metrics further in *Chapter 10* as part of performance management.

Comprehensive validation

Validation uses simulated attacks or other techniques to identify whether your detection systems or individual detections are identifying the associated malicious activity. Validation is commonly used as part of the Test phase of the detection life cycle but can also be used in a continuous comprehensive fashion to perform a larger gap analysis. When beginning a validation process, you will likely set some goal for the validation – that is, what coverage you want to validate. This could be validation of detections against certain frameworks, such as MITRE ATT&CK, or specific threat actors or campaigns. After performing a validation, the results can become a detection requirement source based on where existing detections did not provide coverage.

For example, if validation is performed against the MITRE ATT&CK matrix as a gap analysis and it is revealed that we are unable to detect T1053 (Scheduled Task/Job), that technique may become a requirement for a new detection. The *Phase 2 – Triage* section will briefly introduce the concept of detection coverage. Additionally, *Chapter 10* will cover performance management and assessing your detection coverage in more depth. Before closing out this chapter, let's perform a quick exercise to test your understanding of the Requirements Discovery phase.

Exercise – understanding your organization's detection requirement sources

The following questions will assist you in identifying how each of the concepts applies to your organization. If you do not work in a role or company that provides you with the information to answer these questions, choose a fictional company to use with this book. As this book progress, questions like these will help reinforce the concept that certain aspects of your DE program will be heavily influenced by organization-specific characteristics. Being able to take information about an organization and understand how it affects detection development is an important DE skill:

1. Review the detection requirement sources listed in the chapter. Which of these apply to your organization?

2. Do your current processes enable these stakeholders to easily submit new requirements? How can your processes be improved to increase participation?

By answering these questions regarding your organization, you can establish a foundation that will give you a personalized approach to the rest of the content in this book. This context will guide priorities, limitations, and processes specific to your situation. An example of what this context might look like for an organization is as follows:

1. We have a SOC team as well as various business requirements that could be leveraged for detection requirements. We do not have a Red Team or threat intel team, however, so currently, those are irrelevant sources.

2. At this time, there are no processes for submitting detection requirements. The organization leverages Jira as a ticketing system. We should create templates and procedures for submitting detection requirements with all the required information. We need to identify and notify stakeholders and ensure they understand the process.

With the detection requirements output from this stage, we can now move on to the Triage phase, which will help us identify which of the detection requirements should be prioritized.

Phase 2 – Triage

As the backlog for requirements increases, a Triage phase is required to identify what detection should be focused on next. The following are the inputs and outputs associated with this phase:

- **Input**: Detection requirement created during the previous phase
- **Output**: Triaged and prioritized detection requirement

In most circumstances, dependencies do not exist between detection requirements, allowing the DE team to choose the next appropriate task from the backlog. Using a first-in first-out queue or predefined priority is not preferable as these methods will not consider the changing external threat landscape and internal attack surface. In *Chapter 10*, we will review performance management techniques that influence the Triage phase. The Triage phase can depend upon several factors, including the following:

- The **severity** of the threat
- Your organizational **alignment** with the threat

- Your detection **coverage**
- Active **exploits**

Threat severity

Threat severity relates to the impact of the threat if it is not detected. The greater this impact, the higher the severity. A simple example of this would be the severity difference between detecting reconnaissance versus detecting malware on your network. Most commonly, the further in the kill chain or how far right in the MITRE tactics, the greater the impact. However, the operational environment can affect this rating of severity. Consider the ability to detect a **remote access Trojan** (**RAT**) in your environment. Traditionally, a RAT would be high severity but if found within a closed network, the RAT's inability to contact its C2 would reduce its severity and the detection team may triage to identify malicious users or ransomware as higher severity.

Organizational alignment

In the *Detection requirement sources* section, we discussed the value of threat intelligence in supporting your DE efforts. In *Chapter 9*, we will focus on creating and leveraging threat intelligence to support DE. Threat intelligence is only half of understanding organizational alignment. At a high level, organizational alignment describes how a detection relates to the company or network it is protecting. We start by leveraging threat intelligence to identify external threats' motivations, targets, capabilities, and infrastructure. This external view of the threats can then be overlaid upon the internal view – that is, the industry, organization, infrastructure users, and data that is being protected. If the requested detection falls within the overlap of the external threats and what is being internally protected, it has organizational alignment.

Detection coverage

Understanding your current detection capabilities, both those created by your internal organization and those provided by commercial or open source entities, can inform the triage process. Is this requirement already met by existing detections or is the requestor identifying a gap or fault in the existing detections that were supposed to serve this requirement? This analysis may not be a binary question of whether existing detections identify the malicious activity identified within the request. In addition, you may wish to analyze whether the request is an improvement on existing detections, such as reducing the false positive rate, improving the specificity of the detection, or identifying the activity through additional sources or visibility compared to the current detections.

Active exploits

Quickly protecting against newly identified active exploits may be one of the most visible ways to show the value of the DE team. Rapidly implementing detection in these scenarios helps protect your organization against an active threat and provides value when leadership's attention is squarely on the cyber security team. Consider the Log4j exploit in 2021. *Figure 2.2* shows the increase in attacks over the hours following the exploit's announcement. The ops tempo of adversaries leveraging this vulnerability was hours, not days. Having the ability to match the velocity of the adversary, as well as implementing and deploying detections that identify and block this activity, is a core added value of the DE team:

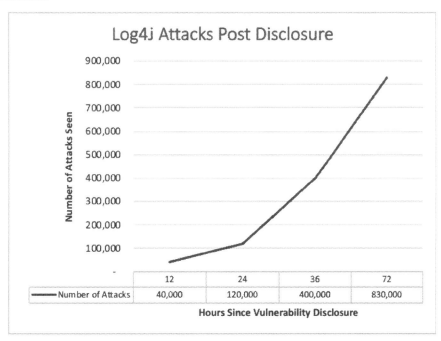

Figure 2.2 – Log4j exploit statistics. Data source: `https://blog.checkpoint.com/ security/the-numbers-behind-a-cyber-pandemic-detailed-dive/`

While it may be tempting to continuously respond to the latest exploits, especially if a request was created to detect it, understanding the exploit and its impact is important. Here are some questions you should consider:

- Is my organization affected by this exploit?

- What is the impact of this exploit?

- Does enough information exist for adversaries to implement the exploit or for a detection to be created against it?

- How easy is it for an adversary to implement the exploit?

- Is the exploit being currently used in the wild, or by adversaries that target your organization?

- How quickly will the affected applications provide an update to patch this exploit?

After using the Triage phase to prioritize detection requirements, the Investigate phase can begin, with the triaged requirements acting as the input.

Phase 3 – Investigate

The Investigate phase has multiple goals, but fundamentally, it needs to prepare a detection requirement for development by converting the detection requirements into more technical ones. Executing this process can identify deficiencies in intelligence or data collection, which will need to be resolved before development can start. The following are the inputs and outputs associated with this phase:

- **Input**: Triaged detection requirement
- **Output**: Detection of technical specifications and data engineering requirements (if applicable)

The Investigate phase can be broken into four steps:

1. Identify the data source
2. Determine detection indicator types
3. Research
4. Establish validation criteria

Let's take a look.

Identify the data source

During this step, you must identify the relevant data sources needed to satisfy the detection requirement. Analysts will need to understand the intent and scope of the detection, to identify the assets in scope. For example, a detection may only be relevant for an organization's **operational technology (OT)** environment, but not their corporate environment. Furthermore, the detection may only be relevant to a specific type of network traffic. This informs you of the specific type of data that will need to be operated on to produce the relevant detection, and therefore the teams that need to be engaged, such as network engineers and operations personnel who understand the specific domain the assets operate in. During this step, any data source deficiencies will also be identified, and where necessary, additional requests will be sent to the appropriate team for resolution (the data engineering requirements mentioned as output). For example, a frequently encountered issue with web server logs is the absence of the X-Forwarded-For request header. If the web infrastructure is not configured to capture this field, detection cannot be written to test for values in that field. Configuration changes need to be made before any dependent detections can be implemented.

Determine detection indicator types

Detection indicator types can be static, behavioral, statistical, or hybrid. Static detections operate on an atomic attribute of a signal. For example, antivirus data may collect MD5 hashes for binaries saved to disk. A detection designed to identify static indicators may have a definition that looks for an MD5 of a specific value. Detections for static indicators tend to be the easiest to implement, but they are also the easiest to evade. They tend to have low long-term value but high short-term tactical value, specifically when scoping an active cyberattack. Behavioral indicators are more complex and can operate on multiple data entity types, with multiple conditions specified. These detections attempt to identify a general definition for a specific tactic being executed. Statistical indicators typically detect aggregate value exceeding some threshold for a given period, or a deviation from an established baseline. *Table 2.1* outlines the indicator types, an example of those indicators, and the requirements that detection systems must satisfy to develop detections of that type:

Indicator Type	Example Requirement	Detection System Requirements
Static	Detect communication with a recently identified phishing site, hosted at `SiteA.com/login.php`, with the IP address *IPAddr1*	The ability to identify a specific IP address, URL, and domain name in any outbound traffic, and the host where the traffic originated
Behavioral	Detect a web server process executing reconnaissance commands	A maintainable list of web server processes, a maintainable list of reconnaissance commands, and the ability to identify processes, child processes, and security contexts for processes
Statistical	The volume of traffic from a single specified host to the internet that rises over a specified threshold within a specified timeframe	The ability to monitor a moving aggregate of bytes sent from a single host, holding a configurable value for a data threshold, and the ability to compare aggregate values against the specified threshold
Hybrid	Communication with a recently identified phishing site, hosted at `SiteA.com/login.php`, followed by an anomalous login activity	The ability to identify a specific IP address, URL, and domain name in any outbound traffic, as well as the host where the traffic originated. The ability to identify login behavior varying from a normal baseline to determine suspicious outliers

Table 2.1 – Detection indicator types

As you can see, detection requirements can become quite complex and require different development strategies. Ideally, these details should be understood and mapped before advancing to the Develop phase.

Research

During this step, analysts need to understand the detection and classify it based on attacker goals and the associated tactics and techniques (often using the MITRE ATT&CK framework). In reviewing the tactics and techniques, this step will reveal whether similar tactic coverage already exists within the detection environment, and how the new detection requirement can be integrated. This might include the following:

- Identifying examples of attacks performed in the past.

- Identifying any similar rules, partial matches, or detections for the same TTPs that should be updated rather than a new detection being created.

- Identifying variations of the attack that could be performed by the adversary. Here, you can deconstruct the attack to identify the underlying capabilities used and determine which of these capabilities are least likely to vary.

Establish validation criteria

The Investigate phase must also identify how detection can be tested. In ideal circumstances, realistic data will always be available to determine whether a detection query runs as expected. However, this is not always the case, for a variety of reasons. Emerging or novel attack techniques may not have many details available, and in these cases, detections are usually theoretical, with no concrete validation. In other cases, assets may not or cannot collect the resolution of data required to build a specific detection, due to a business constraint outside of the control of the security function. Part of the Investigate phase involves sourcing or generating test data that can be used to validate the effectiveness of the detection being reviewed.

Detection requirements can sometimes be expressed in non-technical terms, which require interpretation before they can be translated into specific technical requirements. This process produces a package of relevant technical details that developers need to write detection code, as discussed in the next section.

Phase 4 – Develop

The goal of this phase is to take technical specifications from the Investigate phase, then design, develop, and test a technical implementation for the relevant detection. The following are the inputs and outputs associated with this phase:

- **Input**: Detection of technical specifications

- **Output**: Detection code

As with most development work, this step requires rigorous planning. New detections need to not only satisfy the requirements but must also integrate with the rest of the detections within the environment. Detections are often implemented in the form of a query that is run against a data source or multiple data sources. Depending on your environment and its capabilities, different languages may need to interact with different data sources, and data pipelines and intermediary data stores may need to be built. The development process develops and implements a suitable solution for each new detection requirement, keeping both short- and long-term objectives in mind. This phase can be divided into three sub-processes – **design**, **development**, and **unit testing**:

- **Design**: The **design** process plans the approach for implementing a new detection. In some cases, the detection requirement can be satisfied by simply writing a single query in a system built for managing detections. These can be implemented quickly. However, for more complex requirements, developers often need to devise strategies for collecting, transforming, and processing data from multiple data stores, and writing integrations for different applications and alerting systems. Complex requirements can generate requests for infrastructure changes. These can take significant time to implement, and often, in practice, temporary solutions are implemented until more robust solutions are built.

- **Development**: This **development** process converts the designed solution into a rule or capability that can be run by the detection appliance. In simple terms, this process focuses on writing the code that matches the design outlined in the previous step.

- **Unit testing**: During the **unit testing** process, the detection is executed against a test dataset to ensure the expected results are returned. This step uses the data and criteria outlined by the validation criteria that were produced during the Investigate phase.

With the detection code developed, we are ready to begin testing the code to determine whether it functions as per the requirements.

Phase 5 – Test

Testing is a way to validate the efficacy of your detection and reduce its noisiness before deploying it within a production environment. While we show testing as occurring after development, in reality, it is a continuous process that occurs throughout the detection development process. It should not be relegated to occurring only after development is complete. A best practice within DE is to use testing to guide the development process.

Test-driven development is a software development technique that adapts well to this purpose. Tests are designed before development and are first added to the automated acceptance testing infrastructure. The development process starts with running the tests against your existing detection capabilities. This may result in you identifying already existing detection capabilities or confirming the failure of these tests, which identifies the need to create or update a detection. During the development process, these tests are continuously applied and used to influence the improvement of the detection. Once these tests pass, the detection is refactored (changes are made to the code to improve its implementation and ensure it adheres to best practices without changing its functionality) and retested. Additional tests may also be created throughout the process as the implementer identifies new ways the adversary may try to circumvent the detection.

Types of test data

There are two types of test data: **known bad** and **known good**.

Known bad

Known bad data refers to any telemetry that represents the adversary's activity. This could be anything that's captured while simulating the attack in a sandbox, captured from actual adversary attacks against an environment, or mock data created by altering existing telemetry to represent expected data from an attack.

Known good

Known good data refers to telemetry captured from benign activity within a clean environment. It can typically be curated outside of the DE life cycle and reused to test each detection. In addition to general known good datasets, you may wish to add specific datasets that test the boundary conditions of the detection. This dataset should, if possible, be curated from your operational environment, reducing the risk that the tests are not representative of production.

During this phase, multiple ad hoc tests will be written to ensure the detection performs optimally. In general, these ad hoc tests should keep the following goals in mind:

- Identify possible scenarios for false positives. Each detection can be triggered for scenarios that do not accurately represent the event the detection was designed to capture. One goal of testing is to minimize the false positive rate.

- Identify potential for evading detection. While this step arguably falls under the responsibility of Red Team operators, testers can and should identify more obvious ways to execute techniques that can carry out the action that the detection should identify, while not being detected.

- Identify possibly incomplete detections. These should highlight detection definitions that are too loosely defined and do not correctly identify all permutations of the event to be detected.

After testing and repeating the development phase as required, the detection can move on to the Deploy phase of the life cycle.

Phase 6 – Deploy

The goal of this phase is to take the developed detection from the test environment and migrate it to the production environment. This detection is also monitored to ensure it runs as expected and does not negatively impact the performance of the production system. The following are the inputs and outputs associated with this phase:

- **Input**: Tested detection code
- **Output**: Deployed detection code

Deployment tags are a useful method for representing the maturity stages of a detection, enabling the rapid release of new capabilities while limiting the impact of a malfunctioning detection on analysts reviewing alerts. Here are the criteria for the **experimental**, **test**, and **stable** maturity stages:

- **Experimental**: At this stage, the detection has been designed and converted into code but extensive testing on its performance in a real environment has not been tested. Tweaking will likely need to be done for it to be ready before a peer review. The detection engineer should closely monitor the results to ensure that the rule works as expected. Other analysts, beyond the author, should not review alerts associated with experimental detections. The questions the author should answer at this stage are as follows:

  - Does the detection code execute without errors?
  - Does the detection successfully trigger for the sample(s) provided as part of the detection requirement?
  - Given unrelated samples, do any false positives occur?
  - Is there any negative impact on system performance as a result of the rule?

- **Test**: Once the experimental stage has led to a rule that is believed to be ready for a broader audience, the test stage can occur. The test deployment tag signals that all analysts should review the alerts from the detection, but these alerts are lower fidelity and thereby may be of lower priority than alerts resulting from stable detections. Here are some questions that will assist in this stage:

  - Does the rule trigger under expected conditions?
  - Does the rule conflict with or duplicate existing rules?
  - Is the false positive rate tolerable?
  - Has the broader team identified any ways to improve the detection?
  - Is the broader team comfortable with the quality of the detection?

- **Stable**: Once a rule has been determined to be stable, it is fully deployed to the production environment. Analysts should have high confidence in the accuracy of detections tagged as stable. The rule must have undergone thorough testing in the previous stages; otherwise, you risk affecting business operations. Once operating in production, if changes are needed based on false positives or negatives identified alongside the additional sources of events, a ticket should be submitted to the DE team, who will repeat the life cycle with the existing rule as a starting point.

The Deploy phase is the last phase of the life cycle and at this point, the detection is in production. Updates may need to be made to the rules as further data is collected, which will result in a new detection requirement and a repeat of the life cycle.

Summary

In this chapter, we introduced the DE life cycle and dove into its different phases. To break things down even further, we analyzed the inputs, outputs, and processes of that given stage in the life cycle. These phases will be the basis for the remainder of this book, and in subsequent chapters, we will dive into each of them.

The next chapter will take you through creating your own DE laboratory and the components found within the lab. We will also provide the technical details for investigating, developing, and testing new detections.

3

Building a Detection Engineering Test Lab

In *Chapter 2*, we introduced the **detection engineering** (**DE**) life cycle and provided a high-level overview of each of its phases. In this chapter, we will walk through the process of building a DE lab so that we can practice the concepts that will be introduced throughout the rest of this book.

Before we get started, we need to cover the technical components of a typical detection environment. As mentioned in *Chapter 1*, DE exists to help the cyber security function protect assets. To protect assets at scale, these assets first need to forward event telemetry to a central log store. In more complex configurations, multiple data stores are involved and separate processes are used to compute relevant statistics and aggregate values for detections. Once stored, these events then need to be routinely reviewed to identify those that might be indicative of malicious activity. Furthermore, once a possible malicious activity has been identified, the system must notify the appropriate audiences.

We can break this high-level objective into the following feature sets:

- **Event forwarding**: Forward events from assets
- **Collection**: Collect events in the centralized data store
- **Detection development**: Allow users to define what might be indicative of malicious activity since the definition of malicious activity is constantly evolving
- **Monitoring**: Use those definitions to scan for matching events
- **Alerting**: Notify appropriate audiences if events matching definitions of malicious activity have occurred

Fortunately, multiple solutions exist to address each of these requirements. In this book, we will use Elastic Stack. Its feature set and license make it suitable for building a test lab that we can use to develop and test detections.

In this chapter, we will cover the following main topics:

- Deploying and configuring Elastic Stack
- Setting up Fleet Server
- Adding data sources to the detection lab
- Implementing a simple detection

By the end of the chapter, you will have a fully functioning DE lab to use for the rest of the labs in this book.

Technical requirements

To set up the detection lab, you will need access to a system that can perform virtualization. The supported operating systems for this book's walk-throughs are Linux and Windows.

For a Windows **virtual machine** (**VM**) deployed in a lab, you will require the following resources:

- At least 2 GB of RAM, though 4 GB or more is recommended
- At least 60 GB of disk space

The Elastic Stack

The Elastic Stack is a set of tightly integrated products that are well suited to address the requirements of a DE lab. The Elastic Stack includes the following components:

- **Beats**: A data shipper that is used to collect data from an endpoint and forward it to **Elasticsearch** or **Logstash** for pre-processing. Different packages exist for collecting different types of data from endpoints. While Beats is a core component of the Elastic Stack, in this book, we will use Elastic Agent to forward data from endpoints to Elasticsearch.

- **Logstash**: A powerful tool for transforming data and forwarding it to different destination systems. It offers a high degree of control over re-shaping data and has plugins that support forwarding data to a significant variety of destinations.

- **Elasticsearch**: This is the data storage component. While primarily designed for searching, it has evolved to become a capable data analysis engine.

- **Kibana**: This is the Elasticsearch frontend. Kibana allows users to explore and visualize data stored in Elasticsearch using a web browser. To read more about Kibana's vast feature set, visit Elastic's website: `https://www.elastic.co/kibana/features`.

- **Integrations**: This refers to the large collection of data ingestion components that are enabled by Elastic Agent and managed by Fleet Server. Once an endpoint has Elastic Agent installed on it, administrators can configure the collection of data from a variety of known data sources. Elastic

Agent receives configuration details from Fleet Server about what data should be collected, and which server the data should be output to. These configuration details are defined as agent policies and are stored in Elasticsearch.

Figure 3.1 shows some of the Elastic Stack components and how they can interact with each other to solve many data management problems:

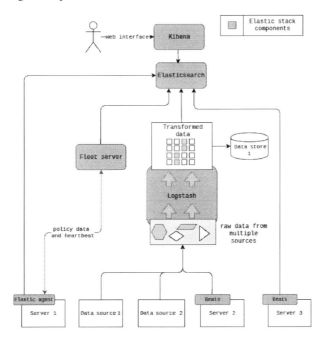

Figure 3.1 – Example Elasticsearch deployment

In this section, we will walk through setting up Elasticsearch and Kibana, specifically for working with detections. Your configurations may vary, depending on the infrastructure you have available. To simplify deployments, we will be making use of Docker and docker-compose.

Important note on security

This book describes a way to deploy a minimal environment for independently developing and testing DE concepts. Many configurations have been simplified and are far too insecure for use in production environments. Thankfully, Elastic Co has provided detailed instructions for setting up the Elastic Stack in production environments on their website. We strongly recommend reviewing this documentation for guidance on planning, deploying, and maintaining the Elastic Stack in a production environment. All of Elastic's documentation, including its installation guide, can be found here: `https://www.elastic.co/guide/index.html`.

In the rest of this section, we will walk through the process of standing up an Elastic Stack, which we will then use for the labs covered in this book. We'll describe one way to provision a simple Elastic Stack environment using Docker. We recommend that you use a Linux-based operating system to act as your Docker host, though the Elastic website (`https://www.elastic.co/guide/en/elasticsearch/reference/current/install-elasticsearch.html`) provides detailed instructions for installing and running the Elastic Stack with and without Docker on Linux, Windows, and macOS systems. As these tools receive updates, their UIs may change slightly, so there may be some differences from the screenshots we have provided.

Deploying the Elastic Stack with Docker

Perhaps the simplest way to get started with the Elastic Stack is by using Docker and the docker-compose plugin. Docker simplifies the deployment of applications by using operating system-level virtualization. This reduces the impact on the configuration of the underlying operating system. While installing the Elastic Stack on the base operating system is a valid and well-documented approach (documented here: `https://www.elastic.co/guide/en/elasticsearch/reference/current/install-elasticsearch.html`), it can sometimes make management and cleanup more difficult. If something goes wrong, you often have to make changes to software and sub-components that might affect other software running on the same system. With containers, we can worry less about managing Elastic sub-components and dependencies. If something breaks, we can simply delete and re-create a container, rather than making changes to components that might impact other software running on the same system. Deep coverage of Docker and container technologies, in general, is beyond the scope of this book, but more information can be found here: `https://docs.docker.com/engine/faq/`.

docker-compose is a powerful utility for orchestrating the creation and configuration of multi-container applications. As input, docker-compose requires a single `docker-compose.yaml` file, which specifies the types of containers to use, their connectivity, volumes, and other configurations. You can read more about using docker-compose on Docker's website here: `https://docs.docker.com/get-started/08_using_compose/`.

We will use docker-compose to orchestrate the deployment of Elasticsearch nodes and a Kibana node. This process is thoroughly documented on Elastic's official website, located here: `https://www.elastic.co/guide/en/elasticsearch/reference/current/docker.html`.

The process described on Elastic's site involves using `docker-compose.yaml` and a `.env` file, which docker-compose then interprets to build the Elastic and Kibana nodes. We will use a slightly modified version of these files to provision two Elasticsearch nodes and a single Kibana node, with some default parameters predefined in the `.env` file.

Installing Docker

Docker provides support for a variety of platforms, including Microsoft Windows, Linux, and macOS. The labs in this book support Windows and Linux. If you are doing these labs on a macOS computer, we recommend using VirtualBox and provisioning a virtual Ubuntu Server to act as your Docker host. You can find instructions for installing Docker on Docker's documentation site (`https://docs.docker.com/`):

- Instructions for installing Docker Desktop on Windows: `https://docs.docker.com/desktop/install/windows-install/`
- Instructions for installing Docker on Linux: `https://docs.docker.com/desktop/install/linux-install/`

More detailed instructions for installing Docker on Windows and Linux are provided in the next section.

Installing Docker on Windows

Follow these steps to install Docker on Windows:

1. Install **Windows Subsystem for Linux version 2** (**WSL2**). This requires Windows 10, version 2004 or later. To start the installation process, open an administrative Command Prompt and type `wsl --install -d ubuntu`. The `-d` parameter specifies the Linux distribution to use for `wsl`. For our lab, we will use the `ubuntu` distribution. If you already have WSL installed, you can check the version that's being used by executing the `wsl -l -v` command. If you already have a `wsl` version 1 distribution, you can upgrade it by issuing the `wsl --set-version <distribution name> 2` command. Once you've done this, you need to restart your computer. Full instructions for installing and upgrading WSL can be found on Microsoft's website: `https://learn.microsoft.com/en-us/windows/wsl/install`.

2. Download and install Docker Desktop from `https://www.docker.com/products/docker-desktop/`.

Installing Docker Desktop on Windows requires minimal user interaction. Once the installation is complete, you should see a window similar to the one shown in *Figure 3.2*:

Figure 3.2 – Docker Desktop on Windows

3. Once the icon in the lower-left corner is green, Docker Engine is running.

4. To check that docker-compose is available, run `docker compose version` from a command-line prompt. You should get an output similar to the following:

```
c:\>docker compose version
Docker Compose version v2.10.2
```

Installing Docker on Linux

If you are running a Debian-based Linux distribution, such as Ubuntu Server, you can find the instructions for installing Docker here: `https://docs.docker.com/engine/install/ubuntu/`. This process will walk you through the process of installing Docker with the docker-compose plugin. Install the following list of packages using the apt package manager via the `sudo apt-get install` command:

- `docker-ce`
- `docker-ce-cli`
- `containerd.io`
- `docker-compose-plugin`

Once those packages have been installed, you can start the Docker daemon using the following command:

```
$ sudo service docker start
```

To test your installation, run `docker --version` from a terminal. You should see an output similar to the following:

```
$ docker --version
Docker version v20.10.12, build 20.10.12-0ubuntu4
```

Running `docker --help` should show the `compose` plugin under the `Management Commands` section, as shown in *Figure 3.3*:

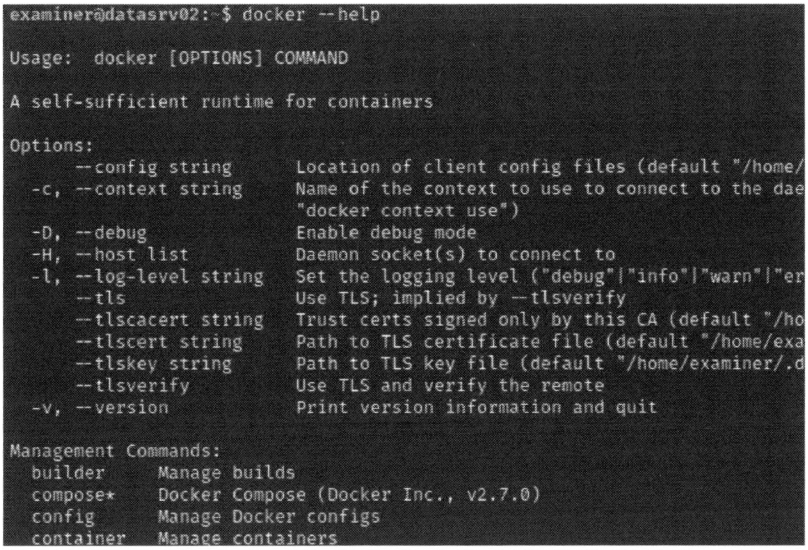

Figure 3.3 – Docker help

With Docker installed, next, we will modify some configuration settings, as required for our Elastic deployment.

Virtual memory configuration

Due to the increased memory requirements of Elastic, the default Docker settings must be modified to handle this.

If you installed Docker on a Linux-based system, as outlined in the Elastic system configuration documentation at `https://www.elastic.co/guide/en/elasticsearch/reference/7.17/vm-max-map-count.html`, then you need to modify the `vm.max_map_count` setting of the Docker hosts via the `sysctl` command. The steps for making this change are different for Windows and Linux systems and are detailed separately in this section.

Windows

If you are running Docker Desktop on Windows, the process is a little different. Since Docker Desktop on WSL2 is a lightweight VM, we need to access that VM or distribution to make those configuration changes. As outlined in Elastic's documentation, we can connect to this distribution using the `wsl` command with the `-d` argument. From a new terminal, run the `wsl  -l` command to list the available distributions, as shown in *Figure 3.4*:

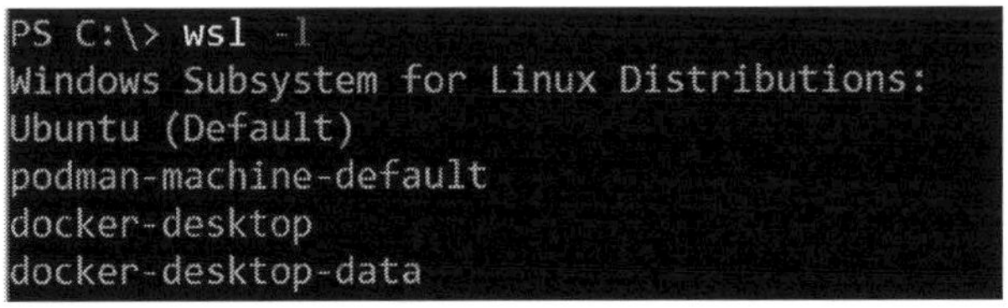

```
PS C:\> wsl -l
Windows Subsystem for Linux Distributions:
Ubuntu (Default)
podman-machine-default
docker-desktop
docker-desktop-data
```

Figure 3.4 – Listing wsl distributions

Intuitively, Docker Desktop uses the `docker-desktop` distribution. You can access this VM directly by issuing the `wsl  -d  docker-desktop` command. From there, you can issue the `sysctl` command to make the required `vm.max_map_count` value change, as shown in *Figure 3.5*:

```
PS C:\> wsl -d docker-desktop
labhost8:/mnt/host/c# sysctl -w vm.max_map_count=262144
vm.max_map_count = 262144
```

Figure 3.5 – Configuring Docker Desktop's virtual memory

To exit WSL2 at any point, type `exit`.

Linux

On Linux, this can be achieved by issuing the following command:

```
sudo sysctl -w vm.max_map_count=262144
```

You can make this change survive reboots by modifying `/etc/sysctl.conf`.

At this point, we have configured Docker as needed to begin installing the Elastic Stack.

Configuring the Elastic Stack

Now that we have Docker installed with docker-compose, we need to download the stack configuration files, specifically `docker-compose.yaml` and `.env`. These files are available in this book's GitHub repository, which is located here: `https://github.com/PacktPublishing/Practical-Threat-Detection-Engineering/tree/main/Chapter%203/Lab%20build/esk`.

In terms of our directory structure, for the rest of this chapter and book, you should create a project folder starting with the structure in *Figure 3.6* for the docker-compose.yaml file and .env files you downloaded previously, as well as certificates that will be required for configuration:

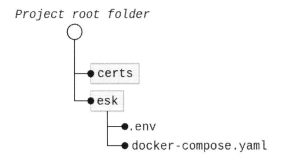

Figure 3.6 – Project folder structure with the Elastic Stack

The docker-compose.yaml file describes the containers, networks, and volumes necessary to run the Elastic Stack. The version used for this book is slightly different from the version available on Elastic's site. The docker-compose.yaml file will create a three-container application comprising two Elasticsearch containers and a single Kibana container, as shown in *Figure 3.7*:

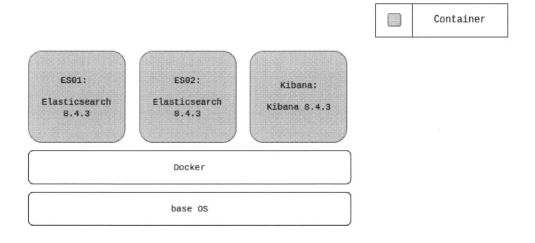

Figure 3.7 – Docker deployment

The docker-compose.yaml file uses a companion file, .env, which specifies default environment variable values used by the stack. You will need to make changes to the highlighted portions of the

.env file shown here. Replace the first two values with secure passwords of your choice. Replace the last three values with randomly generated 32-character strings:

```
ELASTIC_PASSWORD=<<a new password>>
KIBANA_PASSWORD=<<a new password>>
STACK_VERSION=8.4.3
CLUSTER_NAME=docker-cluster
LICENSE=basic
ES_PORT=9200
KIBANA_PORT=5601
MEM_LIMIT=1073741824
XPACK_ENCRYPTEDSAVEDOBJECTS_ENCRYPTIONKEY=<<random 32 character
string>>
XPACK_SECURITY_ENCRYPTIONKEY=<<random 32 character string>>
XPACK_REPORTING_ENCRYPTIONKEY=<<random 32 character string>>
```

Optional storage configuration

Elasticsearch can be quite data-intensive, depending on the volume of data being ingested. If you have a faster or a higher-capacity disk that you prefer to use for Elasticsearch data, you can make changes that instruct Docker to map the Elasticsearch data paths to a path on the high-capacity or high-performance disk:

1. First, create a directory on the disk to hold all your data. Ideally, this disk should be reliably connected to the Docker host – that is, it shouldn't be a removable disk that could potentially be disconnected. Since we will be using it to store our data, if it is ever disconnected while the containers are running, this will cause the containers to terminate ungracefully.

2. Once the data directory has been created, we can make the relevant modifications to the .env file. We will add three additional default environment variables that will hold the paths for the Elasticsearch and Kibana data. For example, if the directory we created was /path/to/large/disk/elasticdata/, we would add the following three lines to the .env file we edited previously:

```
ES1_DATA=/path/to/large/disk/elasticdata/es01
ES2_DATA=/path/to/large/disk/elasticdata/es02
KIBANA_DATA=/path/to/large/disk/elasticdata/kibana_data
```

This will create three environmental variables that we will reference in the docker-compose.yaml file.

3. In the docker-compose.yaml file, we need to modify the volumes section of our Elasticsearch and Kibana containers so that we can configure the container for it to leverage these disks. For es01 and es02, you can add the following lines under volumes:

```
- ${ES1_DATA}:/usr/share/elasticsearch/data
```

```
    - ${ES2_DATA}:/usr/share/elasticsearch/data
```

This should create a `docker-compose.yaml` file that looks like this:

```
es01:
    depends_on:
      setup:
        condition: service_healthy
    image: docker.elastic.co/elasticsearch/
elasticsearch:${STACK_VERSION}
    volumes:
      - ../certs:/usr/share/elasticsearch/config/certs
      - ${ES1_DATA}:/usr/share/elasticsearch/data
...
es02:
    depends_on:
      - es01
    image: docker.elastic.co/elasticsearch/
elasticsearch:${STACK_VERSION}
    volumes:
      - ../certs:/usr/share/elasticsearch/config/certs
      - ${ES2_DATA}:/usr/share/elasticsearch/data
```

4. Similarly, for the Kibana container, you can make the following addition:

```
kibana:
    depends_on:
      es01:
        condition: service_healthy
      es02:
        condition: service_healthy
    image:
docker.elastic.co/kibana/kibana:${STACK_VERSION}
    volumes:
      - ../certs:/usr/share/kibana/config/certs
      - ${KIBANA_DATA}:/usr/share/kibana/data
```

With these changes in place, Docker will use your specified path in place of the relevant data directories for the Elasticsearch and Kibana containers. Ensure these files are saved to the correct hierarchy in the directory structure that was described at the beginning of this section.

5. Using a new terminal or administrative command-line prompt, change your working directory to the `esk` supdirectory of the project root folder and issue the `sudo docker compose up -d` (for Linux) or `docker-compose up -d` (for Windows) command.

> **Debugging tip**
> Running this command without the -d parameter will allow you to see the terminal output from each container. This is extremely helpful when troubleshooting stack setup issues and other errors.

6.   You can check the status of your stack by running the sudo docker compose ps command:

```
examiner@datasrv02:/dev/delab/esk$ sudo docker compose ps
NAME            COMMAND               SERVICE   STATUS             PORTS
esk-es01-1      "/bin/tini -- /usr/l…"  es01      running (healthy)  0.0.0.0:9200→9200/tcp, :::9200→9200/tcp, 9300/tcp
esk-es02-1      "/bin/tini -- /usr/l…"  es02      running (healthy)  9200/tcp, 9300/tcp
esk-kibana-1    "/bin/tini -- /usr/l…"  kibana    running (healthy)  0.0.0.0:5601→5601/tcp, :::5601→5601/tcp
esk-setup-1     "/bin/tini -- /usr/l…"  setup     exited (0)
```

Figure 3.8 – Container status via the terminal

7.   Once the es01, es02, and Kibana containers have a status of **Running** (as shown in *Figure 3.8*), this means your setup has been successful so far. Once no runtime issues arise, you can attempt to access the services.

8.   On Docker Desktop for Windows, you can monitor the startup progress of your stack by using the Docker Desktop app. The **Containers** window should look like what's shown in *Figure 3.9*:

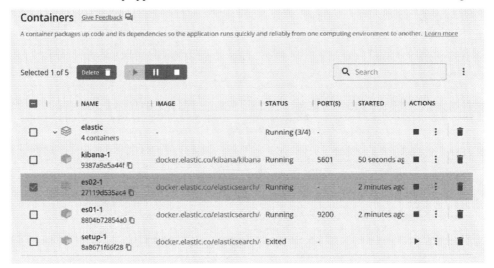

Figure 3.9 – Container status via Docker Desktop

9.   If everything has gone well, you will be able to access your Elastic Stack by going to http:// [ip address of your docker host]:5601, or http://localhost:5601 if you are running Docker on the same machine. You will see a login page similar to the one shown in *Figure 3.10*:

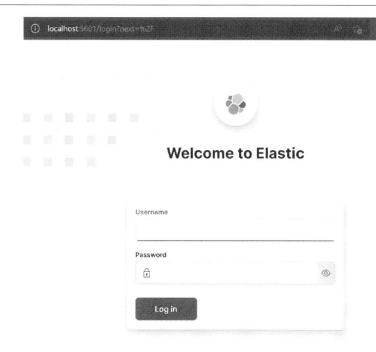

Figure 3.10 – Elastic login page

You can log in by using elastic as the username and the password specified in the .env file for the ELASTIC_PASSWORD value. After logging in, you'll be greeted with a welcome message. At this point, we've successfully set up the Elastic Stack for our detection lab.

The next step in the lab setup process is to set up Fleet Server.

Setting up Fleet Server

In our lab, we will be collecting telemetry from multiple endpoints. To enable this, we will install Elastic Agent on any system we want to collect data from. In larger deployments, agents can get deployed to hundreds or even thousands of endpoints and each of these endpoints can have different data collection requirements. Managing these agents can become complicated as the number and diversity of installed agents increase. Fleet Server is a component of the Elastic Stack that attempts to simplify agent management.

From Kibana, we can create different agent policies, which define what data should be collected, apply those policies to different endpoints, and even uninstall Elastic from these endpoints if we need to. This capability is extremely powerful, especially in larger environments with many endpoints.

We will use Fleet to manage the endpoints that we'll connect to our detection lab. The following section details how to install Fleet Server.

Installing and configuring Fleet Server

For our lab, we will add an additional container to act as our Fleet Server. *Figure 3.11* shows the previous Docker deployment but includes the additional container for Fleet:

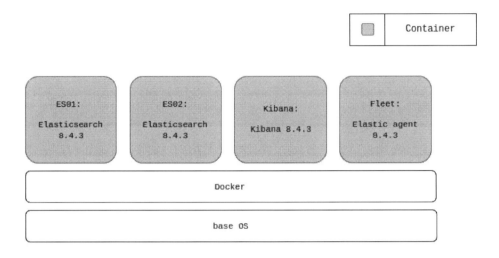

Figure 3.11 – Docker deployment with Fleet

Let's get started with installing Fleet:

1. In our main project folder, add a new directory named `fleet`. In that directory, copy the .env and `docker-compose.yaml` files hosted here: `https://github.com/ PacktPublishing/Practical-Threat-Detection-Engineering/tree/ main/Chapter%203/Lab%20build/fleet`.

    Our project's directory structure should now match the one shown in *Figure 3.12*:

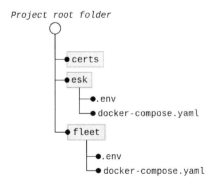

Figure 3.12 – Project folder structure with Fleet

2.   Before we use docker-compose to launch this stack, we need to modify the `.env` file. Specifically, we need to add the service token that Fleet will use to connect to the rest of the stack.

     To get that service token, we can navigate to the Fleet administration page from the Kibana frontend.

3.   Start by logging in to your Elastic Stack (via `https://[ip address of your docker host]:5601`). Then, click the hamburger menu in the top-left corner of the page. Under the **Management** section (near the bottom), click **Fleet**. After navigating there, you will be presented with the screen shown in *Figure 3.13*, which walks us through setting up Fleet Server. For the Fleet Server host field, use `https://[ip address of your docker host]:8220`:

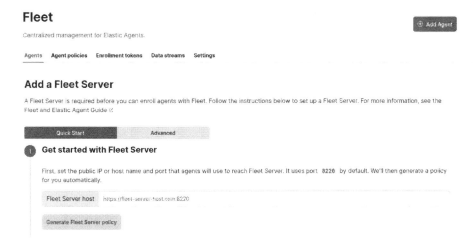

Figure 3.13 – Fleet Server configuration screen (step 1)

4.   Select **Generate Fleet Server policy**. As shown in *Figure 3.14*, a sequence of commands for installing Fleet on a centralized host will be provided:

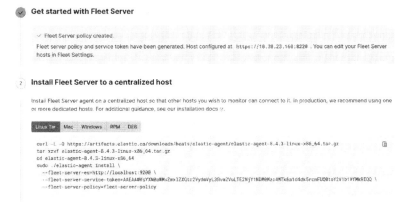

Figure 3.14 – Fleet Server configuration screen (step 2)

5. In our case, we only need the value of `fleet-server-service-token`. Copy this value from that web page and paste it into the `.env` file in the `fleet` subdirectory.

6. You can now start the Fleet container using the `sudo docker compose up -d` command. Shortly after, you should see confirmation that this Fleet Server was successfully connected, as seen in *Figure 3.15*:

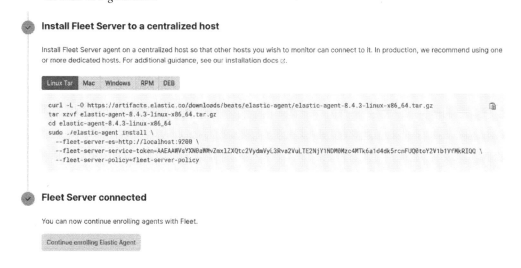

Figure 3.15 – Fleet Server configuration screen (step 3)

With that, Fleet has been configured. Next, we'll perform some additional configurations that are required for full functionality.

Additional configurations for Fleet Server

By default, the Fleet Server policy is configured to send output to the Elastic host (`http://localhost:9200`). Hosts that we later connect to our Fleet Server may not be able to reach the Elasticsearch backend using that address. Therefore, we need to change the default output so that telemetry from additional hosts gets stored in Elasticsearch.

From the **Settings** tab, select the pencil icon next to the default output. An edit window similar to the one shown in *Figure 3.16* will be displayed. For the **Hosts** section, enter `https://[ip address of docker host]:9200`. For **Advanced YAML configuration**, enter `ssl.verification_mode: none`:

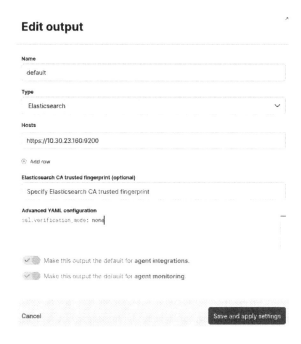

Figure 3.16 – Fleet output configuration

Finally, click **Save and apply settings**. With that, your Elastic Stack has been configured with Fleet so that you can manage Elastic Agent simply.

Adding a host to the lab

For our detection lab, we will deploy a single Microsoft Windows client workstation and install Elastic Agent, which will allow us to monitor security events in Kibana.

Requirements

To get started, we will need the following:

- **Virtualization software**: There are many options available, but the most popular desktop systems are VirtualBox and VMware. If you have access to and prefer using other software, such as ESXi or Hyper-V, these are also reasonable options. Regardless of the software you choose, ensure it is deployed on a host that has connectivity to your Elastic Stack. We will show detailed instructions for setting up the Windows 10 VM on VirtualBox, but the process will be similar to other virtualization packages. VirtualBox is available for multiple operating systems as a single installer file, which simplifies the installation process. You can download VirtualBox here: https://www.virtualbox.org/wiki/Downloads.

- **Windows installation media**: This is distributed as a `.iso` file, which we can use with our virtualization software. You can download the Windows 10 installation `.iso` file from here: `https://www.microsoft.com/en-us/evalcenter/evaluate-windows-10-enterprise`.

VM setup

Let's look at the VM setup:

1. To start, install VirtualBox. Obtain the installation package from the VirtualBox site here: `https://www.virtualbox.org/wiki/Downloads`.

2. Execute the installer and follow the on-screen instructions to complete the installation.

3. Our Windows 10 VM will be configured with the following resources:

   - At least 2 GB of RAM, though 4 GB or more is recommended

   - ˙ At least 60 GB of disk space

4. Open Oracle VirtualBox. Then, from the main VirtualBox interface, click the **New** icon. You will be prompted to enter some details for the VM. *Figure 3.17* and *Figure 3.18* show the settings to be used in the first two VM creation steps:

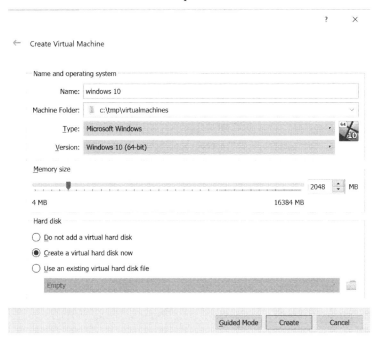

Figure 3.17 – The Create Virtual Machine area in VirtualBox

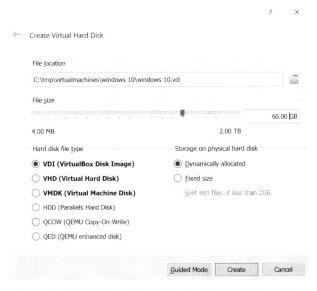

Figure 3.18 – The Create Virtual Hard Disk area in VirtualBox

5. After clicking **Create**, you will see your newly created VM in the listing on the left-hand side of the VirtualBox window. We need to configure this VM to use the Windows 10 installation ISO file. Select the newly created VM and click **Settings** above the VM information.

6. From the **Settings** window (shown in *Figure 3.19*), select **Storage**, then click on the virtualized optical drive. Under the **Attributes** section, click on the CD icon and select **Choose a disk file…**:

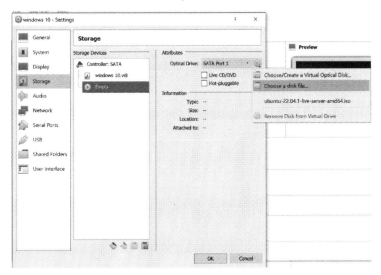

Figure 3.19 – VM settings in VirtualBox

7. A file navigation window will appear. From that window, browse to your downloaded Windows 10 ISO file, then click **Open**.

8. Click **OK** to accept the changes and return to the VirtualBox main window.

9. With that, the VirtualBox VM has been configured and is ready to be launched for the first time. Click **Start** from the main VirtualBox window.

10. Once the VM starts, follow the on-screen instructions to install Windows 10. To get started, click **Install now**.

11. Read and accept the license terms.

12. Then, click **Custom: Install Windows only (advanced)**.

13. Select the disk we created.

14. The installation process will reboot the VM. Once it restarts, you will be prompted for some basic information to complete the installation.

15. You will then be prompted to create a user account. Ensure you use a username and password that you can remember.

Congratulations! You now have a Windows 10 client installed for use in our detection lab. The next step is to install Elastic Agent so that our Windows 10 client can forward events.

Installing Elastic Agent

We can set up Elastic Agent via the Elastic Stack UI by performing the following steps:

1. Log in to our Elastic Stack.

2. Navigate to Fleet from the **Management** section of the navigation menu.

3. We can connect this host to our Elastic Stack by clicking **Add agent** from the **Agents** screen, shown in *Figure 3.20*. For the first prompt, enter `Windows policy`. This will create a policy that the new agent will be assigned to:

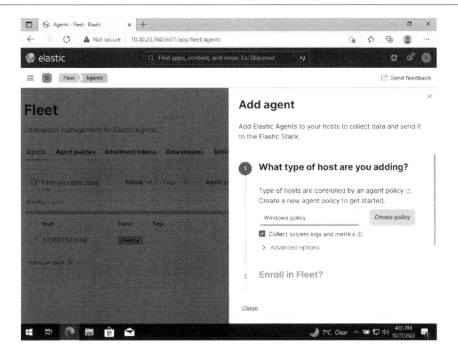

Figure 3.20 – Add agent

4. For *Step 2*, leave the default option, **Enroll in Fleet (recommended)**, selected.

5. *Step 3*, shown in *Figure 3.21*, provides the installation script for multiple environments. Since we are enrolling a Windows workstation, we will click on the **Windows** tab and click the clipboard icon at the top right to copy the inner text:

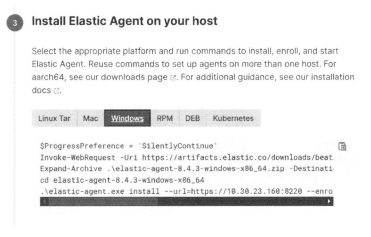

Figure 3.21 – Elastic Agent install script

This script is used to silently download the agent installer ZIP, unzip the archive, and execute it with the appropriate command-line flags. For the agents to work in our environment, we need to make one modification to this installation script. First, let's take a look at the individual commands issued in this installation script. The following table explains these commands:

Command	Description
`$ProgressPreference = 'SilentlyContinue'`	Suppresses the PowerShell progress bar.
`Invoke-WebRequest -Uri https://artifacts.elastic.co/ downloads/beats/elastic-agent/ elastic-agent-<<VERSION>>- windows-x86_64.zip -OutFile elastic-agent-8.4.3- windows-x86_64.zip`	Downloads the Elastic Agent installation files from `elastic.co` to the current working directory.
`Expand-Archive .\elastic-agent- <<VERSION>>-windows-x86_64.zip -DestinationPath .`	Extracts the contents of the Elastic Agent installation files to the current directory, indicated by the `.` shorthand. This command will create a new directory that contains the Elastic Agent installation files.
`cd elastic-agent-<<VERSION>>- windows-x86_64`	Changes the working directory to the newly created Elastic Agent directory to where the installation files were extracted.
`.\elastic-agent.exe install --url=https://10.30.23.160:8220 --enrollment-token=<<ENROLLMENT TOKEN>>`	The Elastic Agent installation command is automatically generated using the URL that was configured for your Fleet Server, as well as your enrollment token for the selected policy. For our lab, since our configurations are not to production standards, we need to append `--insecure` to the end of this command for our agents to connect.

Table 3.1 – Elastic Agent installation commands

6. After updating the script to include the insecure flag, switch to the Windows VM where you want to install the agent. Since this script downloads files, we suggest changing your working directory to the current user's Downloads directory before execution. To get started, launch a new administrative PowerShell window. You can do this by clicking the Windows icon in

the lower left-hand corner of the screen, then searching for `PowerShell`. Hover over the **Windows PowerShell** result, then select **Run as administrator**.

7. Once the PowerShell window opens, change the working directory to your user's Downloads directory by issuing the `cd $env:USERPROFILE\Downloads` command.

8. From there, issue the Elastic Agent installation commands you obtained from your Elastic Stack. For the last command, ensure the `--insecure` parameter is appended.

    A message stating **Elastic Agent has been successfully installed** will be displayed once there are no installation errors.

    Following its successful installation, you should see a confirmation message similar to the one shown in *Figure 3.22*. You should be able to see your host in the list of Fleet agents:

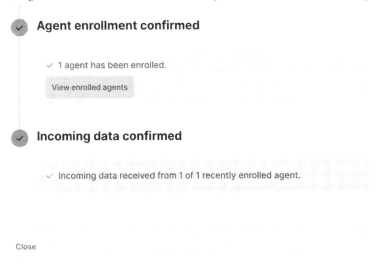

Figure 3.22 – Agent enrollment confirmed

9. Your newly enrolled host will appear in the list of agents. Elastic Agent can be installed on many different operating systems, and this installation process can be repeated for any additional hosts you want to enroll in the Elastic Stack. We encourage adding additional hosts if you have resources available.

10. At this point, you are probably wondering what type of data is being sent back to the Elasticsearch backend. You can view this data by navigating to the **Discover** page, under **Analytics** in the hamburger menu. This should bring you to a page similar to the one shown in *Figure 3.23*:

Figure 3.23 – The Discover view in the Elastic Stack

Elastic is now configured to receive logs from our Windows host. Next, we will look at how we can adjust the configuration of a connected agent to provide better logs.

Elastic Agent policies

Fleet and Elastic Agent allow us to centrally control the type of data being sent from our connected agents using *agent policies*. To view these, click on **Agent policies** via the **Fleet management** page. You should see two policies listed, one auto-generated Fleet policy and the one that was created earlier while we were enrolling our first Windows host, as shown in *Figure 3.24*:

Figure 3.24 – Elastic Agent policies

Each policy can have several *integrations* added to it, which control the type of data being collected. Click on **Windows policy**; you will see that a single *System* integration has been added. To view the configurable details of this integration, click on the name of the integration; you should see a window that looks similar to the one shown in *Figure 3.25*:

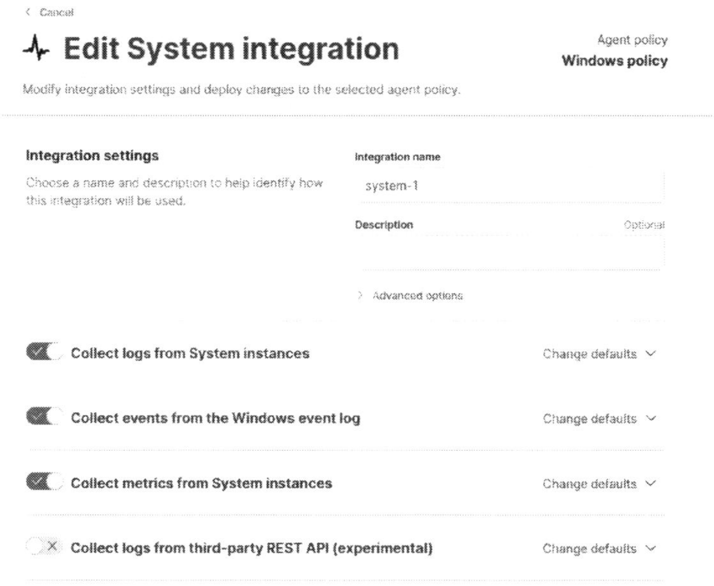

Figure 3.25 – Edit System integration

If this integration hasn't been configured to collect Windows event logs, click **Collect events from the Windows event log**. Clicking on **Change defaults** shows us some more configurable options for each type of data being collected. We can see that this integration is currently configured to collect data from the **Application**, **Security**, and **System** event logs, as shown in *Figure 3.26*:

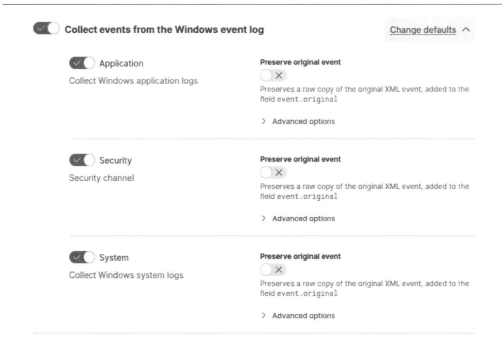

Figure 3.26 – Windows event log collection settings

With that, we have a DE lab deployed that includes the Elastic Stack, Fleet Server, and a single Windows host. Next, we will test the data flow and detection capabilities of the Elastic Stack by building our first detection.

Building your first detection

Detections monitor data stores for specified patterns and then take some action when a pattern match occurs. These actions can be anything from adding data to a queue to triggering an alert that sends a message to a defined audience. To see some of this in action, in this section, we will walk through the process of creating a very simple detection, or *rule*, for failed login attempts that rise over a specified threshold.

It's important to emphasize that this is not a very good detection for reasons we will elaborate on in later chapters, but it will give you an understanding of the general mechanics of detections:

1. First, log in to your Elastic Stack and click the hamburger icon from the top-left corner. Then, navigate to **Manage** under the **Security** section. From there, click on **Rules**. This will take us to the **Create new rule** page.

2. Click **Threshold**, leave the default sources as is, then enter `event.code: 4625 AND winlog.channel: "Security"` in the **Custom query** section.

3. For **Threshold**, enter a value of 4. Click **Continue** once these values have been filled in and match what's shown in *Figure 3.27*:

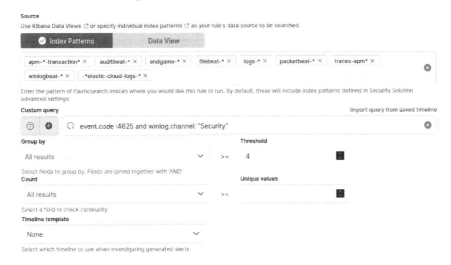

Figure 3.27 – New rule configuration

4. For the **About rule** section, enter `failed logon threshold met` under **Name** and add a **description**. Leave the **Default severity** and **Default risk score** values as is. Click **Continue** once these values have been filled in and match what's shown in *Figure 3.28*:

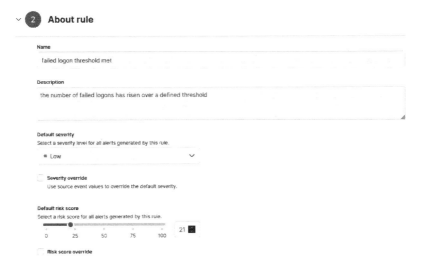

Figure 3.28 – New rule details

5. For the **Schedule rule** section, enter 10 for **Runs every** and 5 for **Additional look-back time**. This means the rule will check the data store every 10 minutes, and at those times, the scope of events for review will be everything recorded 15 minutes before. This is because the time range for search is the rule interval plus the additional look-back time.

6. For **Rule actions**, leave the default value of **Perform no actions** as is, then click **Create and Enable Rule**.

7. With our newly created rule in place, we can run a simple test to ensure the rule operates as expected. In this case, our rule checks for events that have the event.code attribute set to 4625 and the winlog.channel attribute set to security, both of which were recorded in the last 15 minutes. If the number of events rises to 4 or higher, an alert will be recorded. Windows events with event.code = 4625 and winlog.channel= security refer to Windows Security event logs indicating a logon failure. To test this, we can go to our Windows virtual host and log off if we're already logged in, or lock the session.

8. At that point, we can try logging in with an incorrect password four times. This will generate the data necessary to trigger our detection. If successful, we will see a generated alert, similar to what's shown in *Figure 3.29*:

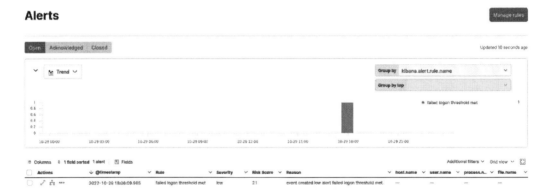

Figure 3.29 – Successful detection result

And with that, we have a fully functioning detection lab!

Additional resources

In this chapter, we demonstrated how to build a detection lab from scratch using the Elastic Stack, Fleet, and Windows hosts, which will allow you to customize it to your needs as well as better understand the underlying technology concepts. However, many open source projects have attempted to provide simplified deployments of entire lab infrastructure, as well as other log aggregation technologies outside of the Elastic Stack. The following list provides some projects to look into if you want to explore other options. The rest of this book's labs will add to this chapter's lab, though:

- DetectionLab (`https://detectionlab.network/`, no longer maintained)

- The Hunting ELK (`https://thehelk.com/intro.html`)

- Matano (`https://github.com/matanolabs/matano`)

- Wazuh (`https://wazuh.com/`)

You can use these projects if you want to automate parts of deploying a DE environment.

Summary

In this chapter, we built out the lab infrastructure that will be leveraged in the rest of the lab exercises within this book. We did this by leveraging Docker to deploy containers. Our lab includes the Elastic Stack, Fleet Server, and a single Windows host.

In *Chapter 4*, we will dive into the data sources we can use to build detection, such as application or endpoint logs. We'll discuss how to identify valuable data sources and add those data sources to the lab.

Part 2:
Detection Creation

Part 2 dives into more technical aspects of detection engineering, focusing on the creation of detections. First, we'll understand the importance of data sources, how to identify relevant data sources, and the challenges you may face. We'll then discuss how we can create, investigate, and triage detection requirements. With an understanding of the early steps of the detection engineering life cycle, we can move on to learning how to develop detections for both static and behavior indicators. To wrap up this part, you'll learn more about the procedural side of things, including how to document detections and automate the development and deployment process.

This section has the following chapters:

- *Chapter 4, Detection Data Sources*
- *Chapter 5, Investigating Detection Requirements*
- *Chapter 6, Developing Detections Using Indicators of Compromise*
- *Chapter 7, Developing Detections Using Behavioral Indicators*
- *Chapter 8, Documentation and Detection Pipelines*

4
Detection Data Sources

In the previous chapter, we built out a detection engineering test lab that will be leveraged for the labs throughout the rest of this book, as well as any testing you want to perform yourself. This lab environment included the Elastic Stack, Fleet Server, and a single Windows host. In this chapter, we will discuss the different data sources that can be leveraged as part of detection engineering. Furthermore, we will provide optional labs that will allow you to expand your lab environment so that you can include some of these additional sources if you want to test them and have the resources available.

The data sources we consume for detection engineering help determine our ability to provide widespread detection coverage for an organization. Without network data, we can't develop network-based signatures, potentially missing web-based threats or C2 communication. Without application data, we might not be able to identify malicious activity taking place within a specific application. Simply put, an increase in the quantity and quality of the data sources we have available to us will provide us with more detection opportunities.

We will cover the following main topics in this chapter:

- Understanding data sources and telemetry
- Looking at data source issues and challenges
- Adding data sources

The first section will help us understand, at a high level, what data sources are and the type of data sources available. At this point, you should be able to identify the data sources relevant to your use cases. We'll then discuss certain issues and challenges to consider when defining and configuring your data sources, allowing you to look at your data sources and identify the impact of such issues. Finally, we'll wrap up by adding a new data source to our lab and creating a detection that would not have been possible without that additional telemetry.

Technical requirements

The labs in this chapter assume you have completed the lab setup in *Chapter 3*; these labs will expand on the existing Elastic Stack deployment. If you have not set up the detection lab, we recommend returning to *Chapter 3* and completing the exercises provided there first.

In this chapter, we will deploy a web server running on a Linux VM. The VM will require the following specs:

- 10 GB of hard disk space
- 2 GB of RAM

The labs in this chapter will not use the existing Windows host, so it can be powered off to save resources during this chapter's labs.

Understanding data sources and telemetry

Covering all potential data sources in a corporate environment or even going into depth on each of the major ones is not feasible given the number of data sources present in an organization's infrastructure. As such, this section will highlight the major data sources and provide a brief explanation of their relevance to detection engineering.

We are going to look at two different types of sources of data for detection engineering. The first is going to be raw telemetry. These are unprocessed logs that simply state an event occurred, without a determination on whether it is malicious or not. This is going to be our focus with detection engineering as we can use these raw events to identify malicious activity without relying on an existing security solution's detection capabilities. The second type of data source that we'll briefly discuss is security tooling. Data from security tooling primarily focuses on processed events but can also include its own raw telemetry data.

Raw telemetry

As mentioned previously, we are using the term raw telemetry to describe unprocessed logs produced by systems and applications. The data source will generate logs containing events with no context regarding whether they may be malicious.

This section will look at the various data sources that fall under the category of raw telemetry, the type of data they provide, and examples of detection designs that leverage those sources.

Endpoints and servers

Endpoints and servers are likely the first resources that come to mind when you think about the components of an organization's infrastructure – rightly so as they typically make up a large majority of the organization's assets and are vulnerable to users' risky behaviors.

Endpoints and servers generate logs detailing activities occurring on the host. This includes important events such as user logins and administrative activities (such as configuration changes or user creations). In this section, we won't differentiate servers from endpoints in terms of the logging details as they both provide similar or the same types of logs. Where the difference comes into place is determining detection requirements. For example, you might want to prioritize detections for suspicious activity on a domain controller over an individual's workstation as the risk to the organization is higher if the domain controller is compromised.

Unfortunately, every operating system has its methods of logging, so we have to consider what OS our endpoints and servers are running. The log locations and types of logs available will vary between the different operating systems. For example, Windows provides its logs via Windows Event Logs. Logs are divided into several different categories and custom logs can even be created. In *Chapter 3*, we added a Windows host and enabled log forwarding via Fleet to bring in application, system, and security logs. These are by far the most relevant logs to ingest. If you have enabled PowerShell Script Block Logging in your environment, we recommend you also turn on log forwarding for those events. Similarly, if you have deployed Sysmon in your environment, those logs should also be forwarded.

The following tables provide the potential log sources by operating system type. It is worth noting that these are not comprehensive lists and that there may be additional logs that will provide value to your use case, but these provide the highest value across all organizations.

Windows

Windows has robust logging features, some enabled by default, others requiring enabling. These events are stored as Windows Event Logs, which are divided into a few sub-categories. *Table 4.1* provides descriptions and examples of the events that are stored in each of these logs:

Event Log Type	Description	Example
Application log	Events generated at the application level. Logs may vary as they depend on developer configurations.	The application crashed due to memory exhaustion An error occurred while starting an application
System log	Events generated at the operating system level related to system operations.	A service was started
Security log	Events generated at the operating system level related to potential security risks.	User account creation

PowerShell log	Any events related to the PowerShell engine (the program), providers, and commands.	PowerShell application started
Sysmon log	Any events generated by the Sysmon service.	Process creation

Table 4.1 – Windows event log types

Note that PowerShell event logs only include full command lines if PowerShell Script Block Logging is enabled. It is disabled by default and must be enabled via a Group Policy Object or the Registry. Without these command lines, we lack the most important context surrounding PowerShell execution. Knowing an attacker executed PowerShell provides little value if we don't know what they used it to do.

It is also important to note that Sysmon is not installed on Windows by default but provides highly valuable data. Sysmon logs include those for process creation (including hashes and command-line details), network connections, and filesystem changes, all of which are either not logged or logged with a minimal context in the default Windows Event Logs. This context can be the difference between knowing that an attacker used a known malware payload to exfiltrate data to a remote server versus knowing an attacker executed an unknown file with an unknown purpose. We recommend that you consider deploying Sysmon in your environment and collect the logs, if possible. To learn more about Sysmon, see https://learn.microsoft.com/en-us/sysinternals/downloads/sysmon. Sysmon is also available for Linux but as it is not as widely used on Linux systems, it will be left out of the next section about Linux sources.

Linux

Linux logs are stored in system files under the /var/log directory. A few logs of relevance exist, as outlined in *Table 4.2*. In some cases, the name of the file differs depending on the specific Linux distribution being used or if the defaults have been changed:

Log Type	Description	Example
/var/log/syslog or /var/log/messages	All global system activity data	Startup messages
/var/log/auth.log or /var/log/secure	All security-related events	Account logins, root account actions
/var/log/cron	Information about scheduled tasks	Command execution resulting from a cron job

`/var/log/faillog`	Information about failed login attempts	Account login failure
`/var/log/audit/` `audit.log`	File modification and syscall activity based on auditd rules	A modification was made to a monitored file or a file was added to a monitored directory

Table 4.2 – Linux log types

It is worth noting that auditd's rule file must be configured by the user to specify the files and syscalls to be monitored, so you will not see those logs unless they've been configured on the system.

macOS

macOS provides a type of single, centralized log storage called macOS Unified Logs. As such, all log entries related to the system being monitored should be accessible via this source. The example detection design in the following note box, along with the others shown throughout this chapter, will show you how to take a particular detection requirement and associated data source and gather the information needed to create detection logic in plain English. This first one is going to look at using both Windows event logs and Linux logs to identify a MITRE ATT&CK technique.

> **Example detection design using an endpoint data source**
>
> Let's assume we are receiving application, system, and security logs from a Windows endpoint. As a detection requirement, we want to know if any non-admin users are creating additional user accounts. This could be a sign of a threat actor establishing persistence via user account creation (MITRE ATT&CK Technique T1136). Researching what evidence exists for Windows account creation reveals that Windows Security Event ID 4720 is used to log account creation events for both local and domain users. So, in plain English, our detection design is "If there is a Windows Security event with event ID 4720, and the *subject username* associated with the event is not an administrator, trigger a detection."
>
> Let's assume you also have a Linux host in the same environment. In that case, you want to monitor the `/var/log/auth.log` or `/var/log/secure` logs (depending on the distribution). In plain English, the detection design is "If there is a `/var/log/auth.log` event containing the `new user:` string, trigger a detection."
>
> Unfortunately, the `auth.log` file does not record which user initiated the event, so we will have to rely on an analyst review to determine whether it was legitimate account creation activity or not.

Network data

Network telemetry can be gathered from numerous data sources and provides highly valuable context. It is going to be unlikely that an incident is 100% isolated to a single local host. There are multiple points in the kill chain during which we are likely to see network activity. For example, a drive-by download will result in web traffic during the initial access stage, the C2 communication will leverage the attacker's chosen C2 protocol, and lateral movement can be seen between devices on the network. As such, solely relying on endpoint logs instead of covering both planes will result in a huge coverage gap.

In terms of how and from where we can gather network data, we have a few options. The first is that we can leverage packet captures from the endpoints themselves. All network traffic is captured and forwarded to the data storage system. These packet captures will provide full details and the content of any network connections. For this, we need to configure endpoints to capture traffic and export the packet captures with a packet capture solution. One such option is Packetbeat, which we will test in an upcoming lab using our lab's Windows host. It is worth noting that packet captures take up a significant amount of storage space, and thus most organizations do not perform network-wide, constant full-packet captures.

The second method of gathering network data is from the network devices themselves. There are a few different device types that can be mined for network data. Networking infrastructure devices, such as routers and switches, can provide some relevant network data in an unprocessed, raw form. It would not be our first recommendation for a network data source but in the absence of more advanced and comprehensive data (such as from a perimeter firewall), it can provide some coverage. Most routers and similar devices have a web portal you can access to administer the device and set up shipping logs via Syslog to a server. Many of these devices may collect flow data, which is essentially metadata about network connections providing details of the source and destination IPs and ports, as well as the traffic size. If the devices support flow data, a flow collector can be used to obtain this data. It may be useful in identifying C2 traffic (abnormal or known-abused ports, for example) or exfiltration attempts (abnormally large amounts of data leaving the network).

As a related data source, firewalls and other network security solutions will have some subset of logs that are events rather than alerts and may provide context worth including in your detection engineering lab. This data source, however, also falls under the *security tooling* type of data source rather than raw telemetry since these devices often implement some sort of processing to enrich or morph the events. For example, a firewall may have traffic logs that are essentially raw telemetry, detailing the source and destination properties of a connection. That same firewall might also have NGFW capabilities and have a log for URL filtering that provides context as to which websites were blocked and why. In the latter case, we are looking more at security tooling data rather than raw telemetry as the NGFW's detections are what generate events.

Example detection design using a network data source

Let's assume we are receiving traffic logs from a firewall device on the network perimeter. As a detection requirement, we want to know if a single source IP is exhibiting repeated failed connections to various destination ports. This could be a sign of a port scan against a host (MITRE ATT&CK Technique T1046). The firewall logs should tell us the source and destination port and IP address, as well as if the connection failed or was successful. So, in plain English, our detection design is "If the firewall is logging a significant number of failed connections with a shared source IP but unique destination ports, trigger a detection."

Cloud assets

The reason we decided to highlight cloud assets as a data source category in this book is due to the growing nature of the cloud. It's highly likely that, as a detection engineer, at some point in your career, you will identify a detection requirement relating to a cloud asset or environment. The cloud is extremely complex in terms of the number of services and resources you'll find available, as well as the variation that occurs between different cloud vendors (that is, AWS versus Azure versus GCP, and so on).

Attackers are more frequently targeting the cloud as its use is widespread but not well understood, so it is often trivial to find misconfigured, vulnerable cloud resources that are publicly accessible. MITRE has even mapped their Enterprise ATT&CK matrix to the cloud: `https://attack.mitre.org/matrices/enterprise/cloud/`. The matrix includes many techniques that overlap with those seen in traditional, on-premises environments. This is because a lot of cloud resources are simply cloud-hosted versions of existing technologies. There are, however, some cloud-specific techniques that have been added to the ATT&CK framework. Regardless of how your organization leverages the cloud, it is important that the detection engineering team is aware of the existence of any cloud assets and understands how they can be used as a data source.

Example detection design using a cloud asset data source

Let's assume we are receiving CloudTrail logs from an AWS account that hosts several VMs used by the organization. CloudTrail records all API and user activities for all services in your AWS account. As a detection requirement, we want to know if an unauthorized user accesses an S3 storage bucket called *sensitive-data*. This could be an indicator of MITRE Technique T1619, Cloud Storage Object Discovery. Research shows that when users are inspecting the contents of a bucket, a ListBuckets API call is recorded in the CloudTrail logs. So, in plain English, our detection design is "If there is a CloudTrail event for a ListBuckets API call to the *sensitive-data* S3 bucket, and the user associated with the event is not authorized to view that bucket, trigger a detection."

Applications

Application logs can vary greatly as they are defined by the developer of the application rather than the operating system itself. Some of the common sources of application logs are mail, web, and database servers. While they may be running on a Linux or Windows server and have the associated OS logs, they'll also have logs specific to the application running on the server. The types of logs will depend on the specific application, but the following is a list of log and event types you may observe:

- Access, authentication, and authorization logs (who logged in/out and when, whether it was a successful login attempt, and what operations were performed)

- Change logs (what configuration changes were made, what users or permissions were added, when the software was last updated)

- Error logs (any errors that occurred during application execution, such as disk space limits, memory exhaustion, and licensing issues)

- Availability logs (system shutdowns and reboots, failover occurrences, backups complete)

From this list, the most valuable to detection engineers are the access, authentication, and authorization logs and the change logs. Error and availability logs may provide some insight for incident investigations but in terms of developing detections, they will provide less value.

Example detection design using an application data source

Let's assume we are receiving logs from an Apache web server. As a detection requirement, we want to know if any SQL injections are being performed against our server. One of the many methods for performing SQL injections involves inserting SQL statements into the URL parameters followed. The results of submitting this request may allow the attacker to reveal information from the backend database. An example of a known string placed in URLs for attempting SQL injection is `or 1=1#`. This might be indicative of an attacker trying to gain access to the environment via SQL injection (T1190), so we need to detect such strings present in web traffic. In plain English, our detection design is "If there is an Apache HTTP access log with a GET event that has a URL containing the `or 1=1#` string, trigger a detection."

Under the category of applications, there are also **Software-as-a-Service** (**SaaS**) data sources. These are going to provide similar data as other application sources but are not hosted on your infrastructure and, as such, may require further exploration to understand what data is available and how it can be retrieved. SaaS can refer to any cloud-hosted application or software leveraged by the organization; however, the most prevalent use of SaaS in organizations is application suites such as Google Workspace and Office365, which provide email and productivity tools.

Example detection design using a SaaS data source

Let's assume we use Google Workspace as our SaaS provider for email and productivity tools and are receiving audit logs from the account. As a detection requirement, we want to know if admin privileges are granted to any additional users. While this could be legitimate admin activity, it could also be a sign that the attacker is trying to get an account they need to perform additional actions or maintain persistence (T1098). Research shows that such activity is recorded as a `GRANT_DELEGATED_ADMIN_PRIVILEGES` or `GRANT_ADMIN_PRIVILEGE` event for the `admin.googleapis.com` service within the Google Workspace admin audit logs.

So, in plain English, our detection design is "If there is a Google Workspace admin audit log event for the `admin.googleapis.com` service with an event name of `GRANT_DELEGATED_ADMIN_PRIVILEGES` or `GRANT_ADMIN_PRIVILEGE`, and it was initiated by a user who should not be creating accounts, trigger a detection."

Raw telemetry provides the most valuable data for detection engineers, but there are uses for logs that are directly generated by security tooling, as we will discuss next.

Security tooling

While we will not heavily discuss the use of security tooling data for detection engineering in this book, it is important to understand what data could be available to you via these sources as they might prove useful for your specific detection requirements. Security tools leverage their proprietary detections within their tool, which is why they may not be as relevant for creating new detections. The alerts from security tooling are often based on the same raw telemetry we discussed in the previous sections, resulting in potential overlap in information. Furthermore, we have to be aware of how multiple security tools may alert on the same behavior, just in different ways. For this reason, you need to be aware of the effect that writing a detection based on this data source may have in terms of generating duplicates. Security tool alerts, however, should not be completely ignored by detection engineers as they can prove useful in gap analysis and identifying attack chains.

The key data sources we are going to touch on in this section are **endpoint protection** and **network protection**, with a brief mention of **security information and event management** (**SIEM**) technologies.

Endpoint protection

Endpoint protection, as the name implies, involves detecting and/or preventing malware on user endpoints. The most common types of endpoint protection are **antivirus** (**AV**) and **endpoint detection and response** (**EDR**). These solutions use a variety of tactics to detect suspicious and malicious activity. While we don't know the exact code running on the backend to perform detections, the most common methods include indicator-based (a known bad IP address) and behavior-based (abnormal activity). Furthermore, more and more companies are adopting solutions that have some component of **machine learning** (**ML**) that will assist in computationally determining what is potentially malicious. One way you might use an endpoint protection data source for detection engineering is by generating alerts on a series of techniques being used or an increase in activity of a certain kind. For example, if an alert for an attachment on an email is followed by malware execution on an endpoint, that might be worth providing a detection for as it implies the kill chain of an attack is continuing instead of being blocked by the endpoint protection.

Network protection

Next, we have network protection. We've already discussed raw telemetry from endpoint and network devices; similarly, tools for endpoint and network security contain vastly different but equally important data sources. In terms of the types of devices we might see in our network, email security appliances and firewalls are probably the most common. Email security appliances provide some level of alerting to malicious email activity, such as detecting known malicious files or URLs observed in emails traversing the network. Firewalls, depending on their capabilities, might provide security alerts such as communication with known bad domains/IPs, abnormal traffic, and malicious files being downloaded.

Along with the vendor-provided devices that you might deploy in your network, there are popular open source options worth mentioning. Zeek and Suricata are open source network security tools that act as network security monitors and/or intrusion detection and prevention systems. Like commercial solutions, they provide alerts based on traffic analysis and threat signatures. Along with built-in rules, users can create their own rules, making it particularly interesting to detection engineers. While using these tools is outside the scope of this book, there are plenty of resources online that can help you learn to leverage them.

Security information and event management (SIEM)

Lastly, we have SIEM systems. These themselves are log aggregators that provide additional enrichment and context, ultimately providing security analysts with a single pane of glass related to what is happening in their environment. Less value will be provided from this concerning detection engineering since it, in theory, is ingesting the same data sources as us. Where it does provide value is if you cannot get access to specific data sources the SIEM already ingests. We can simply forward those events from the SIEM instead of the originating device. Secondarily, if the SIEM is providing any sort of enrichment or correlation that could be leveraged for detection development, it might be worth including as a data source.

Given this high-level overview of possible data sources, we can look further into the approach MITRE ATT&CK has taken to document this information.

MITRE ATT&CK data sources

In *Chapter 1*, we introduced the MITRE ATT&CK framework, specifically the **tactics, techniques, and procedures** (**TTPs**) that they document. There are, however, a couple of other knowledge bases provided by MITRE that tie additional security information and intel to the TTPs. One of these knowledge bases documents data sources that can be leveraged to identify these TTPs. Data sources, from MITRE's perspective, are the categories of information that can be gathered from sensors or logs. MITRE has also mapped its data sources to the ATT&CK techniques they can be used to detect.

Our first example of a detection design in the previous section was for creating new user accounts, which could indicate persistence being established. We associated that technique with MITRE ATT&CK Technique T1136. Looking at the MITRE ATT&CK data sources, we can see that a data source exists for User Account Creation (`https://attack.mitre.org/datasources/DS0002/#User%20 Account%20Creation`). It says that account creation can be detected via event `ID 4720` on Windows or `/etc/passwd logs` on Linux. This is the guidance we needed to create the detection design, provided right alongside the technique we used to develop the detection requirement.

We are not going to look at the data sources provided by MITRE in depth; the full knowledge base can be accessed here: `https://attack.mitre.org/datasources/`. It is worth mentioning this framework briefly as it can be used to map detection requirements for data sources, especially if you are leveraging ATT&CK to plan your detection requirements.

Now that you know what data sources may be available to the detection engineering team, let's work through an exercise that will help you think about how these data sources apply to your environment.

Identifying your data sources

The following list will help you identify which data sources you have available, and which should be prioritized so that they can be integrated into your detection engineering infrastructure. If you are working for an organization in which you are aware of the infrastructure, we suggest that you go through this list and identify what your organization's data sources look like. In future chapters, understanding your data sources will help you understand the detections that are possible and relevant for your organization:

- Assets:
  - User endpoints (laptops, desktop computers, mobile devices)
  - Servers:
    - Are any of these servers public facing?
    - What type of servers are they? Domain controllers, web servers, file servers, and so on.
- Software:
  - Operating systems are running on the various assets
  - Software/applications used throughout the organization
- Network architecture diagram
- Cloud assets:
  - SaaS applications

- Security solutions:

  - SIEM

  - Endpoint protection (AV/EDR)

  - Network protection (IPS/firewall/WAF)

To show what this might look like in a corporate environment, look at the following list as an example of identifying data sources at a high level:

- Assets:

  - Each employee is issued a laptop computer and cell phone. Our local office each has several desktops that are used when assisting customers.

  - We have three servers in a co-located data center. This includes a domain controller, internal file servers, and a public-facing web server.

- Software:

  - All laptops are running Windows 10. All mobile devices are running iOS. The servers are running Windows Server 2016.

  - Atlassian Jira and Confluence are used by employees. Salesforce is used by our sales team. The help desk uses TeamViewer to connect to endpoints remotely for troubleshooting.

- Cloud assets:

  - We leverage Microsoft 365 as our SaaS provider for email and productivity tools

  - We have a development team that uses AWS for various projects, primarily for running virtual machines in the cloud

- Security solutions:

  - We use Splunk as our SIEM.

  - We deploy Sophos to all user endpoints, as well as their cell phones.

  - We have a Palo Alto next-generation firewall protecting the network. Additionally, we have an F5 web application firewall in front of our web server.

All these resources will result in logs being produced, which will become the data sources for our detection development. Using the list of resources identified in your organization, you can start to identify the relevant data sources. For example, there are no Linux hosts in the example organization's list of data sources, so they should focus on detections related to Windows hosts, as time spent on Linux detections would be fruitless. If an email-related threat needs to be protected against, we can see that Microsoft 365 is used for email in this example – this guides us to where we can detect such threats.

Ensure that you can forward logs from the identified devices. If the device is managed by a vendor or another team in the organization that will not support exporting logs, it should not be included as a potential data source.

In terms of prioritizing data sources, this should be guided by the same methods that will be discussed as part of the requirements discovery process, which we will dive into in *Chapter 5*. Essentially, your data sources prioritization will be based on your detection requirements. So, for now, we'll gather the list of possible data sources, and then, as detection requirements are determined, we'll add any data sources that were not included in our initial data lab configuration based on our needs. This will also help ensure we're not consuming compute resources and storage on logs that aren't even leveraged in any of our detections.

The other advantage of having this clear list of available data sources from the start is that you can avoid wasting time planning detections that you don't have the data available for. For example, if you don't have any public-facing applications, you shouldn't be writing detection rules for attacks that attempt to exploit such applications.

Now that we know what a data source is and which are relevant, the next section will cover the issues and challenges that you may encounter when attempting to implement them in your detection lab or organization.

Looking at data source issues and challenges

Unfortunately, a lot of variabilities are involved in what data sources will be available and the quality of those data sources. We'll touch on several of the causes of such variability and the challenges they present in the following subsections.

Completeness

The completeness of the data provided by a data source is based on the value of the attributes captured for any given event. We do not want to waste storage resources and bandwidth on data sources that won't add value to our investigation due to the data they expose. For example, if a system provides logs showing a network connection was established but there are no details on the source/destination of the connection with contextless timestamps and ambiguous time zones, there is likely not much that can be used from that to develop a quality detection. As such, we either ignore or de-prioritize this data source.

As an additional note regarding completeness, some data sources provide varying amounts of information based on logging configurations. There are countless ways to configure Windows, Linux, and macOS logging to capture additional or less information. For example, in the previous section, we mentioned PowerShell Script Block Logging. It is not enabled by default, but if enabled, it can provide PowerShell commands that can be executed on the host. You should be aware of the existing policies but also keep in mind where it might be worth requesting better logging configurations.

Quality

When we discuss the quality of a data source, we want to look at a few key features. We need to ensure our data is reliable, consistent, and trustworthy. First, if we don't have high confidence in the data source itself in terms of the data it reports, we should not be using it as part of our detection development. We need to ensure that the sources we are querying are providing accurate information. If you are unsure of the value a particular data source will provide, consider that uncertainty when prioritizing data sources. It may be worth integrating the data to further investigate its value, but this should not be prioritized over a known-good, high-value data source.

Another aspect affecting the quality of data is the format it is provided in. Third-party tools, such as the Elastic Stack, which we are using in our labs, often expect data to be formatted in a specific way. You need to ensure the data you are shipping to your detection system can be understood by the platform. For example, if the destination system expects a JSON file that can be parsed and you try to send a Windows Event Log, it will not be parsed and will likely just be dropped. It's important that when identifying data sources, you also document what format the logs are in and what methods can be used to export them to your detection system.

Finally, systems can generate large volumes of rich data for every type of event that occurs. However, if the interpretation of these events is unclear, this can lead to inaccurate detections and undue delays during incident response.

Timeliness

When it comes to security, time is of the essence. Our detection platforms must alert us as soon as possible after malicious activity occurs. As such, the timeliness of receiving data is an important factor to consider when approaching the topic of data sources. One of the primary issues surrounding timeliness is that some data sources will not immediately provide data for querying. If the data source performs any post-processing that causes a delay between the activity being recorded and the processed data being available to ship to our detection system, we will potentially see a delay between the event time and the detection time. It is important to be aware of and document any time deltas that may exist between the event's occurrence and its delivery to the detection system.

Coverage

Coverage is going to tell us whether the given data sources we have identified provide the data we need for developing detections. For example, if the detection requirements state we need to detect exploit activity targeting a public-facing web server, but we aren't receiving logs from that server, then our data source coverage is causing blockers for detection development.

Another aspect of coverage is ensuring that the data sources and your data ingestion processes are resilient. This essentially means that if logging is failing for any given data source, it should either be known or there should be a fallback mechanism where needed.

If attacker activity is occurring at the same time there is a disconnect between the victim system and detection platform, we don't want to find out during an investigation when no evidence exists of activity on that system. This is even more critical if the data sources have a short retention period and your logging or detection system is responsible for *archiving* that data with an extended retention period.

Coverage is something you are going to want to revisit regularly as data sources may expand as the organization grows, so your coverage will change over time. Make sure that any teams responsible for deploying new infrastructure and applications are aware of your data source requirements so that your team can be notified when new potential data sources are created.

Exercise – understanding your data sources

If you completed the *Identifying your data sources* exercises in the previous section, you can now use what you've learned about data source issues and challenges. For this exercise, take your list of possible data sources and begin to document the various properties that will potentially affect the value of your data source. The following questions are worth answering for the sources on your list to ensure you fully understand the data source:

- What method is required to retrieve logs from the data source? API, Syslog, or something else?
- What format does the data source provide logs in?
- What timezone is the data source using for their timestamps?
- Who is the point of contact for the data source that we need logs from?
- What are the retention policies of the data source?
- Does the detection engineering team have access to retrieve logs from the source?
- What is the delay between an event occurring and it being received in the detection lab?
- Can the logging configuration be modified to improve the data being received?

Now that we know what data sources exist and what value they provide, let's learn how to integrate additional logging into our detection engineering lab.

Adding data sources

Now that we know more about the data sources available to us, let's work through a few exercises to expand the data sources in our lab. Without the visibility of the data sources we are protecting, we are unable to write detections.

Keep in mind that each data source will involve an additional virtual machine or application to generate the logs. As such, if you have a limited number of compute resources available, focus on those most relevant to your organization.

The Elastic agent simplifies the process of collecting data from different sources, depending on the type of service being hosted on an endpoint. Planning the collection of data typically starts with organizing your endpoints into logical groups, based on shared characteristics, such as operating system, location, and service being hosted. These typically align with data collection requirements. Using Fleet, we can then create policies that collect relevant data for each of these groups.

Lab – adding a web server data source

In the *Raw Telemetry - Applications* section, we mentioned web server logs being a common source used by corporate organizations. In this lab, we will consider a scenario where a web server is added to our detection environment. This first half of this lab will focus on how we can use Elastic to pull logs from a web server. This is vital as the second half of the lab will involve writing a detection for attack activity specifically targeting web servers.

By completing these labs, you should be able to identify data sources relevant to your organization and ensure you are collecting valuable telemetry.

Lab setup

As detection engineers, we need to understand the types of events that can occur on web servers and the common types of attacks targeting web servers. Those inputs can help us design requirements for data collection. At a high level, we know web servers receive requests from clients, process them, then send a response back to the client. *Figure 4.1* shows the transactional flow between web servers and clients. Understanding this request-response transaction helps us understand what data might be available for designing detections:

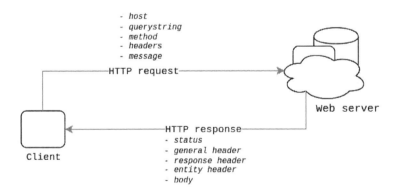

Figure 4.1 – Web server traffic overview

Now that we understand this response-request flow, let's begin setting up our lab to include this data source. We will use a small lab topology for this lab. In addition to the Elastic Stack, we will provision a single Linux virtual machine to host a web application:

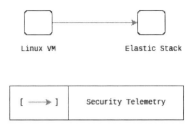

Figure 4.2 – Web server deployment

The Linux virtual machine should have 10 GB of hard disk space and 2 GB of RAM to efficiently support the application. To provide a web server that will be ripe with opportunities to play with detections, we will leverage the **Deliberately Insecure Web Application (DIWA)** project (https://github.com/snsttr/diwa).

Let's start by deploying the DIWA project to a new Linux VM:

1. Create a new Linux virtual machine with Docker installed (follow the instructions for Docker installation from *Chapter 3*, if needed).

2. Clone the DIWA repository using Git via the following command:

    ```
    git clone https://github.com/snsttr/diwa.git
    ```

3. Create a file named docker-compose.yaml one directory above the diwa folder with the following contents. This docker-compose file can also be downloaded from this book's GitHub repository at https://github.com/PacktPublishing/Practical-Threat-Detection-Engineering/blob/main/Chapter%204/docker-compose.yaml:

    ```
    version: "3.8"
    services:
      webapp:
        build:
            context: ./diwa
        ports:
            - 80:80
        volumes:
            - /var/log/apache2:/var/log/apache2
    ```

4. Start the web application using the docker compose up -d command.

> **Important note on security**
>
> There are many ways to deploy this web application. Please keep in mind that the application was deliberately designed to be insecure. That said, do not deploy it in a configuration that allows public access to this server.

Introduction to Apache logs

DIWA uses the Apache web server, one of the more popular web servers available. Apache handles the work of receiving requests from web clients and returning a response for valid requests. Apache is typically configured to log requests to `/var/log/apache2/access.log` using the **common log format** (**CLF**). The configuration of these log files is stored in an Apache configuration file called `/etc/apache2/apache2.conf`. This file tells us what metadata to record for access events. Since the Apache access logs are plain text, they can be viewed without any special programs. A sample log entry is shown here:

```
10.30.23.212 - - [17/Nov/2022:02:56:54 +0000] "GET /js/bootstrap.
min.js HTTP/1.1" 200 10188 "http://10.30.23.137/" "Mozilla/5.0
(Windows NT 10.0; Win64; x64) AppleWebKit/537.36 (KHTML, like Gecko)
Chrome/107.0.0.0 Safari/537.36 Edg/107.0.1418.42"
```

While reading an access log file is a fairly trivial task, attempting to analyze log files can quickly become cumbersome. This is one massive benefit of shipping our Apache logs to a more robust data platform such as the Elastic Stack. Searching, analyzing, and building detections for Apache access logs becomes significantly easier once they've been ingested into Elastic.

Case study – Labcorp's new web portal

To help understand this lab a little better, let's place it within a simple scenario.

Labcorp is a new company and it recently completed a project to build a new web portal. The web portal is deployed on a web server, which they plan to make publicly accessible next week. Amid all the excitement surrounding the development and implementation of the web portal, the project team neglected to involve the security team. The project owners are now working with security to ensure they mitigate as much risk as possible before launch. Preliminary security tests revealed unauthorized users may be able to access a sensitive page, `secret-xu2d7a.php`. Business leadership is adamant that the portal needs to go online, despite the potential vulnerabilities, but asked the security team to put as many security controls as possible in place to mitigate any potential risks. The detection engineering team has been asked to develop detections for any users accessing the sensitive `secret-xu2d7a.php` resource.

Data collection configuration

Before we can build any detections, we need to make sure the web portal has been configured to forward telemetry to a secure data store – in the case of our lab, this is our Elastic Stack. As covered in *Chapter 3*, the data that's collected from each agent is defined in an agent policy. Each agent policy can have multiple integrations attached to it, which control what specific data gets sent to our Elastic Stack. By default, when creating a new agent policy, if **Collect system logs and metrics** is left enabled, a single integration named **System** will be added, which intuitively instructs the agent to collect common system logs and metrics. While this is useful for understanding the general operation of the system and its monitoring performance, it does not capture the data we need to build security detections.

For web servers, the logs with the highest value for detection and investigative purposes are the web server access events and network packet telemetry. Network packet data will record all connections to the web server and any metadata we specify for collection. HTTP access logs will record any access attempts received by the web server process, as well as details such as the resource requested, client details, and the response sent for the resource.

The Elastic agent makes forwarding these events simple. This can be accomplished in three steps:

1. Create an agent policy (as shown in *Figure 4.3*):

    I.   Navigate to the **Agent Policies** section of Fleet, then click **Create agent policy**.

    II. Make this new policy **Apache Web Server Policy**. In practice, it is useful to assign similarly configured systems, with data collection requirements that are identical to the same agent policy:

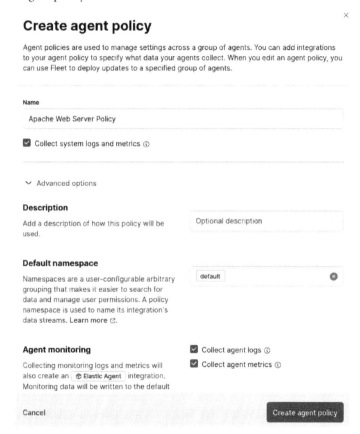

Figure 4.3 – Creating an agent policy

2. Click **Add integration** and then search for the **Apache HTTP server** integration.

3. To get even deeper visibility, we will also add the network packet capture integration. From the **Add Integrations** page for our policy, search for `Network Packet Capture`.

After performing these steps, our new policy should look like the one shown in *Figure 4.4*:

Figure 4.4 – Apache Web Server Policy

By default, the Network Packet Capture integration is configured to collect data that won't be relevant to our web server. To tweak those settings, click on the integration name for the Network Packet Capture integration, then click on **Change Defaults**. Change the HTTP setting from its default value to the new value shown in the corresponding row in *Table 4.3*. All other settings can be set to **Disabled** as they are irrelevant to capturing HTTP traffic:

Setting	Default Value	New Value	Reason
HTTP	Ports: 80, 8080, 8000, 5000, 8002 Send Request: Disabled	Ports: 80 Send Request: Enabled Include Request Body For: `application/x-www-form-urlencoded`	In this exercise, we are focusing on port 80 traffic, so there is no need to capture traffic on the other HTTP ports. We are also interested in seeing the content of requests, so we need to enable the Send Request feature.

Table 4.3 – Network Packet Capture configuration changes

Next, we need to install the Elastic agent on the Apache web server. To do this, we can use the **Add agent** option under the **Actions** menu on our policy page, as shown in *Figure 4.5*:

Figure 4.5 – Adding an Elastic agent

Ensure the following settings are in place for the **Add agent** page:

- What type of host are you adding?: **Apache web server policy**

- Enroll in Fleet?: **Enroll in Fleet (recommended)**

- Install Elastic Agent on your host: Since we provisioned a Linux server for this lab, ensure **Linux Tar** is selected, then copy the installation command shown

Next, we can issue these commands on our Apache web server. Here, we need to make one important edit to the last command in the listing. At the very end, we need to append `-insecure`.

When adding the agent, make sure the new agent policy is assigned. Having configured a web server policy, we can expect web server events to show up in our Elastic Stack. The steps to confirm you are receiving logs are as follows:

1. Navigate to Fleet, then click on the name of your web server agent.

2. Click **Logs**, then **Open in logs**.

   Alternatively, you can navigate to **Discover** under **Analytics**, then search for your web server's hostname.

3. If you don't see any events, try navigating to your web server address so that Apache's access logs get modified.

Elastic also provisions useful dashboards for the integrations that are added to agent policies. To see the dashboards that are available for your environment, navigate to **Analytics | Dashboard**. Let's take a look at the dashboard for network data. From the dashboard's search bar, search for `Network Packet Capture`, then select the dashboard called [**Network Packet Capture**] **HTTP**. You should see a dashboard similar to the one shown in *Figure 4.6*:

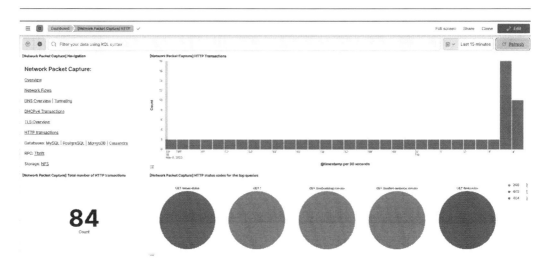

Figure 4.6 – Network Packet Capture HTTP dashboard

These dashboards are excellent for providing a high-level view of the collected data. At this point, we have successfully configured the web server to forward events to the Elastic Stack. This should provide us with the visibility needed to build detections. Next, let's look at building a detection so that we can access that confidential resource:

1. From the case study, we know that the resource we need to monitor is secret-xu2d7a.php. Let's take some time to understand how that resource can be accessed. Use your browser to navigate to the web server (based on the IP address of your VM) that has the DIWA application deployed. You should be greeted with a page similar to the one shown in *Figure 4.7*:

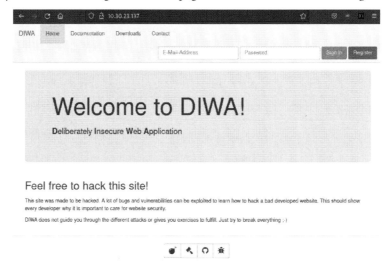

Figure 4.7 – DIWA home page

2. There are a few ways to view the contents of `secret-xu2d7a.php`, but for this scenario, we'll just abuse the site's downloads section. Navigate to **Downloads**, then hover over one of the sample documents. You'll notice a link similar to `http://[your vm]/download.php?file=lorem-ipsum-1000-words.txt`.

3. Let's test what happens when we replace the file parameter with the known-exposed file. Browse to `http://[your vm]/download.php?file=../content/secret-xu2d7a.php`. Sure enough, the `secret-xu2d7a.php` file gets downloaded, as shown in *Figure 4.8*:

Figure 4.8 – DIWA file download

4. Navigate to **Discover** under **Analytics**. Ensure the time filters are configured to show events around the time you made the download request, then enter the following KQL query:

```
url.query: *secret-xu2d7a* OR url.full.text : *secret-xu2d7a*
```

You should see several results show up, with the matching search hits highlighted. You can review the data returned to understand which fields can be used to design a detection. For each row, you can expand the document to see all available attributes, as shown in *Figure 4.9*:

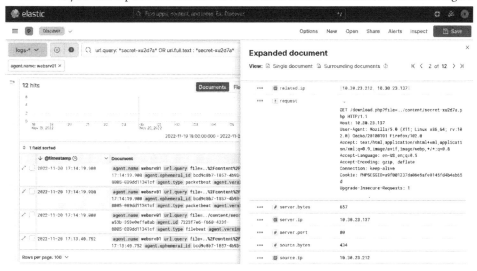

Figure 4.9 – Expanded document view

5. We can use the same query to create a detection for the secret document being accessed. From **Alerts**, under **Security**, click **Manage rules**. Then, click on **Create new rule**. Set the following values in each step in the form that is displayed:

- Step 1:

  - **Rule type: Custom query**

  - **Source**: (leave unmodified)

  - **Custom query: url.query: *secret-xu2d7a* or url.full.text : *secret-xu2d7a***

- Step 2:

  - **Name: Secret Document Accessed**

  - **Description: A user has accessed the secret document**

- Step 3:

  - **Runs every: 5m**

  - **Additional look-back time: 1m**

6. You can now navigate back to the main alerts page and view your results. As shown in *Figure 4.10*, accessing the secret document generates an alert:

Figure 4.10 – "Secret Document Accessed" alerts

As an exercise, consider the detection we've just built and how it can potentially be evaded. Are there any improvements you could make to make it more robust?

With this lab complete, you should now be able to see how certain attacks may be missed if you do not consider the data sources you collect. Originally, we were only bringing in endpoint logs from workstations. This would not have allowed us to see a network-based attack targeting our web server.

By identifying a web server in the environment, as well as understanding that attackers will likely try to remotely target the host via exploit attempts, we were able to bring in the relevant logs and create a detection for the activity.

Summary

In this chapter, we discussed the concept of data sources as they relate to detection engineering. Fully understanding your data sources is an integral part of detection engineering – without good data, you can't develop quality detections. Furthermore, gaps in data sources being received will also result in gaps in detections. We ended this chapter by adding a couple of new data sources to our detection lab, specifically Apache web server logs and network packet capture data.

In the next chapter, we'll dive into workflows and technologies that enable us to efficiently design, develop, and maintain detections.

Further reading

If you want to learn more about the MITRE ATT&CK data sources outside of what we briefly mentioned in the first section of this chapter, there are several blog posts by MITRE themself that specify the goals of the project and how the schema for data sources was created. Check them out here:

- `https://medium.com/mitre-attack/defining-attack-data-sources-part-i-4c39e581454f`

- `https://medium.com/mitre-attack/defining-attack-data-sources-part-ii-1fc98738ba5b`

- `https://medium.com/mitre-attack/dissecting-a-detection-part-1-19fd8f00266c`

- `https://medium.com/mitre-engenuity/researching-data-sources-to-build-a-foundation-for-detections-e9369a8dbb23`

We also recommend diving into the MITRE ATT&CK data sources knowledge base to explore different data sources available for investigating certain techniques.

5

Investigating Detection Requirements

In *Chapter 4*, we discussed the various data sources that may be leveraged for creating and implementing detections. We also provided guidance on understanding what data sources provide the most value to your organization. Lastly, a new data source was added to our Elastic Stack as part of a lab demonstrating the inclusion of additional data sources.

Now that we know how to get data flowing through our detection engineering lab, we can begin discussing the detections themselves. In this chapter, we'll specifically discuss prioritizing detection requirements, establishing a detection repository, and how to deploy detection code.

We will cover the following main topics in this chapter:

- Revisiting the phases of detection requirements
- Discovering detection requirements
- Triaging detection requirements
- Investigating detection requirements

Revisiting the phases of detection requirements

In *Chapter 2*, we introduced the detection engineering lifecycle, shown again in *Figure 5.1*. The first phase of the lifecycle is the *Requirements Discovery* phase. In that section, we touch on the characteristics of a complete detection requirement as well as the sources of detection requirements. The second phase of the lifecycle is the *Triage* phase, which involves taking the detection requirements from the first phase and deciding which should be prioritized. *Investigate* is the last phase before actually turning our detection requirements into detection designs and code. During this phase, we perform four key steps: identify the data source, determine the detection indicator types, research the requirement, and establish validation criteria.

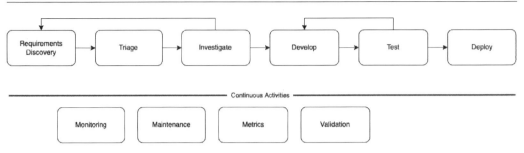

Figure 5.1 – Detection engineering lifecycle

In the following sections, we are going to go into more detail on each of those phases and provide exercises that will assist you in beginning to develop detection requirements specific to your objectives. Detection requirements are our starting point for the rest of the lifecycle, so without our detection requirements established and fleshed out, we have no direction.

Discovering detection requirements

The first phase of the detection engineering lifecycle and our introduction to detection requirements is the *Requirements Discovery phase*. A proper approach to requirements discovery is important because it ensures that we are receiving context from outside our department that can guide development to provide the most value. Without connections to our stakeholders and clear guidance on how they can communicate detection requirements to us, we will spend more time tracking down employees and information than actually developing detections.

To recap *Chapter 2*, for each detection requirement, in order to turn a requirement into a design and, ultimately, into detection code, we need the following information captured as part of our *Requirements Discovery phase*:

- The **Requesting Organization**, that is, where the request originated
- A brief **Description** of what needs to be detected, either in technical or high-level terms
- The **Reason** for the requirement, which will be used to help in prioritization in later phases
- Any **Exceptions** to be taken into account; essentially a list of possible false positives
- The **Scope**, which assists in reducing false positives by only implementing detections where relevant
- **Evidence** should be attached to the request, such as **packet captures** (**PCAPs**) or logs related to the event trying to be detected

These types of requests can come from a variety of sources, both from within the detection engineering team and from outside:

- Threat intelligence
- Internal threat intelligence

- Open source threat intelligence

- Business security requirements

- Red team exercises

- SOC requests

- Continuous activities

Each of these sources is touched on in *Chapter 2* if you need a refresher. Since we've already covered what these sources are, we are going to move on to how we leverage the sources and requirement characteristics to produce requirements.

Tools and processes

An important aspect of detection engineering to discuss and include from the beginning of the lifecycle is the processes that should be created along with the tools to be leveraged in order to efficiently collect and track detection requirements. These processes should be clearly established and shared with all stakeholders upon the establishment of the **detection engineering** (**DE**) program. Processes and tooling will vary from organization to organization based on the existing tools being leveraged, the organizational structure, and other factors. However, we will provide some examples of ideal workflow and vendor-agnostic tool recommendations that can be adapted to your specific use case.

Tools

When referring to tools in this stage, we are looking at productivity tools that can assist in implementing the processes developed by the DE team, rather than technical solutions used for developing detections. We will remain vendor-agnostic by discussing the types of tools that should be leveraged and leave it up to you which vendors your organization chooses to leverage. There are three key technologies that should be implemented as part of your DE team's requirements discovery workflow: a ticketing system, a communication platform, and a wiki.

A **ticketing system** is key to ensuring that detection requirements end up in a centralized location regardless of the source of the requirement. Whether it's a detection engineer creating a ticket for a requirement they've identified or the SOC team reporting the need for a detection based on their observations, we want to know that they will all end up in a single view. Furthermore, the functionality of ticketing systems will help you track a requirement's development progress all the way to the *Deploy* phase. It also acts as a historical archive so that if a rule needs modifications down the road, a reference back to the original request and its context can be made.

When evaluating ticketing system solutions, consider features such as integration with Git and your communication tool (as will be discussed later) that will allow the platform to integrate with the entire detection engineering flow. Furthermore, the ability to create templates and automated workflows will reduce manual effort and decrease the chances of inconsistency between tickets.

The next tool worth highlighting is a **communication platform**. This may seem obvious and most likely your team already uses an internal communication tool. It is recommended that your choice of communication tool includes a way to communicate in real time via voice or text, create groups and channels to segregate discussions by topic, and integrate with other tools, as mentioned with the ticketing system. If integrated with the ticketing system, DEs can receive notifications about new tickets or updates to tickets in real time without monitoring the ticketing system itself. Integration with Git will allow for notifications related to changes in the code base.

Lastly, we recommend creating a **wiki** or similar collaborative documentation tool for your team. We're about to dive into the processes that should be established for kicking off the detection development lifecycle. It's only logical to have a centralized location where these processes are documented and easy to find. Documentation is an integral part of any security team as it will ensure that processes are performed consistently, accurately, and efficiently. The wiki will expand to meet your needs and can include any information that you feel is relevant to the entire team. This could be high-level workflows, detailed technical specifications for code, onboarding procedures, and more. If a process is repeated more than a few times or a question is being asked and answered repeatedly, it's probably worth developing documentation around.

Next, we'll look at high-level processes in the *Requirements Discovery stage* and briefly highlight how the aforementioned tools can be integrated into these processes.

Processes

In this section, we are specifically going to look at a high-level workflow related to the *Requirements Discovery phase* and ending after *Triage*. This process is represented in *Figure 5.2*.

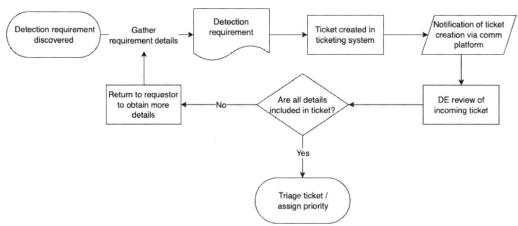

Figure 5.2 – Requirements Discovery phase workflow

First, a detection requirement is discovered. As we discussed, this requirement may come from the DE team itself or could originate from other stakeholders, such as the SOC or red team. Regardless of the source of the requirement, it should include all the information mentioned previously, being the components of a complete detection. This detection requirement should be submitted via the ticketing system following any guidance in the DE team's ticket creation procedures, which should be documented in a wiki or similar tool.

Assuming your ticketing system and communication platform are integrated, per our recommendation, this ticket creation should send a notification via chat to the engineers. This way, regardless of whether the request originates internally or not, all relevant persons will know immediately rather than needing to check email or the ticket system itself for any new requests.

During the review of the incoming request, the engineer should compare the content of the ticket against their criteria for a complete requirement and ensure all information has been provided. If not, the ticket should be returned to the submitter to provide any missing information. If the ticket meets the DE team's requirements, the analyst should triage the ticket (using processes to be discussed later in this chapter) and set an associated priority. At this point, it will be in the queue ready to move on to the *Investigate* phase once it gets assigned to an engineer.

One last thing to mention regarding communication and the exchange of information is the concept of industry standards. There are many frameworks in the cyber security industry designed to help create a common nomenclature for communicating certain technical information. For example, the **Common Vulnerability Scoring System** (**CVSS**) to communicate vulnerability information, MITRE ATT&CK (which we discussed in *Chapter 1*) to describe **tactics, techniques, and procedures** (**TTPs**), STIX to communicate incident artifacts, and others. If your organization leverages any of these frameworks or finds a use case for standardizing such information in communications, take that into account when building your workflows.

Exercise – requirements discovery for your organization

This exercise provides questions and prompts to help you approach requirements discovery and the application of the *Requirements Discovery phase* in your own organization. Specifically, we'll look at the sources of requirements in your organization to help identify stakeholders that should be aware of the processes. Save the results from this exercise as it will be leveraged in future exercises to guide your journey through the detection engineering lifecycle.

Let's start by looking at requirement sources. As a refresher, we looked at threat intelligence, business security requirements, red team exercises, SOC requests, and continuous activities as potential sources of detection requirements. Since continuous activities are part of the detection engineering lifecycle and thus a source internal to the team, we are going to ignore them for the time being and focus on external stakeholders. Use *Table 5.1* to identify which of the four remaining sources are relevant to your team:

Requirement Source	Point of Contact	POC Email Address
Threat Intelligence		
Business Security		
Red Team Exercises		
SOC Requests		

Table 5.1 – Requirement Source Contact Sheet Template

Obviously, if your company does not have an intel or red team, for example, then that requirement source is not relevant to your organization and can be ignored. Identifying a **point of contact** (**POC**) early in this process is important because there will be much communication needed with stakeholders to explain processes and collaborate on the development of detections. We recommend scheduling meetings with each POC and the relevant team members to introduce yourself and your role and explain how their team can play an integral role in the detection engineering lifecycle. Explain the benefits that the external team as well as the whole organization will receive in exchange for becoming part of the DE team's processes. Filling out this table should be simple and should result in something that looks like *Table 5.2* You'll notice in this example the organization doesn't have a red team, so that row has been removed to focus on only the relevant sources. If you have a wiki, as recommended in the *Tools* section, find a place within the documentation to save this information for future reference.

Requirement Source	Point of Contact	POC Email Address
Threat Intelligence	Brenda White	`bwhite@corp.net`
Business Security	Larry Walker	`lwalker@corp.net`
SOC Requests	Bobby Clark	`bclark@corp.net`

Table 5.2 – Requirement Source Contact Sheet Example

You should now have the list of data sources and associated context (which should also be migrated to your wiki), if gathered in *Chapter 4*, as well as this table of requirement sources and context. This will allow you to more quickly identify what capabilities and resources are available to your team when we discuss the *Triage* and *Investigate* phases.

Triaging detection requirements

In this section, we'll discuss the steps that should be taken and the criteria to be considered when prioritizing requirements. Triage is an important phase of the detection engineering lifecycle because not all detection requirements will have the same impact on the organization's defenses, so it is important that we prioritize our efforts toward those that will provide the most value. If engineers are provided an unprioritized list of detection requirements, you risk missing the requirements that may prevent a major attack because everyone is working on what they feel like rather than what is best for the organization.

There are four criteria we mentioned in *Chapter 2* as factors when triaging requirements:

- **Threat Severity**
- **Organizational Alignment**
- **Detection Coverage**
- **Active Exploits**

For each detection requirement that comes in, we need to evaluate how it is affected by the above four factors in order to determine the **return on investment** (**ROI**) of implementing a detection for the requirement. To simplify converting a triage assessment to a ticket priority, we are going to implement a simple scoring scale for each category and sum those up for a cumulative score that can be used to determine which tickets should be worked on first. First, let's introduce the scoring scale of each category.

Threat severity

In *Chapter 2*, we provided the following definition related to threat severity:

"The threat severity relates to the impact of the threat if it is not detected. The greater this impact, the higher the severity."

Therefore, when assessing a detection requirement's threat severity score, we are considering how severe the impact of a threat *not* being detected and the attacker successfully carrying out their activities would be. *Table 5.3* provides scoring criteria for the **Threat Severity** category:

Score	Description	Example
1	The threat is passive but could lead to further malicious activity.	Reconnaissance scans against public-facing servers: Common activity but not inherently malicious until the threat actor abuses findings.

2	The threat is actively in the environment but presents a low risk at this stage in the kill chain.	A phishing email is malicious but without the context of the follow-up actions, is not a critical threat by itself.
3	The threat presents a severe threat to the organization.	Ransomware payload execution: If a ransomware payload executes, it risks taking down critical components of the organization and having a major financial impact.

Table 5.3 – Threat severity scoring

As can be seen from the definitions, we define threat severity based on the specific activity being detected, not the context of a wider attack.

Organizational alignment

Using organizational alignment as a method for triaging threats involves understanding how external threats' motivations, targets, capabilities, and infrastructure overlap with the industry, organization, infrastructure users, and data that is being protected. Threat intelligence should be used to identify which threats align most with your organization's profile.

Score	Description	Example
0	The threat is irrelevant to the organization.	A threat targeting macOS endpoints in a Windows-only environment.
1	The threat is likely not going to target your organization but the risk still exists.	A threat actor primarily focused on targeting a geography outside your own but known to target your industry.
2	The threat is widespread/untargeted.	A mass Emotet malspam campaign.
3	The threat specifically targets your organization.	Known threat based on internal observations or a threat actor known to target your geography and industry.

Table 5.4 – Organizational alignment scoring

Filling out this table is likely going to be more challenging than the one for threat severity as threat severity is determined without the organizational context. Organizational alignment requires you to first understand your environment and then identify based on research how relevant a given threat is given the additional context.

Detection coverage

Prioritizing detection requirements has a clear relationship with which detections would have the greatest return on investment for the organization. Part of this is determining whether we are already covered for all or part of a requirement. Obviously, if we already have in-depth coverage for the requirement, it shouldn't even be in the queue. Creating a detection for something that we can't currently detect will receive a higher score over improving the detection rate of an existing detection since the impact it has on our overall coverage is greater.

Score	Description
0	In-depth coverage is already provided for this specific technique.
1	This technique requires an update to the scope of an existing detection.
2	No coverage for this requirement exists. A new detection is required.

Table 5.5 – Detection coverage scoring

With the detection coverage score documented, we can either move on to calculating the cumulative score priority or, if exploits are involved, we need to also determine the **Active Exploits** score.

Active exploits

The **Active Exploits** score should only be used in the scoring process if the detection requirement involves detecting a specific exploit. For this category, we have to consider a couple of factors, which means we have multiple scoring tables. Specifically, we'll look at the relevance of the exploit to the organization and the prevalence of the threat.

First, identify whether the organization is vulnerable to the exploit based on which technologies and software versions are affected:

Score	Description
0	The organization is not vulnerable to the exploit.
1	The organization is vulnerable to the exploit but the turnaround time of a patch is quick.
2	The organization is vulnerable and a patch is unavailable or will not be deployed soon.

Table 5.6 – Active exploit (relevance) scoring

While scores of 1 or 2 both relate to an organization being vulnerable, we differentiate by whether a patch is available and to be implemented soon as this greatly impacts priority. If we know a patch is coming to mitigate the risk soon, that could be the difference between working on this detection requirement and another one. By the time we develop, test, and deploy a detection, it's possible that a patch will have already been released. As such, we want to ensure that we don't just think about the threat at the exact moment but whether it will still be relevant by the time the detection is released.

One thing not included in the scoring criteria for an organization's vulnerability but worth considering is if only a specific geographic region or industry is being targeted with the exploit, it may be worth considering the requirement irrelevant. You should assess the likelihood of the exploit becoming more widely leveraged based on the next scoring table. Specifically, this table focuses on how likely it is that the vulnerability will be exploited based on public reporting of the availability of exploit code and observed activity.

Score	Description
1	No exploit code or in-the-wild activity has been observed.
2	Some in-the-wild activity has been observed but no public exploit code is available.
3	Exploit code is publicly available and actively being used by threat actors.

Table 5.7 – Active exploit (prevalence) scoring

Now that we understand how to score each of these factors, we can dive into combining the results into a priority to close out the *Triage* phase.

Calculating priority

Assuming you've assigned a score for each category above, we're going to perform a simple sum, as shown in *Figure 5.3*, to assign a priority score for the entire detection requirement.

Figure 5.3 – Priority score formula

Before we calculate the score though, we first want to make sure no there are no categories with a score of 0, as this will indicate the detection requirement should be rejected instead.

The following cases of a 0 score indicate that the detection requirement should be marked as irrelevant with context as to why and returned to the requestor:

- If organizational alignment receives a score of 0, the detection requirement can be rejected as this means that the organization is not at risk for the given threat

- If detection coverage receives a score of 0, this means that the detection requirement is already covered and should be returned to the requestor, referring them to the existing detection

- If the relevance of active exploits receives a score of 0, it means that the organization is not vulnerable to the related exploit so a detection is not required

Assuming there are no zero scores, then the priority can be calculated by summing together all the scores. Let's look at three examples of this being implemented at a tech company in the United States to show how it can help us triage requirements:

- **Detection Requirement #1**: SOC is requesting a detection be put in place for an Emotet malspam campaign they are actively observing. They report a **remote access Trojan (RAT)** is installed on the host at the end of the infection chain:

  - **Threat Severity**: 3. The RAT will allow for remote code execution, which is a severe threat.

  - **Organizational Alignment**: 2. Emotet malspam is a widespread attack and not specifically targeting the organization.

  - **Detection Coverage**: 2. Let's assume no detections currently exist for this threat.

  - **Active Exploits**: N/A.

  - **Priority Score**: 7

- **Detection Requirement #2**: The intel team is requesting a detection for their research into a new threat actor primarily targeting utilities in the United States; however, the intel team believes that this group might change their targeting to include other verticals such as tech. The primary known TTP associated with this group is credential theft via phishing:

  - **Threat Severity**: 2. Credential theft is early in the kill chain and we don't know what the attacker plans to do with the stolen credentials. Without the context of additional kill chain actions, we should leave this threat severity at 2.

  - **Organizational Alignment**: 1. While the threat actor has not directly attacked tech companies in the United States yet, they are active in the region in adjacent verticals and the intel team assesses that they may target the organization in the future.

  - **Detection Coverage**: 1. Let's assume we have a detection for some of the phishing TTPs reported by intel, but there are several threat characteristics they want added to our detections.

  - **Active Exploits**: N/A.

  - **Priority Score**: 4

- **Detection Requirement #3**: The red team is requesting a detection for exploitation of a recently announced vulnerability in Microsoft Exchange. They've assessed that the organization's Exchange servers are vulnerable and an attacker could cause remote code execution if successfully exploited. A patch is available, but it is unclear how long it will take to get deployed in the environment. Widespread in-the-wild exploitation has been observed and public exploit code is available:

  - **Threat Severity**: 3. If successfully exploited, the threat actor will be able to perform remote code execution, which presents a severe threat.

  - **Organizational Alignment**: 2. The exploitation is targeted toward Microsoft Exchange, regardless of the specific organization involved, so it is essentially an untargeted/widespread attack.

  - **Detection Coverage**: 2. No detections currently exist for this threat since it's a new exploit.

  - **Active Exploits**:

    - **Relevance**: 2. The red team has validated that the organization is vulnerable and is unsure of when a patch will be deployed.

    - **Prevalence**: 3. The red team reports that exploit code is publicly available and attacks are being seen in the wild.

    - **Priority Score**: 12

Now let's assess what these priority scores tell us. Put simply, the higher the score, the sooner the requirement should be worked on. In the specific requirements discussed above, our scoring indicates that *Detection Requirement 3* (Exchange exploit activity) should be worked on first, then *Detection Requirement 1* (Emotet malspam campaign), and finally, *Detection Requirement 2* (new threat actor).

This order makes sense when performing a non-mathematical assessment. First, we are going to get a detection in place for a widespread vulnerability actively being exploited for which we have no way to detect it. Once vulnerabilities have public exploit code and major attention, a significant number of threat actors will try to take advantage. After that, we can work on the active Emotet campaign. Emotet is widespread and untargeted but can have an impact, just potentially without the same aggressive and sudden activity we expect from a widely exploited vulnerability. Lastly, we can work on the intel team's request, but it can go into the backlog since we have some relevant detections already and the threat actor has not yet attacked organizations in our vertical, nor do we know what the final impact of their attack would be. While there may be subjectivity in some cases due to additional factors relating to managerial decisions on what to prioritize, the formula above can provide some initial guidance.

In your ticketing system, set the ticket priorities accordingly. Even if an integer-based score is not used, the scores can help you put ticket priorities into the low, medium, high, or critical range. *Table 5.8* provides a mapping of scores to priority levels.

Score	Priority Level
1-3	Low
4-6	Medium
7-9	High
10+	Critical

Table 5.8 – Priority levels by score

This completes the *Triage* phase and allows us to move on to the *Investigate* phase, performing the rest of the lifecycle for each detection requirement in the order determined by the priority scoring.

Investigating detection requirements

The last phase we'll discuss as part of this chapter is the *Investigate* phase. As mentioned in *Chapter 2*, the goal of the *Investigate* phase is to *prepare a detection requirement for development, by converting the detection requirements to more technical requirements*. The four steps involved in this phase are data source identification, detection indicator types, research, and establish validation criteria. These steps were previously described in *Chapter 2* and, as such, we are not going to reiterate the content here. We will, however, look at the detection from the previous section and show how we can take detection requirement #3, our top priority requirement, and investigate the requirement further.

First, we start with the detection requirement information:

The red team is requesting a detection for exploitation of a recently announced vulnerability in Microsoft Exchange. They've assessed that the organization's Exchange servers are vulnerable and an attacker could cause remote code execution if successfully exploited. A patch is available but it is unclear how long it will take to get deployed in the environment. Widespread in-the-wild exploitation has been observed and public exploit code is available.

As will often be the case when detection requirements come from outside teams, they do not have the same perspective as a detection engineer so the requirement they provide may not include everything required to design a detection. Therefore, the *Investigate* phase is important to ensure all information is gathered prior to development starting. Establishing the research that needs to be done is how we can help ensure a quick and effective turnaround of a detection requirement into a detection.

Now let's go through each step of the *Investigate* phase and see how we can gather the information relevant to each step. The first step is Data Source Identification. Looking at the detection requirement description alone, without knowing the details of the particular vulnerability, there are two things that stand out as relevant to data source identification. First, they mention the vulnerability targets Microsoft Exchange. Knowing this, we should gather both the endpoint logs (Windows Event logs) and application logs (Microsoft Exchange logs) from all vulnerable Exchange servers. We could also gather IIS logs, which provide visibility over any POST/GET requests made to the Exchange server. The second key phrase that stands out is "remote code execution." This means that if the attacker exploits the vulnerability, they will able to execute the code remotely, from outside of the server itself. For that to happen, we will potentially be able to observe the attacker's activity traversing the network. Therefore, we should identify any network appliances sitting between the Exchange server and the internet that would have visibility of such traffic, such as a firewall.

The second step of the *Investigate* phase is to determine relevant detection indicator types, that is, whether we will be working with static, behavioral, or statistical indicator types. If we were working with an intel team providing details on known hashes or IP addresses of attackers working with the specific exploit, static indicators might be relevant. In the case of the red team providing details on an exploit, however, we are likely going to be looking at developing behavioral detections, as we want to know what it looks like when the exploit is executed regardless of the specific exploit payload or attacker leveraging it.

Next, we need to research the threat to understand how we can detect this specific exploit. With the description we have, we would likely need to dive deeper into how the exploit works to understand how we can detect it. For the sake of the example, let's say that the red team tells us that `ProxyShell` is the Exchange vulnerability they are concerned about. Having been a widely reported-on vulnerability, a simple Google search for `Detecting ProxyShell` will lead you to numerous blog posts from security vendors and researchers demonstrating the behavior observed when exploiting the vulnerability. Some examples of what you'll find with such research are that there are certain values in POST requests in the IIS logs that indicate an attempt to exploit the vulnerability as well as certain Exchange Management Shell Cmdlets that are executed during the exploitation. Those are both good starting points for how we could detect this behavior. Furthermore, the widespread nature of this vulnerability means that researchers have published open source signatures for projects such as Sigma. We encourage you to search online for ProxyShell detection techniques and identify various activities that we could alert on to potentially stop such an attack.

Given the information gathered during the research step, combined with our knowledge of relevant data sources and indicator types, we can establish validation criteria. Essentially, how do we know that the detection we've written works as expected? At this point in the process, we can create some technical statements that indicate what we expect from the detection. Here is an example of one possible validation criterion:

If successful, then executing the PowerShell `New-MailboxExportRequest` command on Exchange Server should result in the detection being triggered based on the presence of `New-MailboxExportRequest` in the MS Exchange Cmdlet logs.

Notice the preceding statement defines the behavior we want to test (executing `New-MailboxExportRequest`), the result we should see (a triggered detection), and the data source and associated condition to be met (`New-MailboxExportRequest` in the MS Exchange Cmdlet logs). If we aren't executing the right command, seeing the right detection, or gathering the right data from the right source, there is something wrong with our detection.

We recommend reviewing the *Investigate* section of *Chapter 2* if you need a refresher on the above concepts.

Summary

In this chapter, we first looked at the phases involved in creating and documenting detection requirements. We defined a methodology for scoring and prioritizing requirements allowing an organization to triage requests from multiple stakeholders. Lastly, we worked through some example scenarios using this prioritization approach to demonstrate how it can be used to support a detection engineering team.

In the next chapter, we're going to work through multiple example detections to demonstrate the design and creation process of detection rules for various scenarios. Then we'll briefly touch on testing our new detections.

6

Developing Detections Using Indicators of Compromise

In this chapter, we will apply the detection engineering life cycle to investigate and develop detections in our lab. In *Chapter 2*, we identified four sub-steps to the *Investigate* phase and three sub-steps to the *Develop* phase, which we will follow in our exercises in this chapter.

Investigate:

1. Research context

2. Data source identification

3. Detection indicator types

4. Establish validation criteria

Develop:

1. Design

2. Develop

3. Unit test

At the beginning of the book, we introduced the Pyramid of Pain, which can be used to evaluate how easily the adversary can evade our detections. In addition to signifying the difficulty for the adversary to evade detection, the pyramid levels also (mostly) align with how easily a detection can be created. For this reason, we will start with implementing simpler static indicator detections that align to lower levels of the pyramid, and in the next chapter, we will move on to behavior-based detections.

We will cover the following main topics in this chapter:

*   Leveraging indicators of compromise for detection

*   Scenario 1 lab

Technical requirements

The labs in this chapter will involve the use of the detection engineering lab built as part of *Chapter 3*.

Leveraging indicators of compromise for detection

When developing detections, the concept of **indicators of compromise** (**IoCs**) will frequently come up. Threat intelligence sources commonly share information about threats and will often include IoCs, which can take multiple forms. We briefly discussed the concept of indicators in *Chapter 1*.

In this section, we are going to dive further into the concept of IoCs, the Pyramid of Pain, and how they relate to detections. These concepts will be brought up again in *Chapter 8* when we go in-depth into leveraging threat intelligence for detection engineering.

In *Chapter 1*, we saw that static indicators such as hashes, IP addresses, and domain names are at the bottom of the Pyramid of Pain, and are trivial for adversaries to change. Despite being easy to change, they do provide a method for short-term, tactical defense. When talking about detecting IoCs, this is typically our focus: a quick way to detect known threats until the threat actor modifies their attack to evade static detection. While it is often a game of whack-a-mole, it provides a stop-gap solution while more in-depth detections can be written against the **tools and tactics, techniques, and procedures** (**TTPs**), the less mutable elements of the Pyramid of Pain. For that reason, we cannot ignore the concept of creating detections against static IoCs, and in this chapter, we will look at how we can take IoCs published publicly and leverage them to detect known malicious activity.

At the most basic levels on the Pyramid of Pain, we have hash values, IP addresses, and domain names. These are the three layers we are going to focus on with our example scenario in this chapter focusing on detecting IoCs. Although simple for the attacker to change and thus short-lived, these indicators are often quickly identifiable via threat intelligence, whether from internal data sources or **open source intelligence** (**OSINT**), and easy to implement. Furthermore, there are tons of open source feeds and resources that provide these types of indicators.

Typically, when looking at these indicator types, we see two categories, **host-based** and **network-based** indicators. Host-based indicators are those that exist on a host in their final state. *Hashes* are **host-based indicators**. Along with hashes, we could also look at other host artifacts, such as registry keys or directories. These are slightly harder for the attacker to modify but also not as widely distributed in threat intel feeds. As such, we'll be focusing on hashes, but the same concepts and processes apply to all host-based artifacts but against different log fields.

The second category is **network-based indicators**, such as *domains*, *IP addresses*, and *URLs*. Network-based indicators are focused on those that are captured by data sources monitoring network traffic or hosted on network infrastructure. Once again, we can expand on these indicator types to include user agents, URI patterns, and other network artifacts if we have that information available to detect on. This chapter's example, however, will focus on just domains, IP addresses, and URLs, as they are the most common ones you will encounter.

When it comes to creating detections using IoCs, it is one of the easiest and quickest detections that can be developed. At the simplest level, with static indicators, we identify fields matching specific values, for example, looking for any fields associated with MD5 hashes containing a given known malicious hash. The steps for creating a detection based on static indicators are standard regardless of the artifact type and take place in the *Investigate* and *Develop* phases. We start with the *Investigate* phase. The following is a list of the sub-steps in the *Investigate* phase along with a description of their purpose:

1. **Research**: We need to use the information provided in the detection requirement to expand our knowledge of the threat. With regard to detecting IoCs, this will typically involve identifying context related to each indicator (that is, how a given file or domain is related to a threat).

2. **Data source identification**: With the context of indicators known, we can determine which data sources are likely to have visibility over the threat, which will tell us what logs to detect against.

3. **Detection indicator types**: If the indicator types are unknown, they should be documented. At a high level, you will have either static or behavioral indicators. In the case of static indicators, the detection requirement may provide the indicators in a format that includes their specific type, such as IP address, domain, or SHA256 hash. If so, this step becomes negligible as it's part of the detection requirement.

4. **Establish validation criteria**: Before a detection can ever be deployed to production, we need to ensure it works as expected. Establishing validation criteria helps us specify how we can determine that a detection meets the goal of the detection requirement.

Let's look at the *Investigate* phase in more depth as it relates to detecting static indicators. First, we must gather the list of indicators. These indicators will either come from within the organization, such as indicators identified in attacks against the organization, or from OSINT, which could be either blog posts or threat feeds. Once we have the starting list provided by the detection requirement, we can perform the Investigate phase of the detection engineering life cycle to gather additional indicators and context. Typically, when we receive indicators as part of a detection requirement some context is provided as to why these indicators need to be blocked. This context should be noted as it will help us in the next step. Additionally, we should perform research to ensure that there are no additional related indicators of value. For example, we might be able to obtain a file hash associated with a payload URL or the IP address a domain is being hosted at.

Given the indicators and their context, we next need to identify the data sources within the scope for this detection. This is going to depend on both the indicator type and the context. The first way to narrow down relevant data sources is based on indicator type. Simply put, if the data source does not provide logs containing indicators of that type, it is irrelevant. For example, hashes will not appear in Apache access logs, so that they can immediately be ignored as a data source for the detection of hashes. If you are unsure of whether a data source will provide certain information, look at samples to see what fields are available. Make sure to record this information in the **detection engineering** (**DE**) team's documentation for future reference so that it does not need to be evaluated every time.

The second factor in whether a data source is relevant is the context of the indicator. By this we mean, is the indicator likely to appear in a given log based on its context? For example, if we are attempting to detect indicators associated with a social engineering campaign that gets users to navigate to a URL via phishing over phone calls (vishing), then it would not make sense to waste resources building detections for that URL appearing in email data sources, because email was not involved. Similarly, if a malicious payload is being distributed via email, then detecting a file hash observed via web traffic downloads is fruitless.

The last piece of information we need to gather is the relevant field names based on the data sources identified. In this case, since we already have the indicators, this step is equivalent to the *Detection indicator types* step of the *Investigate* phase. There are two key considerations here:

- **Indicator type and context**: You want to first narrow down the list of fields containing the indicator types for which you are writing detections. For example, if you are detecting an IP address in a firewall log, you have two fields to choose from, one for the source IP and the other for the destination IP. At this point, you have to use the context obtained in your research to decide which specific field is relevant to the indicator you are detecting. For example, if you are trying to detect an IP address known to be used for data exfiltration, you want to look for it as a destination IP. If the IP address is the member of a botnet performing brute-force attacks against your organization, then the source IP is more relevant. Sometimes you may want to detect on both the source and destination, but in cases where you want to reduce performance impact or the chance of false positives, the context can often help create a more specific detection.

- **Naming conventions**: Ideally, you are writing detections for a platform that normalizes data from different sources to use a shared field name. For example, if your firewall stores the source IP address in a field called `src.ip` and your **virtual private network** (**VPN**) logs use `src_ip`, you must create a check for the value of the IP in all possible versions of source IP fields. In the case of a system that normalizes data, all source IPs, regardless of data source, will be stored in a field as named by the system administrator.

To help solidify these concepts, we will look at an example of how an OSINT provider that provides indicators can be leveraged for developing detections.

Example scenario – identifying an IcedID campaign using indicators

In this example scenario, we will look at an OSINT provider on an IcedID malware campaign in order to understand how we can use this intel to identify static indicator detection opportunities. Furthermore, it's important to identify the data source requirements related to such a detection requirement.

There are many vendors and websites dedicated to the sharing of threat intel. One of these websites is AlienVault's **Open Threat Exchange** (**OTX**), which provides a collection of IoCs associated with campaigns that AlienVault refers to as **pulses**. For this example, we are going to look at a pulse associated with a malvertising campaign distributing IcedID via fake Google ads. The pulse can be viewed here: `https://otx.alienvault.com/pulse/639b10240d0534275ddbdea1`.

The indicators gathered were based on a *SANS* **Internet Storm Center** (**ISC**) diary, which can be read here: `https://isc.sans.edu/diary/rss/29344`. At a high level, this campaign involves the following steps:

1. A user visits an SEO-poisoned Google ad.

2. A series of redirects leads the user to a fake AnyDesk download page.

3. A ZIP archive is downloaded from this page that contains an MSI file.

4. The MSI file, if opened, drops and runs a malicious DLL to install IcedID, and C2 communication is established.

Included in the pulse are IPv4 addresses, domains, URLs, and file hashes, all of which can be leveraged for static indicator detection. While the attacker may create new infrastructure or modify payloads, these indicators provide a quick method to block the immediate threat while more comprehensive, behavioral detections can be developed.

The first step in creating a detection for these static indicators is to identify which data sources provide events containing the data we want to detect – in this case, file hashes, IPv4 addresses, domains, and URLs. Let's start with file hashes. There are several data sources from which we might receive hash values. The primary source is going to be endpoint-level logs, including both raw telemetry (such as Windows event logs) and security events (such as **anti-virus** (**AV**) and **endpoint detection and response** (**EDR**) logs). Security tools will typically capture file hashes as part of their events. File hashes are less common within raw telemetry, although sometimes logging configurations can be used to capture additional information. For example, in the following exercise, we will review how to install and configure **Sysmon**. Sysmon will provide you access to several events that record the hash of a file, including process creation and driver load events.

In some cases, we may observe file hashes in logs from network-based security tools. Two key examples of this are **email security appliances** (**ESAs**) and **next-generation firewalls** (**NGFWs**). ESAs may include the hashes of any observed attachments. Although not a capability of all NGFWs, some of them will calculate the hash of files traversing the network.

Along with file hashes, we have IPv4 addresses, domains, and URLs, all of which are network-based indicators. Just like with file hashes, we have multiple sources related to such indicators. In this case, however, network logs are going to be our primary source with some endpoint logs available as a secondary source. IPv4 addresses are going to be the most common of the three indicator types, whereas domains and URLs are going to appear only where either **Domain Name System** (**DNS**) resolution or web traffic is involved.

Table 6.1 outlines the data sources most relevant to this scenario as well as the indicator types associated with those data sources. The indicator types will vary based on event type, so only a subset of logs from each source may contain that indicator type. The **Notes** column of the table provides some context surrounding the limitations of certain indicator types:

Log Type	Indicator Types	Notes
Raw telemetry – endpoints (e.g., Windows event logs)	File hashes IPv4 addresses Domains	File hashes depend on specific logging tools or configurations, such as Sysmon. Non-internal IP addresses are only going to appear in logs involving network activity. Domains depend on logs that perform DNS resolution.
AV/EDR alerts	File hashes IPv4 addresses Domains URLs	File hashes should be present in many AV/EDR alerts, although the hash type may vary. Network indicators are going to depend on the type of event. AV/EDR are endpoint-focused but if the source of a malicious payload is an external website, the network info may be captured.
Firewalls	File hashes IPv4 addresses Domains URLs	Network indicators are going to be more common. Stateless firewalls are only going to provide IPs and maybe domains if some sort of DNS resolution is in place. NGFWs typically include URL filtering capabilities and will record URLs being visited. File hashes will only be present if an NGFW provides some sort of file analysis that also computes the hash.

Log Type	Indicator Types	Notes
ESAs/email logs	File hashes IPv4 addresses Domains URLs	Sender and recipient IP addresses and email domains will be present in ESAs and email logs. File hashes and URLs may be present in these logs if the ESA is performing an analysis of attachments and embedded URLs. Some email providers will also record file hash attachments or extract URLs. It is all dependent on the vendors being leveraged.

Table 6.1 – Relevant data sources for scenario 1

As can be seen, all of our data sources have the potential to provide most of the indicators relevant to our detection requirement, but it all depends on the configurations and capabilities of the systems being leveraged. This is where understanding your environment becomes important. If you don't know whether your firewalls perform URL filtering, you won't know whether you can leverage those appliances for detecting suspicious/malicious URLs.

The other consideration here is that we have multiple places where indicator types match those in our detection requirement, but we need to identify which data sources it makes the most sense to implement detections against. This involves fully understanding the activity you are trying to detect, and which systems will have visibility based on the attack chain.

As part of the detection engineering life cycle, we must go through the *Investigate* phase. In this phase, we attempt to gather additional context related to our detection requirement in order to most effectively develop a detection. For our example scenario, that means understanding the context related to the indicators so that we can determine what data sources would be of most value. We'll begin by looking at the file hashes provided in the pulse. While the pulse solely provides a list of indicators, we can look at the reference article to determine how these hashes came into play.

The source article provided all hashes in SHA256 format, while the pulse included the associated MD5 and SHA1 hashes as part of the pulse. Since the source article solely provided SHA256, we will focus on those for this purpose. If a system you are developing a detection for only supports SHA1 or MD5 and the sample is publicly available, **AlienVault OTX** or other OSINT providers can be used to obtain the SHA1 and MD5 hashes associated with each SHA256 hash. *Table 6.2* contains a list of hashes and notes about each hash based on reviewing the SANS ISC diary that was referenced.

Luckily for us, the article lists the indicators with details about the associated file, so we just need to parse out the provided information:

Hashes	Investigation Notes
19265aac471f7d72fcddb133e652e04c03a54 7727b6f98a80760dcbf43f95627	File description: ZIP archive downloaded from malvertising redirects. Filename: `Setup_Win_14-12-2022_18-36-29.zip`
63a7d98369925d6e98994cdb5937bd8965066 65be9f80dc55de7eb6df00f7607	MSI (installer) contained within the downloaded ZIP archive. Filename: `Setup_Win_14-12-2022_18-36-29.msi`
7e5da5fcda0da494da85cdc76384b3b08f135 f09f20e582e049486e8ae2f168e	DLL dropped by MSI installer. Used to install IcedID payload. File path: `C:\Users\ [username]\AppData\ Local\MSI5da0ddad.mst`
53639070024366d23c3de5ba1d074cbd1d8b9 e78d46f75c32ef02fc20c279fc3	GZIP binary download by the installer DLL from a remote URL.
205fbc52fafd456388d3ef80ff00498c90295 791a91811725fea94052dc4fe7a	Data binary used in combination with the IcedID DLL for persistence. File path: `C:\Users\ [username]\AppData\ Roaming\GenreAttract\ license.dat`
bfa3eb36beeaa65334abe81cdd870e66b37da3 e478d1615697160244fd087b48	Persistent IcedID DLL payload. File path: `C:\Users\ [username]\AppData\ Roaming\{12A3307B-B372-BBC6-7E4B-4992C7C7842B}\ {6127EF7F-696C-8BDF-5350-88ECC5774CA5}\ uwurtb4.dll`

Hashes	Investigation Notes
7486c3585d6aa7c2febd8b4f049a86c72772fd a6bd1dc9756e2fb8c5da67bafa	Cobalt Strike PowerShell script downloaded from remote URL.

e8f2c929e1b84a389fede03bff9a4ee951cf563a
64809b06f2f76201536fddf7
	Cobalt Strike EXE downloaded from remote URL.
	
	File path:
	
	`C:\Users\[username]\`
	`AppData\Local\Temp\`
	`Dimuak.exe`

40194a07a5afa1ef8e0ea4125a62d4ff5b70a148 49b154a4694cfd08e40eb22b	Binary related to Sliver-based and/or DonutLoader malware.
08dd1a4861f4d2b795efb71847386bd141caa0a7 ce141798e251db8acd63d3a9	Executable related to Sliver-based and/or DonutLoader malware.

Table 6.2 – Scenario 1 hashes with investigation notes

We now have some context about what each hash represents and where it originated from. This will make sure we are targeting the detections we build toward the systems where that activity might be observed. The **Investigation Notes** column of the table also includes notes about file paths and names that could also be used within detections.

The SANS ISC diary can be reviewed to obtain even more intel relevant to detection engineering, such as command lines executed, the specific URL at which the payloads were hosted, and more. For the purposes of this exercise though, we are going to focus on how we can use the hashes in particular. To do this, we are going to leverage *Table 6.1* and *Table 6.2* in combination to see which data sources should be leveraged for creating detections for these hashes. *Table 6.3* adds an additional column to our last table in order to show the relevant data sources:

Hashes	Investigation Notes	Relevant Data Source(s)
19265aac471f7d72fcddb133e65 2e04c03a547727b6f98a80760dc bf43f95627	File description: ZIP archive downloaded from malvertising redirects.	Endpoint telemetry AV/EDR Firewalls
63a7d98369925d6e98994cdb5937 bd896506665be9f80dc55de7eb6d f00f7607	MSI (installer) is contained within the downloaded ZIP archive.	Endpoint telemetry AV/EDR

Hashes	Investigation Notes	Relevant Data Source(s)

`7e5da5fcda0da494da85cdc76384`
`b3b08f135f09f20e582e049486e8`
`ae2f168e`
	DLL dropped by MSI installer. Used to install IcedID payload.	Endpoint telemetry
		AV/EDR

`53639070024366d23c3de5ba1d07`
`4cbd1d8b9e78d46f75c32ef02fc2`
`0c279fc3`
	GZIP binary download by the installer DLL from a remote URL.	Endpoint telemetry
		AV/EDR
		Firewalls

`205fbc52fafd456388d3ef80ff00`
`498c90295791a91811725fea9405`
`2dc4fe7a`
	Data binary is used in combination with the IcedID DLL for persistence.	Endpoint telemetry
		AV/EDR

`bfa3eb36beeaa65334abe81cdd87`
`0e66b37da3e478d1615697160244`
`fd087b48`
	Persistent IcedID DLL payload.	Endpoint telemetry
		AV/EDR

`7486c3585d6aa7c2febd8b4f049a`
`86c72772fda6bd1dc9756e2fb8c5`
`da67bafa`
	Cobalt Strike PowerShell script downloaded from remote URL.	Endpoint telemetry
		AV/EDR
		Firewalls

`e8f2c929e1b84a389fede03bff9a`
`4ee951cf563a64809b06f2f76201`
`536fddf7`
	Cobalt Strike EXE downloaded from remote URL.	Endpoint telemetry
		AV/EDR
		Firewalls

`40194a07a5afa1ef8e0ea4125a62`
`d4ff5b70a14849b154a4694cfd08`
`e40eb22b`
	Binary related to Sliver-based and/or DonutLoader malware.	Endpoint telemetry
		AV/EDR
		Firewalls

`08dd1a4861f4d2b795efb7184738`
`6bd141caa0a7ce141798e251db8a`
`cd63d3a9`
	Executable related to Sliver-based and/or DonutLoader malware.	Endpoint telemetry
		AV/EDR
		Firewalls

Table 6.3 – Scenario 1 hashes and relevant data sources

Due to the fact that all the files are dropped on the endpoint at some point, in all cases, any endpoint telemetry or AV or EDR alerts that log file hashes are relevant to our detection development. In the cases where the payload was downloaded from a remote URL, firewall logs also become relevant if some sort of URL filtering and file analysis is occurring as we should be able to observe the payload traversing the network. Packet captures would provide the most value in this case, but a full packet capture infrastructure is not common in most enterprises, so we are going to focus on the more common data sources. We also mentioned ESAs as a potential data source to detect IoCs, but in our example, we are not dealing with an email-based threat, so it becomes irrelevant to our specific use case.

At this point, we know what hashes we want to detect, why we want to detect them, and where/how we want to detect them. The next step is to make sure that the data sources we have identified provide the required information in your specific environment. For example, if you don't have Sysmon configured on Windows hosts, you are not going to find hashes in endpoint telemetry. Most AV/EDR platforms provide hashes, but the hashing algorithm varies so you need to identify whether your system supports MD5, SHA1, or SHA256. If it doesn't support SHA256, then in this example scenario you would need to use OSINT to see whether you could find the associated MD5 or SHA1 associated with the given SHA256. Lastly, you need to determine whether your firewall records hashes of downloaded payloads. In most cases, this is considered a more advanced feature so will likely only be found in NGFWs. As you are identifying which sources record which indicator types, you should consider documenting the information so that for future development you can quickly reference your previous findings.

With an understanding of detecting hashes, we can now move on to our network-based indicators. We are going to create a table similar to *Table 6.3* but for the network-based indicators this time.

It is important to keep in mind that for the network indicators, many of them are related in the sense that they involve a URL, which contains a domain, which resolves to a specific IP address. This means that we have three indicators of the same threat. As we've discussed though, some systems record one indicator type but not others, so having this flexibility in how we can approach the detection is valuable.

For brevity's sake, we will focus on the domains and IPs. The URLs within the pulse are all paths on one of these servers. You'll also notice that there are some IPs associated with multiple domains, indicating that the domains are resolving to or were once resolving to a shared IP. Furthermore, there are some IP addresses that did not resolve to a domain. The data sources listed may only be relevant for a subset of the indicators. *Table 6.4* shows the network indicators, investigation notes, and relevant data sources in an organized fashion:

Domain	IP Address	Investigation Notes	Relevant Data Sources
wwwanydesk[.]top	45.8.229[.]109	Fake AnyDesk website distributing malware	Endpoint telemetry AV/EDR Firewalls
trashast[.]wiki	158.255.211[.]126	IcedID C2 traffic over port 443	Endpoint telemetry AV/EDR Firewalls

Domain	IP Address	Investigation Notes	Relevant Data Sources
primsenetwolk[.]com	94.140.114[.]40	IcedID C2 traffic over port 443	Endpoint telemetry AV/EDR Firewalls
onyxinnov[.]lol	94.140.114[.]40	IcedID C2 traffic over port 443	Endpoint telemetry AV/EDR Firewalls
oferialerkal[.]online	31.41.244[.]54	Malicious **traffic distribution system (TDS)** domain	Endpoint telemetry AV/EDR Firewalls
klepdrafooip[.]com	143.198.92[.]88	Traffic from IcedID installer DLL over port 80	Endpoint telemetry AV/EDR Firewalls
kingoflake[.]com	172.67.130[.]194	Cobalt Strike C2 traffic over port 443	Endpoint telemetry AV/EDR Firewalls
bukifide[.]com	108.177.235[.]187	Cobalt Strike C2 traffic over port 443	Endpoint telemetry AV/EDR Firewalls
N/A	199.127.62[.]132	Cobalt Strike C2 traffic over port 80	Endpoint telemetry AV/EDR Firewalls
N/A	176.105.202[.]212	Cobalt Strike C2 traffic over port 80	Endpoint telemetry AV/EDR Firewalls
N/A	190.61.121[.]35	Sliver and/or DonutLoader traffic over port 80	Endpoint telemetry AV/EDR Firewalls

Domain	IP Address	Investigation Notes	Relevant Data Sources
N/A	`46.4.182[.]102`	Sliver and/or DonutLoader post-infection traffic over port `80`	Endpoint telemetry AV/EDR Firewalls
N/A	`51.195.169[.]87`	IcedID VNC traffic over port `8080`	Endpoint telemetry AV/EDR Firewalls

Table 6.4 – Scenario 1 network-based indicators

Once again, we see that we have various points of logging in our network that can capture network indicators, just like hashes. We see a couple of payload distribution sites, C2 traffic, and other post-infection traffic. In all cases, the context is always communication between victim hosts and the internet, in both directions. Therefore, depending on logging configurations, it's possible to see these indicators appear at each logging data source, both at the endpoint and network level.

As a reminder, this table includes the most universally common data sources, but in your network, you might have other network-related data sources, such as VPN servers or HTTP access logs, so make sure you are leveraging the data source inventory from when we identified data sources in *Chapter 4*.

Something to think about when looking at network indicators is the confidence level we can put behind an indicator. Hashes are completely unique per file, so when we say a file is malicious, we can detect its hash with a high degree of confidence.

The dynamic nature of IP addresses and their relationships to domains makes it much more difficult to assume maliciousness. Threat actors will often go through hosting providers or cloud vendors to host their attack infrastructure. The provider of the infrastructure is likely, by default at least, to dynamically assign IP addresses. This means that one day an IP address could be assigned to a domain hosting a malware distribution site and the next it could be assigned to a legitimate business. For that reason, it is preferable to detect a domain rather than an IP address if possible.

If only an IP address is available, it needs to be researched to determine the level of confidence that it will remain associated with the malicious activity to avoid a high number of false positives.

Now that we have performed our Investigate phase and documented our findings, including indicators, indicator types, context, and relevant data sources, we can move on to the *Develop* phase, where we will plan out and implement detections in our lab environment. We've provided a hands-on lab to walk you through the steps in the following lab, using the same IcedID campaign example.

Scenario 1 lab

As a hands-on exercise for *scenario 1*, you are going to implement detections for both the hashes and network indicators based on the context we identified in the previous section during the *Investigate* phase. We are going to specifically focus on Sysmon as a data source for the sake of simplicity. We've already mentioned that there are other places where these detections could be created, both listed in the prior tables and specific to your own environment, but the process of designing and implementing the detection remains the same regardless of the data source. After walking through this exercise, you should be able to understand how to apply the same process to your use cases.

Installing and configuring Sysmon as a data source

In this part of the lab, we will integrate Sysmon as a data source in our detection engineering lab and use it to create a detection based on the list of hashes we've obtained from OSINT. Sysmon is not installed and configured by default but provides high-value telemetry and we recommend integrating it into your own environment if possible.

Sysmon enables fine-grained control over what events can be recorded on a Windows host, and the attributes recorded with those events. For comparison, while the advanced audit policy Event ID 4688 shows us process creation events, it does not show us the hash of the executable or the working directory for the newly created process. Sysmon has the capability to record these attributes and more.

To get started with Sysmon, we need to first download it from Microsoft's site, here: `https://learn.microsoft.com/en-us/sysinternals/downloads/sysmon`. A single `.zip` archive containing some executable files and the license agreement will be provided. Installing Sysmon is as easy as running `sysmon.exe` with the `-i` parameter. Run the `sysmon.exe -i` command and you should get an output similar to the following:

```
System Monitor v14.13 - System activity monitor
By Mark Russinovich and Thomas Garnier
Copyright © 2014-2022 Microsoft Corporation
Using libxml2. libxml2 is Copyrig©(C) 1998-2012 Daniel Veillard. All
Rights Reserved.
Sysinte-nals - www.sysinternals.com

Sysmon installed.
SysmonDrv installed.
Starting SysmonDrv.
SysmonDrv started.
Starting Sysmon..
Sysmon started.
```

Once installed, events will start being populated in the `Microsoft-Windows-Sysmon/` `Operational` log. To get these events forwarded to the Elastic Stack, we need to add an additional integration for the given agent policy:

1. Navigate to the relevant agent policy, click **Add Integration,** and select **Custom Windows Event Logs**.

2. Click **Change defaults** under the **Custom Windows event logs** section, shown in *Figure 6.1*, and enter the following values:

    -   **Channel Name**: `Microsoft-Windows-Sysmon/Operational`

    -   **Dataset name**: `winlog.sysmon`

3. Save the changes by selecting **Save and Continue** followed by **Save and deploy changes**.

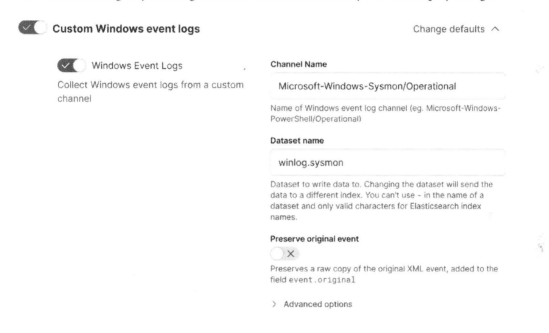

Figure 6.1 – Add Sysmon integration

With this integration in place, Sysmon events will show up in our data store. With logs being ingested, we can begin the implementation of our detections. It's important to mention that Sysmon has powerful configuration functionality, allowing us to tightly control which events are being captured.

> **Note**
> At the time of writing, forwarding Sysmon logs to the Elastic Stack can also be accomplished by using the default Windows integration. Both methods fundamentally achieve the same outcome; however, some data fields are mapped with slightly different names.

Detecting hashes

Once again, we'll start by looking at how we can detect the hashes. Reviewing the Sysmon documentation (`https://learn.microsoft.com/en-us/sysinternals/downloads/sysmon`), we can see that there are a few types of events that will record hashes:

- **Event ID 1**: Process creation
- **Event ID 6**: Driver loaded
- **Event ID 7**: Image loaded
- **Event ID 15**: FileCreateStreamHash

Based on the context we've researched, if we see malicious hashes in our environment, it is likely going to be in the context of process creation since we are discussing executable files. However, since we are centralizing all the events in our Elastic Stack and normalizing field names, combined with the uniqueness of hashes, we will write a detection directly against the hash field of Sysmon logs, regardless of the event ID.

Let's look at an example of event `ID 1` within `SOF-ELK` so we can identify what fields we should be matching against. *Figure 6.2* shows a document (event) in Kibana for event `ID 1`, specifically the raw event.

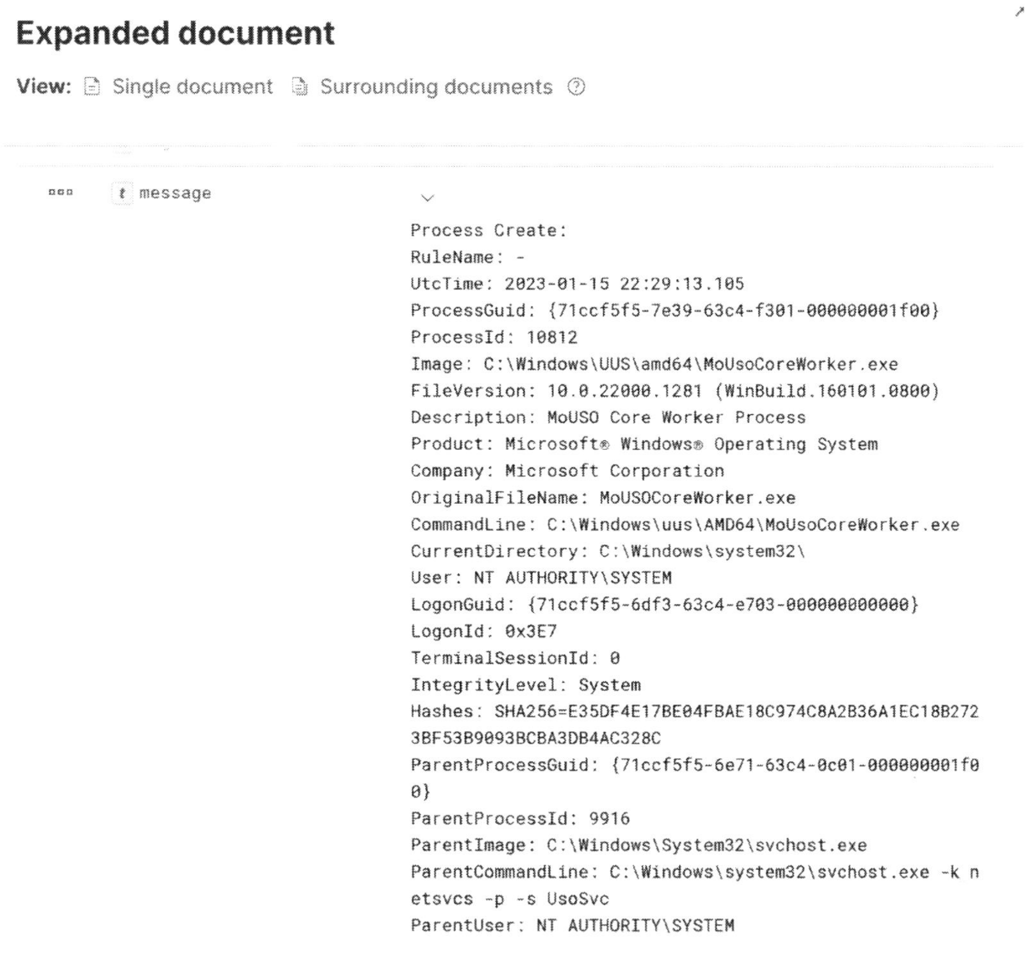

Expanded document

View: 📄 Single document   📄 Surrounding documents ⑦

```
┌──────────────────────────────────────────────────────────┐
```
⚏⚏⚏   𝑡 message   ⌄

```
Process Create:
RuleName: -
UtcTime: 2023-01-15 22:29:13.105
ProcessGuid: {71ccf5f5-7e39-63c4-f301-000000001f00}
ProcessId: 10812
Image: C:\Windows\UUS\amd64\MoUsoCoreWorker.exe
FileVersion: 10.0.22000.1281 (WinBuild.160101.0800)
Description: MoUSO Core Worker Process
Product: Microsoft® Windows® Operating System
Company: Microsoft Corporation
OriginalFileName: MoUSOCoreWorker.exe
CommandLine: C:\Windows\uus\AMD64\MoUsoCoreWorker.exe
CurrentDirectory: C:\Windows\system32\
User: NT AUTHORITY\SYSTEM
LogonGuid: {71ccf5f5-6df3-63c4-e703-000000000000}
LogonId: 0x3E7
TerminalSessionId: 0
IntegrityLevel: System
Hashes: SHA256=E35DF4E17BE04FBAE18C974C8A2B36A1EC18B272
3BF53B9093BCBA3DB4AC328C
ParentProcessGuid: {71ccf5f5-6e71-63c4-0c01-000000001f0
0}
ParentProcessId: 9916
ParentImage: C:\Windows\System32\svchost.exe
ParentCommandLine: C:\Windows\system32\svchost.exe -k n
etsvcs -p -s UsoSvc
ParentUser: NT AUTHORITY\SYSTEM
```

Figure 6.2 – Event ID 1 sample event

Figure 6.3 results from searching the document for the Hash.

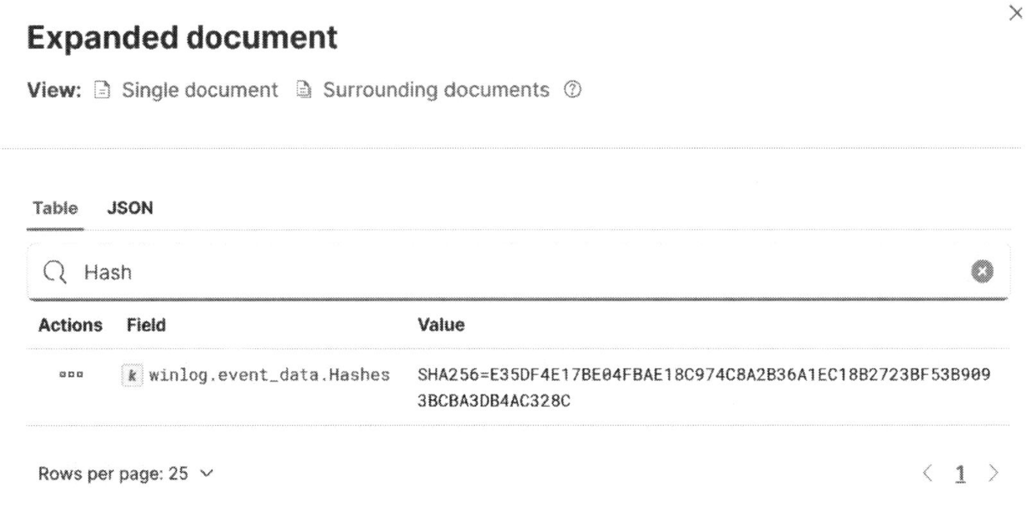

Expanded document   ×

View: 🗋 Single document   🗋 Surrounding documents   ⑦

Table   **JSON**

🔍 Hash   ⊗

Actions	Field	Value
▫▫▫	*k* winlog.event_data.Hashes	SHA256=E35DF4E17BE04FBAE18C974C8A2B36A1EC18B2723BF53B909 3BCBA3DB4AC328C

Rows per page: 25 ∨   ⟨ 1 ⟩

Figure 6.3 – Event ID 1 hashes field

Earlier in the example, we documented SHA256 hashes in particular, so winlog.event_data. Hashes is the field that we need to match against. At this point, we can begin to design our detection using all the information we've gathered to this point.

In the case of detecting atomic indicators, we simply need to map the field name we identified previously to values that we want to alert on. Before looking at the technical implementation, let's first document the conceptual design. This can be done in a variety of ways; it'll be vendor-agnostic in format and provide an understandable blueprint for our detection moving forward. The following is an example of how we could write this out:

```
if winlog.event_data.Hashes is one of
[19265aac471f7d72fcddb133e652e04c03a547727b6f98a80760dcbf43f95627,
63a7d98369925d6e98994cdb5937bd896506665be9f80dc55de7eb6df00f7607]:
```

```
then generate an alert
```

For brevity's sake, this example includes only the first two hashes, but the list can contain all the hashes that need to be detected.

We've finally reached the point of implementation, where we can take our design and put it in our development environment. The following steps will allow us to implement a detection based on a list of hashes:

1. Log in to your Kibana server and go to **Security | Alerts**.

2. Select **Manage Rules** in the top right. On the following page, select **Create Rule** in the top right.

3. In the first step of the rule creation process (**Define rule**, shown in *Figure 6.4*), select **Custom query** as your rule type. We are going to use KQL for this rule since it's the easiest solution and we only need to detect key-value pairs.

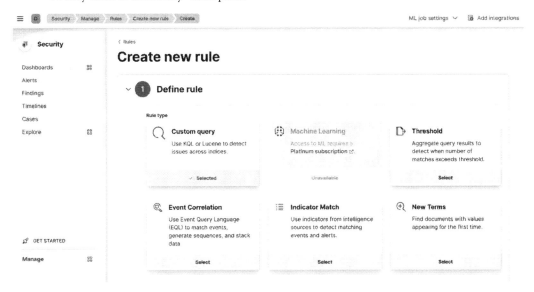

Figure 6.4 – Define rule configuration

4. Under **Custom query**, enter the following search:

```
event.code: 1 and winlog.event_data.Hashes:
(*19265aac471f7d72fcddb
133e652e04c03a547727b6f98a80760dcbf43f95627* OR
*63a7d98369925d6e
98994cdb5937bd896506665be9f80dc55de7eb6df00f7607*)
```

The first parameter looks specifically for event ID 1 (process creation). The second parameter looks for the presence of a hash in the `winlog.event_data.Hashes` field that matches one of the hashes in the list.

Additional `or` statements can be added within the parentheses to include more of our sample hashes.

5. Click **Continue**.

6. In the second step (**About rule**, shown in *Figure 6.5*), choose a descriptive title and description. For example, a good title might be `IcedID Campaign Process Creation`.

Figure 6.5 – About rule configuration

7.   Set the risk to **High**. Since hashes are unique and have high fidelity, we can assume if a process is created with that hash, it is most likely actually IcedID or a related payload running on the endpoint.

8.   Click **Continue** and leave the options as the defaults in the rest of the steps until you select **Create & enable rule** at the end.

With this rule deployed, if any processes associated with the files we discussed in this scenario are created, we will receive an alert.

Detecting network-based indicators

As with the previous exercise, we are going to continue to leverage Sysmon logs to detect our indicators. Reviewing the documentation, we can identify two event IDs to reference for network-related activity:

-   **Event ID 3**: Network connection

-   **Event ID 22**: DNSEvent (DNS query)

The most valuable of these in the context of this scenario is event ID 3. When enabled, it records network connections made by processes and records the process ID, source and destination host names, IP addresses, and ports. The default Sysmon configuration does not record event ID 3, so before continuing to develop the detection, we need to update the Sysmon configuration in our lab environment.

More information about Sysmon configuration files can be found here: `https://learn.microsoft.com/en-us/sysinternals/downloads/sysmon#configuration-files`. Configuration files enable an impressive degree of control over the type of events you can capture and how they get recorded in the Sysmon event log. For an excellent example of what well-developed Sysmon configuration files can look like, we recommend looking at SwiftOnSecurity's sample configuration file, located here: `https://github.com/SwiftOnSecurity/sysmon-config`.

To capture the network connection events, we need to make a modification to the Sysmon configuration. To do this, create a configuration file and add the following content:

```
<Sysmon schemaversion="4.82">
  <EventFiltering>
    <RuleGroup name="Network connection over port 80 or 443 or 8080" groupRelation="or">
      <NetworkConnect onmatch="include">
        <DestinationPort>443</DestinationPort>
        <DestinationPort>80</DestinationPort>
        <DestinationPort>8080</DestinationPort>
      </NetworkConnect>
    </RuleGroup>
  </EventFiltering>
</Sysmon>
```

To apply the new Sysmon configuration, save the file, then issue the following Sysmon command:

```
sysmon.exe -c [path to config file]
```

This command will update the running configuration of Sysmon to capture network connection events over port 80, 443, or 8080, all mentioned in the IcedID report.

Since we know based on the SANS ISC diary that there are malware payloads establishing C2 connections, we expect to see communication from the related process between the victim host and the C2 servers over a given port.

As you may recall, we have domains, URLs, and IP addresses operating outside of the scope of what a Sysmon network connection event would observe, but this same procedure can be reused with any data source providing fields with the chosen indicator type within the right context.

First, we are going to do as we did with the hash-based detection procedure. We need to look at an example of event ID 3 to determine which fields are relevant to our set of indicators. *Figure 6.6* provides an example of event ID 3 as it appears in Kibana, and *Figure 6.7* shows some of the fields of interest related to our example scenario, specifically destination traffic fields.

Expanded document

View: ▤ Single document ▤ Surrounding documents ⓘ |< < **1** of **12** > >|

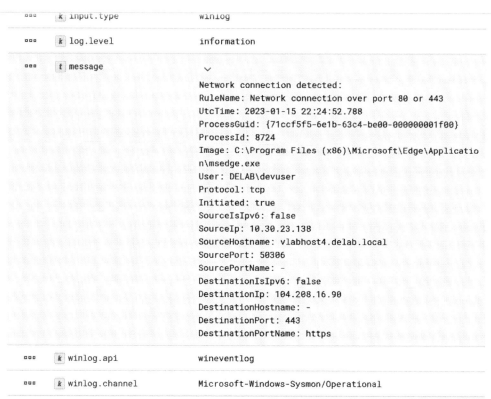

◦◦◦	**k** input.type	winlog
◦◦◦	**k** log.level	information
◦◦◦	**t** message	⌄

```
Network connection detected:
RuleName: Network connection over port 80 or 443
UtcTime: 2023-01-15 22:24:52.788
ProcessGuid: {71ccf5f5-6e1b-63c4-be00-000000001f00}
ProcessId: 8724
Image: C:\Program Files (x86)\Microsoft\Edge\Applicatio
n\msedge.exe
User: DELAB\devuser
Protocol: tcp
Initiated: true
SourceIsIpv6: false
SourceIp: 10.30.23.138
SourceHostname: vlabhost4.delab.local
SourcePort: 50306
SourcePortName: -
DestinationIsIpv6: false
DestinationIp: 104.208.16.90
DestinationHostname: -
DestinationPort: 443
DestinationPortName: https
```

◦◦◦	**k** winlog.api	wineventlog
◦◦◦	**k** winlog.channel	Microsoft-Windows-Sysmon/Operational

Figure 6.6 – Event ID 3 sample event

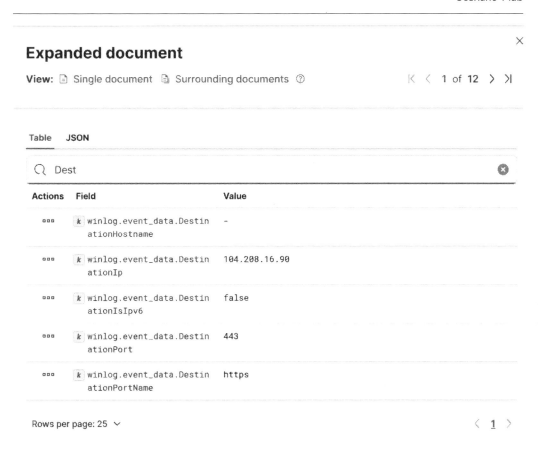

Figure 6.7 – Event ID 3 destination traffic fields

We have both IP addresses and domains so the following fields could be relevant, depending on the context of each indicator:

- `winlog.event_data.DestinationHostname`
- `winlog.event_data.DestinationIp`

When looking at samples in our lab, we observed domain resolution was not occurring for the external IP addresses; as such, detecting based on domains with this specific data source will be fruitless. For that reason, we will focus on the IP addresses. If you have a data source that is generating domains though, the Pyramid of Pain shows us those are going to be more long-lasting indicators. Try to implement similar detections based on additional data sources if you have them. Source hostname and IP address may be interesting too if the traffic is originating from the attacker server, but we should be able to catch any C2 communication as a destination.

The steps for creating our detection rule based on the network indicators will be the same as the hashes but with different search queries:

1. Log in to your Kibana server and go to **Security | Alerts**.

2. Select **Manage Rules** in the top right. On the following page, select **Create Rule** on the top right.

3. In the first step of the rule creation process (**Define rule**), select **Custom query** as your rule type. We are going to use KQL for this rule since it's the easiest solution and we only need to detect on key-value pairs.

4. Under **Custom query**, enter the following search:

   ```
   event.code: 3 and winlog.event_data.DestinationIp:
   (*45.8.229.109* OR *158.255.211.126*)
   ```

   The first parameter looks specifically for event ID 3 (network connection). The second parameter looks for the presence of a hash in the `winlog.event_data.DestinationIp` field that matches one of the IP addresses in the list.

   Additional `or` statements can be added within the parentheses to include more of our sample IP addresses.

5. Click **Continue**.

6. In the second step (**About rule**), choose a descriptive title and description. For example, a good title might be `IcedID Campaign Network Connection`.

7. Set the risk to low. We don't want to trigger high-severity alerts for IP addresses. IP addresses are lower fidelity and highly dynamic, so the IP that was once associated with IcedID may be reassigned to a legitimate website by the time it is detected.

8. Click **Continue** and leave the options as the defaults in the rest of the steps until you select **Create & enable rule** at the end.

With this rule deployed, if any network connections are made to the IP addresses in this scenario, we will receive an alert.

Lab summary

In this hands-on exercise, we took a series of IoCs obtained via OSINT and used them to develop detections for the presence of those values in relevant event types, specifically Sysmon.

While we used a specific set of indicators and Sysmon as the data source, the exact process and steps followed in this section can be used to develop detections for any key-value pairs. Next, we will move up the Pyramid of Pain, beyond static indicators, and see how to detect the tools adversaries may be using.

Summary

In this chapter, we focused on the lower levels of the Pyramid of Pain by creating detections focused on static indicators. These kinds of detections are quick and easy to implement but are more of a short-term measure. For more robust detections with wider coverage, we want to leverage tool- and behavior-based detections, which we'll discuss and create in the next chapter.

Further reading

While out of the scope of the context of this book, it may prove useful to learn more about both Sysmon configurations and **Elastic Query Language** (**EQL**).

To learn more about Sysmon configuration files, go to `https://learn.microsoft.com/en-us/sysinternals/downloads/sysmon`.

To learn more about EQL syntax, go to `https://www.elastic.co/guide/en/elasticsearch/reference/current/eql.html`.

Developing Detections Using Behavioral Indicators

In the previous chapter, we took our first look at building detections. Specifically, we used **indicators of compromise** (**IoCs**) to detect known malicious artifacts from threat intelligence. In this chapter, we are instead going to focus on how we can create more robust detections by focusing on the adversary's tools and behaviors.

First, we'll look at how we can detect a threat actor based on the tools they use. This will involve a lab where we identify what PsExec usage looks like from a detection engineering perspective. Then, we'll move on to focus on specific **tactics, techniques, and procedures** (**TTPs**) and how we can take a specific technique and identify associated evidence that can be used to build a detection.

Technical requirements

The labs in this chapter will involve the use of the detection engineering lab built as part of *Chapter 3*.

Detecting adversary tools

In this section, we will move further up the Pyramid of Pain to focus on detecting an adversary's behavior. The exercise will look at multiple tools that are used by an adversary to perform remote execution. Rather than detecting the tool directly, we instead detect the behaviors performed by the tool or performed by the adversary by using the tool. Since the behaviors align with a technique used to achieve the adversary's tactical objective, these types of detections can be more difficult for the adversary to evade.

Example scenario – PsExec usage

PsExec is a legitimate remote execution tool developed by *Sysinternals*, a *Microsoft* subsidiary. It is part of a collection of tools called **PsTools**. PsExec offers a lightweight means for authenticated users to execute commands on systems remotely. This functionality is extremely valuable for system administrators but is often abused by threat actors to advance malicious objectives. Using this tool, threat actors can execute discovery commands, deploy command and control tools, or deploy ransomware.

Before approaching the task of detecting PsExec usage, we need to research the tool to understand how it works, and what telemetry is generated as a result of its usage. We also need to be aware that the functionality of PsExec is implemented by a few other tools, such as **Impacket** and **Remcom**.

Researching PsExec

Given the task in this scenario is to detect the use of PsExec as a remote admin tool, we will take some time to understand how it works. An archive containing all PsTools, including PsExec, can be downloaded from Microsoft's website at `https://learn.microsoft.com/en-us/sysinternals/downloads/psexec`. After downloading and unzipping the contents of the file on a Windows workstation, you will have `PsExec.exe` available for execution. For our tests, it is best to interact with PsExec using an elevated command prompt or PowerShell session. When you run PsExec for the first time, you will be prompted to accept the license agreement. As indicated in the documentation, you can also accept this license agreement by passing the `/accepteula` command-line argument.

Some additional configurations may be needed when running PsExec remotely. To get around most roadblocks, we recommend making the following configuration changes to the target system:

1. Click on the Windows Start button, search for **Windows Defender Firewall**, and open the application. Click **Allow an app or feature through Windows Defender Firewall**. Click **Change Settings**, then ensure the checkboxes for **File and Printer Sharing** are enabled, as shown in *Figure 7.1*.

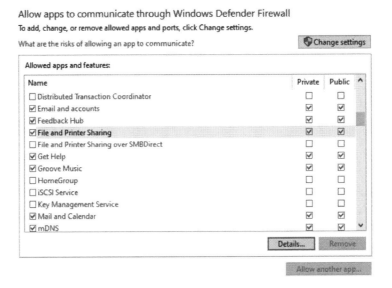

Figure 7.1 – Allow File and Printer Sharing

2. Disable **User Account Control** (**UAC**). From an elevated command prompt, issue the following commands:

```
reg ADD HKLM\SOFTWARE\Microsoft\Windows\CurrentVersion\Policies\
System /v EnableLUA /t REG_DWORD /d 0 /f
reg ADD HKLM\SOFTWARE\Microsoft\Windows\CurrentVersion\Policies\
System /v EnableLUA /t REG_DWORD /d 0 /f
```

3. Reboot the system.

After following those steps, PsExec should work for our lab scenarios.

Issuing the `psexe.exe` command with no parameters shows the full list of valid parameters for executing PsExec. You can review these options to get an understanding of its capabilities. Detailed documentation is also available on PsExec's Sysinternals page provided previously.

Issuing the `psexec.exe -s ipconfig` command produces output similar to the following:

```
PsExec v2.4 - Execute processes remotely
Copyright (C) 2001-2022 Mark Russinovich
Sysinternals - www.sysinternals.com

Windows IP Configuration

Wireless LAN adapter Wi-Fi:

   Connection-specific DNS Suffix   . : lan
   Link-local IPv6 Address . . . . . : fe80::7f0d:f779:ff0:27a6%25
   IPv4 Address. . . . . . . . . . . : 172.17.28.67
   Subnet Mask . . . . . . . . . . . : 255.255.255.0
   Default Gateway . . . . . . . . . : 172.17.28.50
ipconfig exited on LABHOST8 with error code 0.
```

You can retrieve a similar result remotely by issuing the following command from a connected system (replacing the values in the square brackets):

```
Psexec.exe \\[ip address of target] -s -u [privilege account on target
system] -p [password for privileged account] ipconfig
```

Now let's look at some of the functions we can carry out with PsExec. The `-s` argument instructs `psexec` to run the provided commands as a built-in SYSTEM account. This can be useful for administrators as well as threat actors. Using this parameter allows the launching of processes with the highest possible level of privileges on the target system. As shown in the following output, the command issued produces the output of `ipconfig.exe`. We can expand our testing to explore how this might work when targeting a remote system.

> **Note**
>
> For the following example, the command was issued from a domain-joined workstation. A command prompt was launched using a privileged domain user account.

The following code block shows `whoami` being executed against a host at `10.30.23.80` using the SYSTEM account via PsExec and the resulting output:

```
c:\tmp\pstools>psexec \\10.30.23.80 -s whoami -s -u administrator -p
weak-password! whoami

PsExec v2.4 - Execute processes remotely
Copyright (C) 2001-2022 Mark Russinovich
Sysinternals - www.sysinternals.com
nt authority\system
whoami exited on 10.30.23.80 with error code 0.
```

In this example, we pass three arguments:

- The address of the remote system, `\\10.30.23.80`.

- The `-s` parameter, to indicate we want to run this command as SYSTEM.

- The command we want to execute on the remote system. In this case, we want to run the `whoami` command.

Prior to the final output being displayed, you would see a message being displayed, similar to the following:

```
Starting PSEXESVC service on 10.30.23.80...
```

This is because PsExec creates a Windows service on the target system as part of its process for running commands remotely. We can validate this by looking at the service creation events (system event ID `7045`) on the remote system. You should see an event with the details shown in *Table 7.1*:

Event Log Attribute	Value
`EventID`	`7045`
Provider	Service Control Manager
UserName	Administrator
Image Path	`%SystemRoot%\PSEXESVC.exe`

Message	A service was installed on the system. Service Name: `PSEXESVC` Service File Name: `%SystemRoot%\PSEXESVC.exe` Service Type: `user mode service` Service Start Type: `demand start` Service Account: `LocalSystem`

Table 7.1 – Windows event ID 7045 for PsExec activity

Each time we run `PSEXEC` targeting this remote system, it creates a new service creation event with very similar attributes. The service name is always `PSEXESVC` and the service filename is always `%SystemRoot%\PSEXESVC.exe`.

Having understood how PsExec can work from the user standpoint, we can take a closer look at the data sources relevant to its detection. PsExec usage leaves an imprint on multiple data sources, and using different implementations of PsExec modifies data sources in slightly different ways.

We can get a preliminary idea of the data sources we should be interested in by using MITRE ATT&CK. Taking a look at MITRE ATT&CK technique *T1569.002*, *Service Execution* (for the enterprise tactic *Execution*), we can see it lists the following data sources:

- **Command**: Command execution
- **Service**: Service creation
- **Process**: Process creation
- **Windows Registry**: Windows Registry key modification

There is some data source configuration that must occur in order to capture the data we need.

Configuring data sources

Before we get started looking for events we can use for detections, we need to make sure our Windows clients are properly configured to capture these events, and that they get forwarded to the Elastic Stack. We already know that service creation events are being recorded by default (system event ID 7045). So, let's look at how we can capture command execution and process creation.

In this section, we will apply the concepts first introduced in *Chapter 4* regarding data sources. Specifically, we will configure the data sources relevant to identifying malicious PsExec activity, Windows Security auditing logs, and Sysmon. While, as mentioned, Sysmon provides more details than Windows Security auditing logs, not all organizations will be willing to mass install Sysmon, so we will show how the built-in logs can be used in the scenario where Sysmon is not available.

Windows Security auditing

This topic is quite vast and well beyond the scope of this book; however, it is important to understand that many events that Windows is capable of capturing do not get captured by default. This can impair our ability to build certain detections. One example is process creation (`https://learn. microsoft.com/en-us/windows/security/threat-protection/auditing/ audit-process-creation`).

In default configurations, new process creations do not get logged. To record valuable process creation events, without using any additional software, we can make a simple configuration change to our Advanced Audit Policy as shown in the following steps:

1. Using **Group Policy Management Editor** (shown in *Figure 7.2*), navigate to **Windows Settings | Security Settings | Advanced Audit Policy Configuration**, then double-click **Audit Process Creation**.

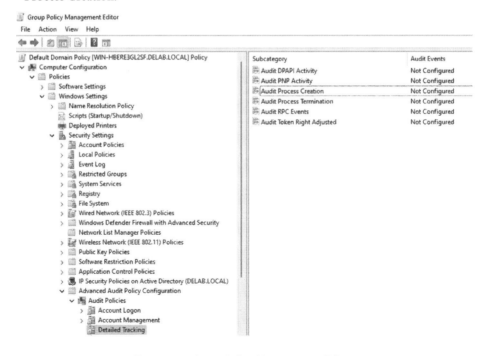

Figure 7.2 – Group Policy Management Editor

2. Double-click **Audit Process Creation**, then select **Configure the following audit events** then **Success**, and finally **Apply** or **Ok**.

3. To apply these settings, we can issue the `gpupdate` command via the command line.

Once the new settings are in place, we will start seeing security event ID 4688 appear in the logs. An example of one of these events is shown in *Table 7.2*:

Event Log Attribute	Value
`EventID`	`4688`
Provider	Microsoft-Windows-Security-Auditing
UserName	Administrator
Message	A new process has been created.
	Creator Subject: …
	Security ID: `S-1-5-21-4192533688-2314721672-1549011681-500`
	Account Name: `Administrator`
	Account Domain: DELAB
	Logon ID: 0x14192BC
	Target Subject:
	Security ID: S-1-0-0
	Account Name: –
	Account Domain: –
	Logon ID: 0x0
	Process Information:
	New Process ID: 0x1d8c
	New Process Name: C:\Windows\System32\mmc.exe
	Token Elevation Type: TokenElevationTypeDefault (1)
	Mandatory Label: S-1-16-12288
	Creator Process ID: 0x1a8c
	Creator Process Name: C:\Windows\System32\cmd.exe

Table 7.2 – Windows event ID 4688

This event shows that the `mmc.exe` process was launched by the DELAB\Administrator account. Since these events get recorded in the security event log, they will be automatically forwarded to the Elastic Stack. To validate, we can issue the following KQL query:

```
event.code : 4688
```

While this information has significant detective value, an even more powerful option exists, which can be rapidly implemented at no additional cost. Keep in mind that in our isolated lab, we were able to collect this event ID without worrying about the quantity of traffic it would produce. In a production environment, you would want to assess the number of logs generated from this auditing and filter out unnecessary data.

Sysinternals Sysmon

In one of the examples in *Chapter 6*, we reviewed Sysmon and its uses in detecting certain types of host events and artifacts. Refer to the section titled *Installing and configuring Sysmon as a data source* in that chapter to install and use Sysmon as a data source for this exercise. In this section, we will look at new event IDs and apply additional configurations to capture the information we require for this scenario. Specifically, we will look at two categories of events: the Windows Registry and named pipes.

The Windows Registry is a core part of the Windows operating system. It is a set of hierarchical databases that store configuration information for nearly every application and system component. Unsurprisingly, most interactive and non-interactive system operations can end up modifying the registry in way. This means this data source is also significantly busier than most. Sysmon logs registry events as event IDs 12, 13, and 14.

To capture the registry events relevant to service execution, we need to make a modification to the Sysmon configuration. For our purposes, we simply want to be able to record the registry changes that get made when a new service is created on a system. These changes are made to the `HKEY Local Machine\System\CurrentControlSet\Services registry path`. To make sure modifications to that path get captured by Sysmon, we can add the following rule group to our existing Sysmon configuration file by inserting it between the existing `<EventFiltering>` and `</EventFiltering>` tags after our previous rule group(s):

```
<RuleGroup name="Service modifications" groupRelation="and">
    <RegistryEvent onmatch="include">
        <TargetObject condition="contains">HKLM\SYSTEM\
CurrentControlSet\Services</TargetObject>
    </RegistryEvent>
    <RegistryEvent onmatch="include">
        <TargetObject condition="end with">\ImagePath</TargetObject>
    </RegistryEvent>
    <RegistryEvent onmatch="exclude">
```

```
        <TargetObject condition="excludes">\ImagePath</TargetObject>
    </RegistryEvent>
</RuleGroup>
```

To apply the new Sysmon configuration, save the file, then issue the following Sysmon command:

```
sysmon.exe -c [path to config file]
```

This command will update the running configuration of Sysmon, to capture registry changes for service creation. We can test this by rerunning PsExec and seeing what happens. If the new configuration is successfully applied, you will receive a registry value set event with data similar to that shown in *Table 7.3*:

Event Log Attribute	Value
`EventID`	`13`
Provider	`Microsoft-Windows-Sysmon`
UserName	SYSTEM
Message	Registry value set:
	RuleName: `Service modifications`
	EventType: SetValue
	UtcTime: `2023-01-11 03:13:16.343`
	ProcessGuid: `{71ccf5f5-20bf-63be-0b00-000000001d00}`
	ProcessId: `688`
	Image: `C:\Windows\system32\services.exe`
	TargetObject: `HKLM\System\CurrentControlSet\Services\PSEXESVC\ImagePath`
	Details: `%%SystemRoot%%\PSEXESVC.exe`
	User: `NT AUTHORITY\SYSTEM`

Table 7.3 – Sysmon event ID 13

PsExec makes use of **named pipes** for communication between the source and target system. We need to also make sure that our client is collecting events associated with named pipe creation. Sysmon captures these as event ID 17 (pipe created) and event ID 18 (pipe connected). We need to update our configuration file by appending our named pipe configuration to the previous file, as shown in the previous configuration steps. Here is the group that needs to be added to the event filtering:

```
<RuleGroup name="Named Pipes" groupRelation="and">
  <PipeEvent onmatch="include">
    <PipeName condition="contains any">\</PipeName>
  </PipeEvent>
  <PipeEvent onmatch="exclude">
    <PipeName condition="contains any">msedgeview</PipeName>
    <PipeName condition="is">\wkssvc</PipeName>
    <PipeName condition="is">\srvsvc</PipeName>
    <PipeName condition="is">\lsass</PipeName>
  </PipeEvent>
</RuleGroup>
```

For context, the new section instructs Sysmon to record the creation of named pipe events but to ignore the creation of some default named pipes that don't have value for the event we're trying to detect.

Testing PsExec again reveals the capture of the following named pipe events. You'll see there are three separate named pipe creation events that were created, each listed in the Message section of *Table 7.4*:

Event Log Attribute	Value
EventID	17
Provider	Microsoft-Windows-Sysmon
UserName	SYSTEM

Message	———————————————————
	Pipe Created:
	RuleName: Named Pipes
	EventType: CreatePipe
	UtcTime: 2023-01-14 03:16:18.045
	ProcessGuid: {71ccf5f5-1e81-63c2-5603-000000001e00}
	ProcessId: 12048
	PipeName: \PSEXESVC-LABHOST8-17532-stdin
	Image: C:\Windows\PSEXESVC.exe
	User: NT AUTHORITY\SYSTEM
	———————————————————
	Pipe Created:
	RuleName: Named Pipes
	EventType: CreatePipe
	UtcTime: 2023-01-14 03:16:18.045
	ProcessGuid: {71ccf5f5-1e81-63c2-5603-000000001e00}
	ProcessId: 12048
	PipeName: \PSEXESVC-LABHOST8-17532-stdout
	Image: C:\Windows\PSEXESVC.exe
	User: NT AUTHORITY\SYSTEM
	———————————————————
	Pipe Created:
	RuleName: Named Pipes
	EventType: CreatePipe
	UtcTime: 2023-01-14 03:16:18.045
	ProcessGuid: {71ccf5f5-1e81-63c2-5603-000000001e00}
	ProcessId: 12048
	PipeName: \PSEXESVC-LABHOST8-17532-stderr
	Image: C:\Windows\PSEXESVC.exe
	User: NT AUTHORITY\SYSTEM

Table 7.4 – Sysmon event ID 17

Additionally, there is an event ID 18 for the pipe connection event, as summarized in *Table 7.5*.

Event Log Attribute	Value
EventID	18
Provider	Microsoft-Windows-Sysmon
UserName	SYSTEM
Message	Pipe Connected: RuleName: Named Pipes EventType: ConnectPipe UtcTime: 2023-01-14 03:03:22.124 ProcessGuid: {71ccf5f5-b005-63c1-eb03-000000000000} ProcessId: 4 PipeName: \PSEXESVC-LABHOST8-17584-stdin Image: System User: NT AUTHORITY\SYSTEM

Table 7.5 – Sysmon event ID 18

At this point, we should be collecting enough data to detect service execution with PsExec. From the previous steps, we have a fair understanding of some events that get recorded when PsExec gets used. However, we should take a look at some additional tools that utilize the same technique (service execution), to see how the telemetry might change. This step is important to avoid writing a detection that is too tightly defined for a few event scenarios.

For an example of why this can be an issue, let's look at a sample event and an inappropriate detection:

- **Requirement**: Detect execution of evil.exe on all systems. (For the purposes of this example, ignore the fragility of executable names.)

- **Event sample**:

  - Event time: 2023-05-01 20:32:01

  - Event Type: File execution

  - Executable name: evil.exe

  - System name: DBServer01

  - Outcome: 0 - started successfully

One plainly wrong approach would be to build a detection that looks for exact matches for all the event attributes. The reason this won't work is that we expect certain attributes to change. The event time will almost always be different, and since we want to be able to detect events on multiple systems, the system name cannot be part of the definition. Inversely, if we develop a rule that only relies on *Event Type = File Execution*, then we will likely capture every execution of evil.exe, but also the execution of many other files that do not have the name evil.exe.

Since attributes can change for events representing the same underlying activity, the rules we develop need to be similarly tuned to account for these changes. If rules are too tightly defined, they will likely not match every occurrence of the event; if rules are too loosely defined, they will generate false positives. A safe goal is to write a rule that minimizes false positives. Let's take a look at how the telemetry changes when using different tools that are functionally similar to PsExec in order to identify which fields will remain consistent.

Impacket

Impacket (https://github.com/fortra/impacket) is described as a "*collection of Python classes for working with network protocols.*" The repository contains an implementation for PsExec (https://github.com/fortra/impacket/blob/8799a1a2c42ad74423841d21ed5f4193ea54f3d5/examples/psexec.py), which very closely resembles Sysinternal's PsExec, in terms of its functionality. The following excerpt shows the output of running impacket-psexec:

```
┌──(examiner Ⓢ labhost3)-[~]
└─$ /usr/bin/impacket-psexec delab.local/
administrator:secret!pw21123@10.30.23.138
Impacket v0.10.0 - Copyright 2022 SecureAuth Corporation

[*] Requesting shares on 10.30.23.138.....
[*] Found writable share ADMIN$
[*] Uploading file HRrcwYpJ.exe
[*] Opening SVCManager on 10.30.23.138.....
[*] Creating service kFWn on 10.30.23.138.....
[*] Starting service kFWn.....
[!] Press help for extra shell commands
Microsoft Windows [Version 10.0.22000.1455]
(c) Microsoft Corporation. All rights reserved.

C:\Windows\system32> whoami
nt authority\system

C:\Windows\system32> exit
[*] Process cmd.exe finished with ErrorCode: 0, ReturnCode: 0
[*] Opening SVCManager on 10.30.23.138.....
```

```
[*] Stopping service kFWn.....
[*] Removing service kFWn.....
[*] Removing file HRrcwYpJ.exe.....
```

On the target system, the system event shown in *Table 7.6* was generated for the created service:

Event Log Attribute	Value
EventID	7045
Provider	Service Control Manager
UserName	Administrator
Image Path	`%systemroot%\HRrcwYpJ.exe`
Message	A service was installed in the system. Service Name: kFWn Service File Name: %systemroot%\HRrcwYpJ.exe Service Type: user mode service Service Start Type: demand start Service Account: LocalSystem

Table 7.6 – Event ID 7045 for Impacket execution

Additionally, the Sysmon registry event shown in *Table 7.7* was recorded:

Event Log Attribute	Value
EventID	13
Provider	Microsoft-Windows-Sysmon
UserName	SYSTEM

Message	Registry value set: RuleName: Service modifications EventType: SetValue UtcTime: 2023-01-14 03:29:21.620 ProcessGuid: {71ccf5f5-b00d-63c1-0b00-000000001e00} ProcessId: 700 Image: C:\Windows\system32\services.exe TargetObject: HKLM\System\CurrentControlSet\Services\kFWn\ImagePath Details: %%systemroot%%\HRrcwYpJ.exe User: NT AUTHORITY\SYSTEM

Table 7.7 – Event ID 13 for Impacket execution

And finally, in *Table 7.8* we can see some associated named pipe creation events (four named pipes created):

Event Log Attribute	Value
EventID	18
Provider	Microsoft-Windows-Sysmon
UserName	SYSTEM
Message	Pipe Created: RuleName: Named Pipes EventType: CreatePipe UtcTime: 2023-01-14 03:29:21.667 ProcessGuid: {71ccf5f5-2191-63c2-7303-000000001e00} ProcessId: 12852 PipeName: \RemCom_communicaton Image: C:\Windows\HRrcwYpJ.exe User: NT AUTHORITY\SYSTEM

Message	Pipe Created: RuleName: Named Pipes EventType: CreatePipe UtcTime: 2023-01-14 03:29:21.683 ProcessGuid: {71ccf5f5-2191-63c2-7303-000000001e00} ProcessId: 12852 PipeName: \RemCom_stdinCQHe2366530 Image: C:\Windows\HRrcwYpJ.exe User: NT AUTHORITY\SYSTEM Pipe Created: RuleName: Named Pipes EventType: CreatePipe UtcTime: 2023-01-14 03:29:21.683 ProcessGuid: {71ccf5f5-2191-63c2-7303-000000001e00} ProcessId: 12852 PipeName: \RemCom_stderrCQHe2366530 Image: C:\Windows\HRrcwYpJ.exe User: NT AUTHORITY\SYSTEM Pipe Created: RuleName: Named Pipes EventType: CreatePipe UtcTime: 2023-01-14 03:29:21.683

Message	ProcessGuid: {71ccf5f5-2191-63c2-7303-000000001e00}
	ProcessId: 12852
	PipeName: \RemCom_stdoutCQHe2366530
	Image: C:\Windows\HRrcwYpJ.exe
	User: NT AUTHORITY\SYSTEM

Table 7.8 – Event ID 18 for Impacket execution

Notice that while we used the same technique, the generated telemetry looked slightly different. We need to keep these changes in mind as we develop our code to detect these events.

Rule development

Looking at the details we have so far, it seems as though we have enough to develop a simple detection. The effect of using PsExec leaves an imprint on three sets of data that are successfully being forwarded to our data store. *Table 7.9* summarizes our observations so far:

Tool name	Service registration – event logs	Service modification – registry	Named pipe creation
PsExec	The service name is `PSEXESVC`, and the service filename is `%SystemRoot%\PSEXESVC.exe`.	These attributes match the service creation event.	Three named pipes get created after the creation of the PsExec service, one for standard input, one for standard output, and one for errors. The named pipe names all start with `\PSEXESVC`.
Impacket-psexec	The service name seems to be randomly generated, as well as the filename. The service file gets copied to `c:\windows\`.	These attributes match the service creation event.	Three named pipes get created after the creation of the PsExec service. The named pipe names all start with `\RemCom`.

Table 7.9 – Tool log generation comparison

Our detection definition should include a check for a service creation event; however, by itself this isn't enough to detect PsExec usage. By profiling the data, we can see that multiple service creation events happen as part of normal Windows operations. (Search for Windows Defender service creation events.) We also can't rely on a service or executable name, since Impacket seems to generate unique names. While registry events do get generated when services are created, for our current environment, the recorded attributes do not give us any new information, or a strong indication of PsExec usage. Relying on only Windows event logs to identify newly created services is therefore reasonable. Our **Elastic Query Language** (**EQL**) for searching for newly created Windows services looks something like this:

```
any where event.code==7045 and winlog.channel=="System"
```

The testing we've just walked through also shows that named pipe creation is a valuable indicator of PsExec usage. The prefixes of these named pipes are predictable, and they always get created after the creation of the Windows service. The following EQL can find named pipe creation events, where the pipe name starts with \RemCom or \PSEXEC:

```
any where event.code==17  and winlog.channel=="Microsoft-Windows-
Sysmon/Operational"  and (winlog.event_data.PipeName like~
"*PSEXESVC*" or winlog.event_data.PipeName like~ "*\\RemCom*")
```

A note about Sysmon field mappings

As mentioned earlier, depending on how the Fleet agent policy integration was set up, the Sysmon fields would get mapped differently. If you used the Sysmon collection as part of the default Windows integration, your query will look slightly different, since the `winlog.event_data. PipeName` attribute is stored as `file.name`. The EQL in this case will look like the following:

```
any where event.code==17 and winlog.channel=="Microsoft-Windows-
Sysmon/Operational"  and (file.name  like~ "\\RemCom*" or file.name
like~ "\\PSEXESVC*")
```

EQL sequences can search for and match a given sequence of events, within a specified timeframe. We can use this feature to match a service creation event, followed by the creation of relevant named pipes:

```
sequence with maxspan=1m
  [any where winlog.event_id==7045 and winlog.channel=="System"]
  [any where event.code==17  and winlog.channel=="Microsoft-
Windows-Sysmon/Operational"  and (winlog.event_data.PipeName like~
"*PSEXESVC*" or winlog.event_data.PipeName like~ "*\\RemCom*")]
```

Testing

In this phase, we want to keep track of the number of events returned, the fidelity of those events, and the time taken for the query to complete. This will help us understand how well our query performs, and how often the detection rule should be executed against live data.

Armed with the EQL from the development process, we need to make sure it returns the data we expect, with as few false positives as possible.

Navigate to **Management | Dev Tools** in the Elastic Stack. Under **Console**, you can enter the query we developed, to ensure only PsExec events show up. Enter the following request:

```
GET /logs*/_eql/search
{
  "query": """
  sequence with maxspan=1m
  [any where event.code==7045 and winlog.channel=="System"]
  [any where event.code==17 and winlog.channel=="Microsoft-Windows-
Sysmon/Operational"  and (winlog.event_data.PipeName like~ "\\RemCom*"
or winlog.event_data.PipeName like~ "\\PSEXESVC*")]
  """
}
```

With the cursor within the request text, click the green play button to see the results. Ideally, this should only return records that indicate PsExec usage.

To make the returned data easier to look at, we can use the `filter_path` argument to only return values we want to review:

```
GET /logs*/_eql/search?filter_path=hits.total.value,hits.sequences.
events._source.agent.name,hits.sequences.events._source.winlog.
channel,hits.sequences.events._source.event.code,hits.sequences.
events._source.winlog.event_data
{
  "query": """
  sequence with maxspan=1m
  [any where event.code==7045 and winlog.channel=="System"]
  [any where event.code==17 and winlog.channel=="Microsoft-Windows-
Sysmon/Operational"  and (winlog.event_data.PipeName like~ "\\RemCom*"
or winlog.event_data.PipeName like~ "\\PSEXESVC*")]
  """
}
```

Review the data returned as you may have events unique to your environment. Does the query return the expected results? If not, how can the false positive rate be reduced?

Implementing the detection

The final step is to implement the detection in the Elastic Stack. To do this, follow these steps:

1. Log in to your Kibana server and go to **Security | Alerts**.

2. Select **Manage Rules** at the top right. On the following page, select **Create Rule** at the top right.

3. Since we are attempting to identify a sequence of events, select **Event Correlation** as the event type.

4. For the query, specify the one we wrote previously, at the end of the *Rule development* section:

- Query:

```
sequence with maxspan=1m
    [any where event.code==7045 and winlog.channel=="System"]
    [any where event.code==17 and winlog.channel=="Microsoft-
Windows-Sysmon/Operational"  and (winlog.event_data.PipeName
like~ "\\RemCom*" or winlog.event_data.PipeName like~ "\\
PSEXESVC*")]
```

- Name: `Possible PsExec Usage`

5. Schedule the rule to run every 10 minutes.

6. For rule actions, leave the default **Perform no actions** action unchanged. Finally, click **Create & enable rule**.

Testing the execution of PsExec should now cause an alert to be raised that looks similar to that in *Figure 7.3*.

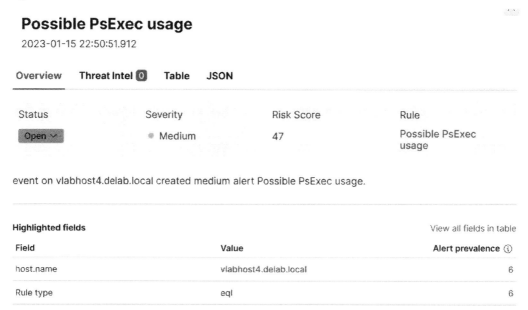

Figure 7.3 – Triggered Possible PsExec usage alert

At this point, we've seen implementations of detections at the indicator level and tool level. The final and top part of the Pyramid of Pain is **TTPs**. The last example scenario in this chapter will walk through an example of implementing a detection based on TTP.s

Detecting tactice, techniques, and procedures (TTPs)

In our last example scenario, we are going to move to the top of the Pyramid of Pain and discuss the detection of TTPs. We are specifically looking at the detection methodology for MITRE ATT&CK technique *T1553.005, Subvert Trust Controls: Mark of the Web Bypass*. First, we'll carry out the Investigate phase to understand the threat we are trying to detect and then we will move to the Develop phase to create the detection for such activity.

Example scenario – mark of the web bypass technique

Our goal in this scenario is to detect the mark of the web bypass technique and reconnaissance used by Qakbot as described here: `https://www.trendmicro.com/en_us/research/22/j/` `black-basta-infiltrates-networks-via-qakbot-brute-ratel-and-coba.html`

From the article, we can see this specific Qakbot campaign uses the technique *T1553.005, Subvert Trust Controls: Mark of the web bypass*. An email is delivered to a victim's mailbox, with a link to an encrypted `.zip` file. The email also contains a password to extract the contents of the `.zip` file, which in this case is an ISO file that contains the Qakbot payloads. For our initial investigation, we'll test some of these actions to study the telemetry that gets generated, so we can plan a method for detecting this activity.

Investigate

Mark of the web tags exist on Windows operating systems to inform the user and system when certain files were downloaded from the internet. *Figure 7.4* shows this tag as it's displayed to the user when accessed via the properties of a file on Windows systems. This tag attempts to block or otherwise subvert certain potentially unsafe actions from being performed.

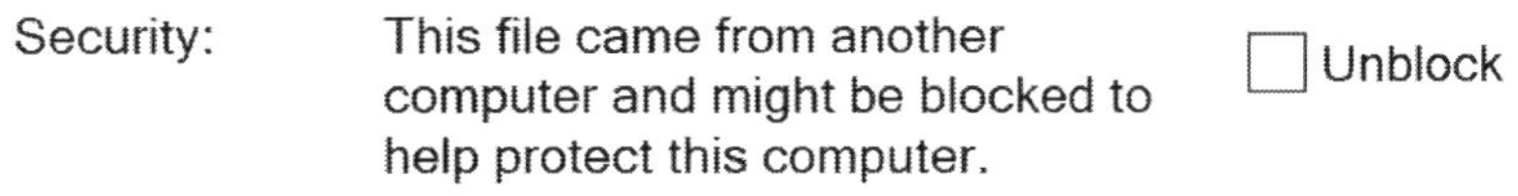

Security: This file came from another   ☐ Unblock
             computer and might be blocked to
             help protect this computer.

Figure 7.4 – Mark of the web tag on Windows

Mark of the web bypass techniques (`https://attack.mitre.org/techniques/T1553/005/`) attempt to deliver files to the end user without this tag set, allowing potentially unsafe actions to be taken.

We don't necessarily need a live Qakbot sample to test these behaviors. For our investigation, we can take any ISO file, add it to a password-protected `.zip` file, then interact with it on a Windows workstation. Opening the `.zip` file and then double-clicking the contained ISO file should produce the same telemetry we expect to see when an end user interacts with a Qakbot `.zip` file.

That being said, looking at sandbox reports for publicly available samples is extremely valuable since it provides a safe method for reviewing detailed behaviors of malware. For our investigation, we can take a look at a sample with an `SHA256` hash of `08e2bf60f946708bc43f842b44a72af-8349c6eeb515d17db96e45a7ef5ee5420` found on *MalwareBazaar*: `https://bazaar.abuse.ch/sample/08e2bf60f946708bc43f842b44a72af8349c6eeb515d17d-b96e45a7ef5ee5420/`

Qakbot comes in many flavors, but this sample closely resembles the version mentioned in the Trend Micro intel report linked to at the beginning of this section. The article depicts the following behaviors, which lead up to the Qakbot infection:

- **User action**: Link to `.zip` file clicked
- **System action**: `.zip` file downloaded, commonly to the user's downloads folder
- **User action**: `.zip` file opened
- **User action**: ISO within the `.zip` file double-clicked
- **System action**: Prompt for `.zip` password
- **User action**: Password entered
- **System action**: ISO file mounted and a new Windows Explorer window is presented to the user, set to the directory of the mounted ISO file
- **User action**: `lnk` file on the ISO file is double-clicked/invoked

Fortunately, Windows records events when ISO files get mounted. These are recorded in the `Microsoft-Windows-VHDMP-Operational` channel. This gives us access to the events shown in *Table 7.10*:

EventID (Microsoft-Windows-VHDMP-Operational)	Description
1	Stop event: Surface Virtual Disk. Recorded when a virtual disk has been successfully brought online and is available for use.
2	Stop event: Unsurface Virtual Disk. Recorded when a virtual disk has been successfully taken offline.

| 25 | Start event: Surface Virtual Disk. Recorded when the OS starts bringing a virtual disk online. |
| 26 | Start event: Unsurface Virtual Disk. Recorded when the OS starts to take a virtual disk offline. |

Table 7.10 – ISO file mount Windows events

As can be seen, some of these event IDs overlap with those we've seen in Sysmon but are associated with very different activities. It is important to understand the context of the events you are looking at when determining what the event ID means.

Testing the mounting of an ISO file from a ZIP file generated for our testing gives the event shown in *Table 7.11*:

Attribute	**Value**
Event ID	25
User.name	devuser
VhdFileName	C:\Users\devuser.DELAB\AppData\Local\Temp\Temp2_qakbot_test.zip\fake_qbot.iso
Message	Beginning to bring the VHD C:\Users\devuser.DELAB\AppData\Local\Temp\Temp2_qbot_test.zip\fake_qbot.iso online (surface).

Table 7.11 – Event ID 25 for ISO extraction from ZIP

Note that the path of the ISO file is in the user's temporary directory. This is because opening and interacting with .zip files on a Windows system extracts the contents to a temporary directory.

The Sysmon documentation shows that it has the capability to record the FileCreateStreamHash event type, which gets recorded when a browser downloads a file. To record these events, we need to make some more modifications to our Sysmon configuration file. As shown in the previous section, we can add an additional rule group to capture these events:

```
<RuleGroup name="zip file created or downloaded" groupRelation="or">
    <FileCreateStreamHash onmatch="include">
       <TargetFilename condition="end with">.zip</TargetFilename>
    </FileCreateStreamHash>
</RuleGroup>
```

This rule will now record an event when `.zip` files are downloaded. If a user clicks a link that downloads a `.zip` file, we now have an event that shows when it happens. *Table 7.12* shows a sample of this event, generated by downloading Sysinternals' `RootkitRevealer.zip`:

Attribute	Value
Event ID	15
event.action	File stream created (rule: FileCreateStreamHash)
TargetFilename	C:\Users\devuser.DELAB\Downloads\RootkitRevealer.zip
User	DELAB\devuser
Message	File stream created: RuleName: zip file created or downloaded UtcTime: 2023-01-15 23:30:15.409 ProcessGuid: {71ccf5f5-8c87-63c4-3302-000000001f00} ProcessId: 2288 Image: C:\Program Files (x86)\Microsoft\Edge\Application\msedge.exe TargetFilename: C:\Users\devuser.DELAB\Downloads\RootkitRe-vealer.zip CreationUtcTime: 2023-01-15 23:30:13.607 Hash: SHA256= E43CDDA38B9D3BA1BCCA25049 60FA921CDF071DA9A046F1 Contents: - User: DELAB\devuser

Table 7.12 – Event ID 14 for ZIP archive download

Following the infection, Qakbot processes and then initiates reconnaissance commands, after injecting itself into the innocent-looking Windows error reporting binary, `wermgr.exe`. Thanks to our Sysmon process events, these should be easy to spot. We would need to look for process events where the parent process is `wermgr.exe` and the subject process is one of the reconnaissance commands listed in the article.

Now that we understand how the attack technique works and the data that will be generated, we can move on to the Develop phase, during which we will actually build a detection for the activity.

Develop

From what we discovered in the previous section, we can build queries to identify the following activity:

- The download of ZIP files
- The mounting of `.ISO` files
- Reconnaissance commands being executed from `wermgr.exe`

Each of the following subsections will provide queries for these purposes that, when put together, can help identify this attack technique.

ZIP file download

An EQL query to detect ZIP files being downloaded looks like the following:

```
any where event.code=="15" and winlog.channel=="Microsoft-Windows-
Sysmon/Operational" and winlog.event_data.TargetFilename like~ "*.zip"
```

Currently, our Sysmon configuration only captures `FileCreateStreamHash` events for files ending with `.zip`, so our inclusion of the `TargetFilename` restriction might seem unnecessary. However, this restriction might become relevant later on, in the event we modify our Sysmon configuration to capture any additional `FileCreateStreamHash` events. We may find in profiling our events that downloading `.zip` files might occur frequently, making this a low-value query. It is very likely this query will generate many events with minimal security relevance.

Mounting of ISO files

An EQL query to detect ISO files being mounted from a ZIP file looks like the following:

```
any where event.code=="1" and winlog.channel=="Microsoft-Windows-
VHDMP-Operational" and winlog.event_data.VhdFileName like~
("*Temp*","*.zip*","*.iso")
```

Similarly, this could be done via KQL using the following query:

```
event.code: 1 and winlog.channel :"Microsoft-Windows-VHDMP-
Operational" and winlog.event_data.VhdFileName: (*Temp* AND *zip* AND
*iso*)
```

This should capture any successful mounting of virtual disks, where the path contains both .zip and Temp, indicating that the disk is possibly being mounted from a .zip file.

Reconnaissance commands executed via wermgr.exe

To detect the execution of reconnaissance commands via wermgr.exe, the following EQL query can be used:

```
any where event.code=="1" and winlog.channel=="Microsoft-Windows-
Sysmon/Operational"  and winlog.event_data.ParentImage like~ "*wermgr.
exe" and winlog.event_data.CommandLine like~ ("*arp -a*","*ipconfig*",
"*nslookup*", "*route*","*net view*","*whoami*","*net
localgroup*","*netstat -nao*","*route print*","*net share*")
```

If preferred, the same search can be done via KQL using this query:

```
event.code: 1 and winlog.channel :"Microsoft-Windows-Sysmon/
Operational" and winlog.event_data.ParentImage: *wermgr.exe and
winlog.event_data.CommandLine: (*arp -a* OR *ipconfig* OR *nslookup*
OR *route* OR *net view* OR *whoami* OR *net localgroup* OR *netstat
-nao* OR *route print* OR *net share*)
```

This captures events where the parent image is wermgr.exe, and the subject process command-line attribute is one of the reconnaissance commands we know Qakbot executes following execution.

At a minimum, we can use two of these queries. We can attempt to use a sequence as we did in the PsExec example; however, the timing is less reliable. Between mounting the ISO file and Qakbot getting invoked, the user still needs to double-click the .lnk file on the ISO file. This can happen immediately or much more slowly. The implementation of the detections can instead be a combination of rules, with different severities. This will communicate to the analyst the fact that something suspicious happened, and the urgency with which it should be addressed.

Testing the queries

As with the testing phase for our PsExec detection, we need to test our queries to determine whether they perform as expected. Ideally, they should return only events related to the behavior we are trying to identify. In our detection lab, we can run our developed queries via **Analytics | Discover** from the Kibana navigation menu and examine the events returned. Keep track of the number of events returned, the fidelity of those events, and the time taken for the query to complete. This will help us tune the queries to improve their performance and fidelity and determine how often the rule should be executed.

If a query returns too much data, this could indicate that we are missing a restriction in our query. If a query returns no data at all, this could indicate that there is not enough sample data to test the behaviors we're looking for, or there is a restriction that is filtering out the events we want to see. Be sure to also check your time filters.

Implementing the detection

Like the previous scenario, we can navigate to **Security | Alerts | Manage Rules | Create new rule** from the Kibana navigation menu to create the rules shown in *Table 7.13*. Configure them to run every 15 minutes and perform no actions:

Rule Name	Rule Type	Query
ISO mounted from `.zip` temporary directory	Custom query	event.code: 1 and winlog.channel :"Microsoft-Windows-VHDMP-Operational" and winlog.event_data. VhdFileName: (*Temp* AND *zip* AND *iso*)
`Wermgr running` reconnaissance commands	Custom query	event.code: 1 and winlog.channel :"Microsoft-Windows-Sysmon/ Operational" and winlog.event_data. ParentImage: *wermgr.exe and winlog. event_data.CommandLine: (*arp -a* OR *ipconfig* OR *nslookup* OR *route* OR *net view* OR *whoami* OR *net localgroup* OR *netstat -nao* OR *route print* OR *net share*)

Table 7.13 – Scenario 3 rule creation parameters

As can be seen, we're using the `Custom Query` rule type and specifically leveraging our KQL queries, not EQL. Previously, we used the `Event Correlation` rule type, which only understands EQL. Therefore, it's important to understand what technologies support what query languages to properly prepare for deployment.

With both these rules in place, we will now receive an alert when the behavior we defined is detected, and have done so from a technique-level perspective so that if a hash or filename, or other static indicator, changes, the technique can still be detected.

Summary

This chapter continued from the previous chapter in introducing the practical implementation of the first phases of the detection engineering life cycle, following the identification of detection requirements, this time focused on behavior-based detections. We discussed how to take a detection requirement associated with a tool or TTP and perform research into how the requirement can be met.

After performing research into each requirement, we performed hands-on exercises to show how the information gathered can be used to implement detections in your lab environment, including performing additional logging configurations to capture the events needed.

Now that we've seen how the detection engineering life cycle can get you from a detection requirement to an implemented detection, *Chapter 8* will look at how we can document detections in a way that will allow for easier tracking and organization. Additionally, we will discuss how detection pipelines and detection-as-code can lead to a more efficient method of testing and deploying detections.

8
Documentation and Detection Pipelines

In *Chapters 6* and *7* of the book, we learned how to create a set of detections. As your team begins to build out your detection repository, it is important to maintain quality by enforcing standards upon the team, and yourself.

In this chapter, we will begin by looking at how to document detections. Proper documentation standards are key to maintaining knowledge within your detection team and supporting SOC analysts reviewing alerts created by the detections. We will demonstrate the type of information that should be documented and methods to standardize and keep the documentation.

Another way to enforce quality is through the use of a detection pipeline. Leveraging a detection pipeline is a good way to implement and automate processes within your team. We'll show what it looks like to leverage detection-as-code and continuous deployment to take code through various stages of texting. We'll also introduce the concept of building blocks and composite detections.

Through the various concepts learned in this chapter, you should have a starting point to build out your team's own operating procedures and standards in order to keep a consistent and high level of quality.

The following main topics will be covered in the chapter:

- Documenting a detection
- The detection repository

Documenting a detection

In the previous chapter, we designed detections to identify **indicators of compromise (IoCs)**, *lateral movement*, and a **mark of the web (MOTW)** *bypass*. While these rules work successfully, they are incomplete because they are not accompanied by documentation supporting the **security operation center (SOC)** analyst's ability to understand the resulting alert, respond to it, or maintain the detection.

In this chapter, we will review how a detection should be documented, and what information it may be valuable to include to properly document a rule developed in *Chapter 7* for the mark of the web bypass technique.

Properly documenting a detection can be as important as the detection rule itself. If the analyst does not understand why the detection fired, what it was detecting, or what steps to take when the detection does fire, the alert may not be properly actioned or actioned at all. If an alert fires and no one is there to review it, does it make a sound? How much documentation is required should be determined by your team and it will evolve as your SOC identifies new pain points or identifies extraneous information not leveraged by your team. We will break down the detection file information into four categories:

- **Information used to maintain the detection**: This can typically be thought of as the detection's metadata and should encompass anything your team requires to track the detection. Some of this information may overlap with what is captured by your repository, such as Git, but it may be useful to have the information stored with the detection itself. The SOC analyst using your detection may not have access to your source repository but may have access to the detection rule itself or the information may be included in the alert created by the detection. Here are examples of some of the information you may gather for maintaining the detection:

  - **Author**: That's you.

  - **Creation Date and Revision History**: When the detection was first created and the date of any updates, along with a short description of what was updated.

  - **Maturity**: Your SOC can define what maturity levels to use. In this book, we will use **Experimental**, **Test**, and **Stable**, which will be defined later in this chapter.

  - **License**: If this detection will be released beyond your organization, a license is required so recipients know of any restrictions you may have. If possible, use an open source license, so the recipient isn't forced to send it on to their legal team. As an example, the MIT License is great if you're fine with people reusing your work.

  - **Ticket**: The issue or ticket number that the detection was created in response to.

  - **References**: Sources such as threat intelligence, blogs, or other analysis the detection was based upon.

- **Information about what the detection is alerting on**: This is the primary information that should be displayed when an alert from the detection fires:

  - **Name**: A descriptive name of what activity is being detected.

  - **Description**: A couple of sentences or a paragraph on what is being detected.

  - **MITRE Tactics, Techniques, and Procedures (TTPs)**: The tactics and techniques that categorize what is being detected.

- **Tags**: Any other keywords about the detection that should be easily searchable.

- **The Detection**: The file should include the detection rule, along with any other information required to run it.

- **The Rule**: The actual thing you want to run. See the previous chapter for more details.

- **Rule Format**: Some devices may support multiple detection formats, which must then be specified.

- **Data Sources / Indexes**: Log files or events the rule runs against and what log sources produce them.

- **Information used to analyze the alert**: This section should include anything that would support the SOC analyst in quickly triaging, analyzing, and responding to the alert. In some systems, much of this information will be grouped together in a *notes* section but it is still useful to address each separately:

  - **Related Detections**: Any additional alerts the analyst should look for that would confirm the detection as being a true positive.

  - **Investigation Suggestions**: Notes explaining to the SOC analyst what additional activity should be examined when reviewing this alert.

  - **Responses or Remediations**: A description or list of responses that should be taken in the event of a true positive. What actions should be taken to clean up this activity and remove the adversary?

  - **False Positives**: What legitimate activity would result in a false positive when the alert fires?

  - **Severity**: Describes how high of an impact a true positive would have.

  - **Confidence**: Describes the probability of an alert firing from the detection being a true positive.

Including this information within the detection documentation will allow for easier tracking of coverage as well as the ability to understand the context of where a rule came from when tuning is required.

Lab – documenting a detection

In this exercise, we will take one of the detections developed in the previous chapter and identify the required properties to document it. We will then use that information to create a fully documented detection. In *Chapter 7*, we developed detections to identify activity that could be indicative of a MOTW bypass used by Qakbot. These detections did not identify the MOTW bypass directly but instead identified unusual activity that commonly would occur with this technique. Take a moment to review that detection exercise and attempt to fill out *Table 8.1* below for the ISO being mounted from a ZIP file in a temporary directory procedure. Your primary audience for this information should be SOC analysts attempting to review alerts created by this detection or other detection engineers updating or reusing the detection:

Property	Value
Author	
Creation Date	
Revision History	
Maturity	
License	
Ticket	
References	
Name	
Description	
MITRE TTPs	
Tags	
Rule	
Rule Format	
Data Sources	
Related Detections	
Investigation Suggestions	
Responses or Remediations	
False Positives	
Severity	
Confidence	

Table 8.1 – Detection documentation template

Now compare your inputs to those captured below in *Table 8.2*. Were there areas that you missed that are listed below, or data that you captured more completely than what we identified? One thing to note is the MITRE TTPs. In *Chapter 7*, we discussed identifying technique **T1553.005: Mark of the Web Bypass**. Our actual rule though indirectly identifies this activity through two other techniques, **T1027: Obfuscated Files or Information** and potentially **T1204.002: User Execution of a Malicious**

File. Taking the time to properly research and identify the correct techniques is important in ensuring SOC analysts properly triage and understand the threat:

Property	Value
Author	Jason Deyalsingh
Creation Date	1/30/2023
Revision History	Initial Release
Maturity	Test
License	MIT
Ticket	N/A
References	`https://www.trendmicro.com/en_us/research/22/j/black-basta-infiltrates-networks-via-qakbot-brute-ratel-and-coba.html`
Name	ISO mounted from ZIP file in temporary directory
Description	Mark of the web tags exist on Windows operating systems, to inform the user and system when certain files were downloaded from the internet. These tags attempt to block or otherwise subvert certain potentially unsafe actions from being performed. Mark of the web bypass techniques attempt to deliver files to the end user without this tag set, allowing potentially unsafe actions to be taken. This detection identifies an ISO mounted from a ZIP file existing in a temporary directory, which is a procedure used by Qakbot after performing a MOTW bypass.
MITRE TTPs	T1027, T1204.002, T1553.005
Tags	Qakbot, MOTW Bypass

Rule	`any where event.code=="1" and winlog.`
	`channel=="Microsoft-Windows-VHDMP-Operational" and`
	`winlog.event_data.VhdFileName like~ ("*Temp*","*.`
	`zip*","*.iso")`

Rule Format	EQL
Data Sources	`winlog.*`
Related Detections	Wermgr running reconnaissance commands

Investigation Suggestions	The ISO run within the temporary directory should be investigated as possible malware. Attempt to identify and evaluate the carrier email message that delivered the ISO as a possible phishing email or investigate the domain or website the ISO was downloaded from. Continue to monitor the endpoint for the Wermgr running reconnaissance commands alert, which identifies suspicious activity that has been seen occurring after this activity and can be used to confirm the threat as a true positive.
Responses or Remediations	If confirmed as malicious activity, contain the endpoint before remediating. Check all outgoing network connections from the endpoint to identify possible C2. This activity has been associated with ransomware activity and lateral movement using Brute Ratel and Cobalt Strike.
False Positives	Users can legitimately download a zipped ISO file as a developer or network admin role.
Severity	Medium
Confidence	Medium

Table 8.2 – Detection documentation example

This data can now be used to populate your alert file. The format of the file and whether certain fields are required or optional may change based on your internal processes or which detection system you are using. It can be difficult to enforce quality detections and processes within your organization to ensure detection engineers are documenting their work as shown above. In the remainder of the chapter, we will show how detection pipelines can be used to provide rigor in your detection engineering processes, review some advanced multi-stage pipelines to illustrate how pipelines can be adapted to maintain quality and velocity in more complex use cases, and we will use an open source repository framework to use the skills learned in the preceding example to document, test, and deploy a detection in Elastic.

Exploring the detection repository

A detection pipeline should support the rapid creation, testing, maintenance, and deployment of new detections in your environment. While the pipeline should be customized to your own usage, forking an existing pipeline is a good way to start. Multiple organizations have open-sourced their detections and associated pipelines for the broader community. Some examples of this are included in this book's *Appendix*. As a starting point, you may wish to see if your chosen product vendor(s) has open-sourced their detections and pipeline, providing a natural starting point. If this does not exist, the Sigma repository and engine is an open source library of detections and a compiler to convert the rules to run in multiple detection environments.

Your detections should be organized to support easy creation and maintenance as your repository continues to evolve. The project layout outlined in *Figure 8.1* aims to provide common software development conventions that have been adapted for use by detection engineering teams. The project will contain rules, support scripts, tests, test data, documentation, and anything else your team needs to maintain their detections.

```
detection_rules
    README.md
    rules
        windows
        macos
        linux
        network
        ...
    tests
        general
        windows
        macos
        linux
        network
        ...
    targets
        qradar
        elasticsearch
        ...
```

Figure 8.1 – Detection repository layout

The `./rules` directory contains a set of subdirectories with the raw detection rules created by your team. Each subdirectory should be organized based upon the platform the rule supports, such as `windows`, `macos`, `linux`, `network`, and so on. Additional subdirectories should be added as the team supports new platforms.

Each rule should follow a predefined naming convention allowing team members to easily identify the rule without opening the file. For this book, we will use the approach of the technique followed by the procedure: `technique_name_procedure_name.yml`.

The `./tests` directory contains any test files and scripts used to check the validity of specific rules or general tests applied across the ruleset. The `./tests` directory sub-structure should mimic the `./rules` directory containing individual unit tests. Additional subdirectories can contain general test scripts that are used as broader tests. When implementing your automated tests within the build process, be specific about which tests should fail the build and which should fail an individual rule. The failure of a single rule should not affect the build process of the remaining rules within the repository. Python is our tool of choice due to its wide availability and ease of use. Testing suites such as Groovy or other language-specific suites should be evaluated if your environment is a heavy user of one of those languages.

The ./targets directory contains the built rules. The Sigma compiler can be used to convert rules to a specific target. Each target type is a subdirectory within the ./targets directory using the same naming convention as the Sigma compiler. This allows multiple appliances to be supported within your detection project.

> **The Sigma compiler**
>
> Sigma is an open source project focused on creating a common signature format for expressing a detection rule. Sigma rules can be compiled into the detection format required for a specific appliance, such as a SIEM or EDR. The Sigma project includes a wide variety of publicly sourced detections in addition to tests and other support utilities. You can download or browse the repository at https://github.com/SigmaHQ.

While almost all detection platforms contain a user interface for deploying new detections, using them can result in issues with larger teams. If your team is implementing detection-as-code processes, rules should only be deployed into their respective environment using an automation pipeline. This creates repeatable tests and processes and ensures that the detection project contains the source of truth for all rules. An orchestrator or deployment tool can be used to manage your deployments.

Later in the chapter, we will discuss allowing your branching methodology to enforce where new detections are deployed and who reviews them. This allows for partial deployment to low-risk environments or testing new rules against live data without concern that the detection will flood your analysts with false positives.

Since Sigma compiles each rule specific to a target detection platform, your team may wish to have a child pipeline that validates the compiled rule for that specific environment and deploys it to the appliance. You can also have your pipeline directly deploy the compiled detection rules to the environment. Child pipelines can be valuable if your team is supporting multiple detection platforms or if you wish to leverage tools or capabilities specific to that platform as part of the deployment process. *Figure 8.2* shows the pipeline for a Sigma rule being deployed through a continuous deployment pipeline.

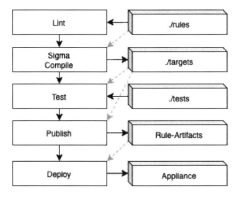

Figure 8.2 – Continuous deployment pipeline for Sigma rules

Let's look at the different stages of this pipeline:

1. **Lint**: Linting is used to perform stylistic and programmatic tests that provide early identification of errors as well as enforcing naming conventions and other coding style properties through static analysis. Since Sigma rules are written as YAML files, a YAML linter can be used to perform this static analysis of the rules and enforce the quality of the writing style of the rules.

2. **Compile**: We are using Sigma to compile Sigma rules in their native format. The `Sigma-cli` command will convert rules from a common language over to the specific format required by individual appliances.

3. **Test**: The testing phase can be used to perform broad tests that run against all rules or tests that are specific to the individual functionality of that rule. By adhering to the same directory structure and naming format in both the `rules` and `tests` directories, we can write a general automation script that identifies which tests should run against which rules.

4. **Publish**: The publish phase outputs the rule or rules in the native format required by the appliance. You may wish to have an artifact repository that stores these outputs. An artifact repository provides a single source of truth for what was deployed for each version of the rules deployed to an appliance and allows the easy rollback of versions of a rule to a previously known good state.

5. **Deploy**: The deploy stage takes the published artifacts and deploys them to the appliance. At this stage, the rules are actually running within the environment.

The use of these various stages allows us to ensure that a detection being deployed to production has undergone thorough testing and reduce the risk of bad code being introduced into the environment.

Detection-as-code

Detection-as-code is a set of processes and capabilities focused on applying software development best practices to those used to build and maintain detections within your security environment. These processes will continue to evolve (as software development processes do). We will start by identifying principles within software development that we would like to emulate or avoid, identify the tools and practices to implement them, and then look at how we can evolve our test bed to support these practices.

Software engineering has evolved over time to improve reliability, the velocity of development, collaboration, testing, and deployment. While this seems to mirror our own detection engineering needs, it is important to recognize some key differences between software development and detection engineering that may affect the processes we choose to adopt. Most prominently, software development is focused on the creation and maintenance of large software systems, with hundreds of thousands of lines of code, that may continue to exist and evolve for decades. Detections though can sometimes be represented in a single line, or perhaps a dozen lines, and can be replaced more quickly as adversaries change their attacks and detection capabilities continue to evolve. It is rare for us to create a detection that is anywhere near the size of a software development project, without it becoming a software development project itself. Software development projects also have interdependencies that interact between the subsystems. Detections, in contrast, are smaller and more atomic. Changing one detection, in many cases, does not impact others. The size and complexities of software systems can result in processes that are necessary to maintain quality software systems but may be overly cumbersome for detections.

These differences are useful to remember. An individual developer, in many cases, will not stand up a CI/CD pipeline for a small script and likewise, a smaller security organization with shared analyst responsibilities may not want to take on the overhead of detection as code processes if the number of custom detections or analysts with detection engineering responsibilities is small. With these caveats in mind, let's review some of the benefits of detection-as-code processes.

Quality maintenance

It can be difficult to keep good documentation and clean code hygiene when there is no enforcement mechanism. Common branching and check-in processes allow the enforcement of peer review of new detections. By adopting code check-in processes within your detection engineering environment, your team becomes each other's detection repository guards for quality enforcement.

Code repositories, such as Git, provide mechanisms for implementing a branching strategy. By implementing a branching strategy for your detections, you can maintain the quality of your detection repository while enabling team collaboration. A typical code repository will have multiple types of branches. The `Main` or `Master` branch is the central repository where all *production-level* (*stable*) detections will reside. On the opposite end of the spectrum are the `Feature` branches. These are created by individuals to work on new detections or updates to existing detections without impacting the production detection repository used by your organization to detect adversaries. Your branching strategy is how your detection engineering team creates `Feature` branches and the steps or additional branches required to merge those features into production.

In order to support our detection engineering workflow, we will introduce additional types of branches to support our detection engineering branching strategy. These additional branch types allow us to enforce gates and processes associated with those types. This branching strategy is provided as a starting point. Your organization should review and customize these processes to best support the team's workflows.

The feature branch

As mentioned above, our `Feature` branch is where new work by the detection engineer is performed. A detection, associated test data, tests, and documentation are developed or updated in this branch. Once these artifacts are developed or updated and the detection is working against the test dataset, it is migrated to the `Experimental` branch.

The Experimental branch

The Experimental branch allows the detection engineer to test the detection within the production environment with the associated alerts tagged for experimental use. You may wish to have the Experimental branch only deploy to a subset of the environment. For example, deploying an **Endpoint Detection and Response (EDR)** detection to a subset of systems that have been identified as non-critical systems.

The test branch

Once the detection has been additionally tuned and meets an appropriate false-positive rate in the production environment, it is migrated to the Test branch. While there should not be a peer review gate to migrate to the test phase, the detection engineer should have all appropriate documentation in place and the detection should have a production-level (stable) quality level. When the detection has migrated to the Test branch, the detection and its associated alerts are reviewed by the broader organization. After the detection has been peer reviewed, it is then migrated to the Main or Master branch and considered to be stable.

Table 8.3 defines the purpose, requirements (gates), and reviewers at each branch:

Branch	Purpose	Gates	Reviewed By
Feature	Individual or collaborative work to build or update a detection	Detection passes against known good datasets and test datasets specific to the activity being detected.	Detection engineer(s) building the detection
Experimental	Test the detection within a production environment	Detection performs appropriately against production data. Detection passes automated linting and contains appropriate documentation.	Detection engineer(s) building the detection
Test	Detection is peer reviewed in the production environment	Detection performs appropriately against production data. Detection documentation and resulting alerts are peer-reviewed.	Full detection engineering team

Stable	Production environment detections	Peer-reviewed. Fully documented. Passed quality review checks. Correct false/positive rate associated with the confidence/criticality.	SOC analysts

Table 8.3 – Repository branches

Now that we understand the process of how code goes from creation to production, let's look at how we can improve the overall performance of our detections by leveraging concepts such as building blocks and composite detections.

Building blocks and composite detections

Many detection platforms have the concept of **building blocks or reusable libraries**. Some may require repeatedly embedding this information within each detection or may have other limitations on how detections may be developed. Building block detections can also be useful to generate low-level alerts that can be used as the basis for other alerts. Let's look at a couple of examples of more complex composite detections and how our detection pipeline can help support the maintenance of these detections within our environment. The purpose of this section is to examine some complex detection pipelines, but more importantly, to review the processes and tools required to create or adapt these pipelines to meet your team's unique circumstances.

Composite alerting

We will define composite alerting as one alert that is based upon one or more other alerts. These alerts may be low-level alerts that on their own would not be reviewed by an analyst but become the basis for more high-fidelity reporting. In this circumstance, we have one or more detections that can generate a low-level alert for a type of activity. These detections are expected to generate alerts with certain properties that can be used in composite detections.

These dependencies could break as your detections continue to evolve. For example, suppose a detection is updated to provide better fidelity or account for a new procedure used by the adversary. Our detection engineer may test that the detection is firing when appropriate but their updated detection is not producing all the necessary properties for the composite detection, or those properties may not be formatted correctly. In this circumstance, the tests for that individual detection would pass, and the standalone tests for the composite detection would pass, but in production, our composite detection would fail because the building block detection no longer produces all the correct properties. Implementing a detection-as-code pipeline allows us to test that these dependencies are met. This use case is demonstrated in *Figure 8.3*. As a note, the label LL1-Tag is an arbitrary tag assigned to associate the two low-level detections as a composite detection.

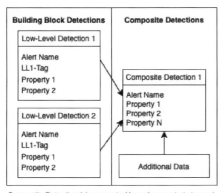 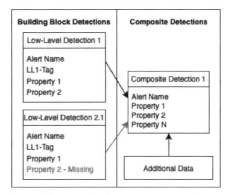

Figure 8.3 – Building Blocks and Composite Detections – Example 1

In our second example, illustrated in *Figure 8.4*, a new composite detection is created that requires new properties to be captured within our low-level building block detection. The detection engineer identifies a low-level detection creating that building block but fails to identify other detections that also create similar building blocks and therefore fails to update these detections with the additional required properties.

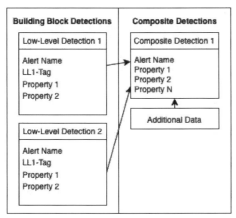 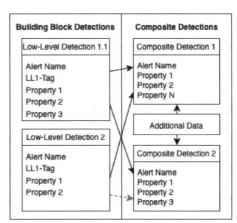

Figure 8.4 – Building Blocks and Composite Detections – Example 2

How can we update our detection engineering pipeline to identify these issues?

We could have our low-level detection tests feed into our composite-level tests. This would seem like a practical solution. Unfortunately, not all low-level detection results would result in a composite detection being generated and therefore our tests would not automatically identify this issue.

In both circumstances, there is an expectation of data that one detection was expected to produce or receive. In some circumstances, your rules engine will identify a missing property and provide an error message that can be identified during the experimental or test phases, when the new or updated detection is tested in the live environment. By including these error checks either directly within your CI/CD pipeline or through your processes, these incorrect configurations can be detected.

If your detection appliance does not provide error messages for these conditions or if your team would like to proactively identify such issues, there are solutions. Data quality tools are a useful mechanism, primarily deployed within data engineering enterprises, for creating checks on how data should be formatted. There are many solutions available but one popular open source option is **Great Expectations [greatexpectations.io]**. **Expectations** are ways to monitor your data for the existence of properties within messages, expected types of data (for example, this property should always be non-zero), or other ways to categorize your data. Great Expectations is designed to work on a data pipeline, which allows us to identify issues with our data as it flows into our SIEM or other data lake. This capability can be leveraged in responding to the above issues or can be applied to identify issues with the logs or other data sources used by our detections. For example, if a log source changes its format, rendering our detections ineffective, expectations can be used to identify these changes proactively and respond.

Embedding tools within detections

Detection engineers may depend upon other parts of their organization to help build more complex detections. For example, the detection engineering team may wish to leverage YARA signatures created by the malware analysis team of the organization within their own detections. After all, your malware team has created these signatures to detect malicious executables or detect potentially malicious activity. The malware analysis team may have its own pipeline where they are testing new and updated malware signatures that evolve as new variants are identified. Unless these signatures are directly designed for detection, there may be issues with embedding the signatures within your detections. Some of the potential issues are provided in the following list:

- The malware analysis team has only tested the signatures against malware. They have not tested the signatures against known good files, resulting in large false positive rates in a non-malicious environment.

- The YARA signatures may depend upon modules that make them impractical to run on an endpoint for detection.

- The YARA signatures may not be optimized to run in a live environment. The signatures may be appropriate for the malware analysis pipeline but the speed and efficiency of the signature may not align with the needs of the detection environment.

- The YARA signature may not detect badness. Malware analysis teams can use YARA signatures to identify certain capabilities or behaviors of a file that are not necessarily malicious but are helpful in speeding up their analysis.

The detection pipeline can be used to optimize and automate these processes. We strongly suggest not automatically deploying to production detections containing capabilities from other teams without a manual quality check from the detection team. The issues identified above can be used as requirements for our ideal detection pipeline. Our malware analysis team creates and updates new YARA signatures. Our detection engineering team has created a detection template where we can embed YARA signatures within the detection. This signature is dependent upon the YARA signature matching our malware analysis team's defined output format.

This workflow creates a detection for each YARA signature within our malware analysis team's repository. It does not, though, account for the issues we identified above. Let's continue to evolve our detection pipeline to account for these issues. *Table 8.4* provides an overview of the aforementioned issues along with potential solutions.

Issue	Potential Resolution
Signature Testing / Efficacy	New signatures are manually tested by the detection team for efficacy or are tagged by the malware analysis team as potential detection signatures. New signatures are automatically tested for false positive rates against a known good dataset.
YARA Signature module dependency	Signatures are dynamically tested for success or failure within the detection pipeline, mirroring the production environment. The pipeline script statically checks signatures for the inclusion of modules.
Speed and Resource efficiency	Signatures are dynamically checked for runtime efficiency within the detection pipeline. Detections embedding the signature are dynamically checked for runtime efficiency within the detection pipeline.
Signature Purpose	The malware analysis team tags signatures that could potentially be used for detection. The detection engineering team whitelists YARA signatures identified as valuable for detection.

Table 8.4 – Potential YARA usage issues

With these issues and solutions in mind, let's look at what a pipeline with YARA signatures embedded might look like. *Figure 8.5* shows a sample detection as a code pipeline for embedding YARA signatures within the detections for deployment. The pipeline assumes the malware analysis team has its own CI/CD pipeline for deploying new signatures for their own usage or into automated malware analysis infrastructure. By implementing the detection engineering pipeline as a child pipeline to the malware analysis team's pipeline, we can decrease the time between when the signatures are updated by the malware analysis team and when the signatures are available for use as detections. Without the pipeline, breakdowns in communicating new updates or risks with testing new updates would likely prohibit the signatures from quickly becoming utilized.

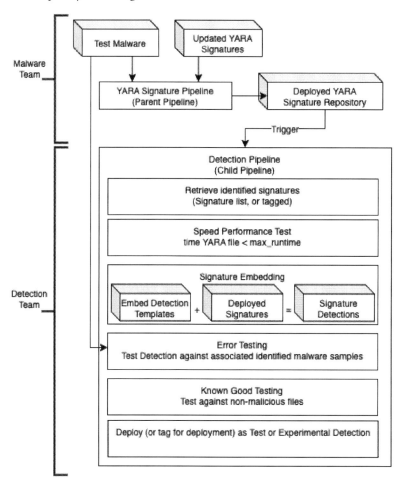

Figure 8.5 – Sample Detection-as-Code Pipeline with YARA Signature Embedding

The pipeline is started based on a trigger created by the parent pipeline. New signatures are either checked for a tag maintained by the malware analysis team or from a whitelist maintained by the detection team signaling its usage for detection. A speed test is performed, checking the time taken to execute the signature. If this passes, a script embeds the signature within the detection "code" creating a new detection. The error testing phase checks the detection against known malware associated with the signature (this repository is usually maintained by the malware analysis team). This phase would also check for any issues with included modules or incompatibility between the signature and the embedding script that would cause the detection to fail. Once the signature passes this phase, it is tested against known good files (this can also be combined with the deploy stage by deploying the signature to a test endpoint). Notice that the pipeline ends with deploying as a test or experimental update. As a detection engineering team, you should not automatically deploy signatures to production that have not been reviewed by a team member.

Challenges creating a detection pipeline

Standing up and maintaining a CI/CD pipeline within a software development team is not a simple task. Duplicating these software processes within a detection engineering team, while beneficial, comes with its own set of complications. It is something that the leadership needs to buy into and be willing to invest in. This can be difficult considering that detection tools contain user interfaces and tooling within their application to allow new detections to be created and deployed. Devoting precious resources to implement custom capabilities for managing detection deployment when someone can add a new detection through a user interface can be a tough sell. It will take time before the advantages of a detection engineering pipeline are noticeable to leadership. Issues with quality control or understanding and managing a detection repository may be good drivers for teams to take this leap.

Many of the tools discussed in this section were not designed to support detection engineering. They were designed to support software development or data engineering. While these tools should continue to work well for detection engineering workflows, their new features and roadmap will focus on serving their primary user base. These tools require integrating with your security platforms, which may lack the correct API functions to support detection as code processes. Prior to investing in researching these techniques, make sure to check that your security tools support the necessary integrations.

Managed service teams and product detection engineering teams have their own set of unique challenges. While these teams will usually have a lower risk tolerance and thus would gravitate to some of the processes documented in this chapter, they may be missing some important features that would benefit from implementing a full detection-as-code pipeline. Specifically, the security tools they are supporting may lack the ability to release silent detections. While a detection engineering team within a SOC can simply tag a detection as "experimental" or "test," a third-party team usually will not want to deploy "test" detections into a customer's environment, clogging up the customer's alert list. Silent detections are a way to deploy detections in a customer environment that are never sent to the customer's alert panel. Instead, they are only viewed by the managed services or product team that created them. This allows the team to test new detections against their customer's real-world situations without adverse effects.

Product detection engineering teams may also lack the ability to see the results of their detections within customer environments. On-premise installations or customer agreements may prevent product detection engineering teams from receiving feedback on the performance or false positive rates of their detections. This lack of visibility can make it difficult to automatically roll back detections with high false positive rates or check the performance in customer environments.

One partial solution to these issues is to use the managed service or product company's own network as the test environment. This approach provides the necessary visibility to test and deploy new detections and receive the associated feedback. This only partially addresses the issue since there will always be deviations between the customer environment and the internal team's network. One example of this approach is Facebook. Prior to releasing new features within the Facebook app, the features are released on the app instances used by their employees. Employees sometimes joke that your first day at Facebook is the last day the Facebook app will work on your phone. There may be some truth there, but it's a great way to catch bugs prior to releasing features to the general public.

Lab – Publishing a rule using Elastic's detection-rules project

In this lab, we will review **Elastic Search's detection-rules** project to leverage a set of capabilities that would be valuable to a detection pipeline. This exercise builds upon your work in previous chapters. In this exercise, we will take the detection we documented in *Chapter 7* and commit it to the repository using some of the tools and processes we examined earlier. We will use the `Elasticsearch` and `Kibana` instances instantiated in *Chapter 3*.

The detection-rules project is maintained by Elastic's detection engineering team. The project aligns with many of the detection-as-code principles that were discussed earlier in this chapter. It contains both the tools for maintaining the repository and Elastic's detection signatures as well. In previous labs, we used Elastic's user interface to write and test new detections. This lab will use command-line interfaces to implement many of the stages we discuss within the CI/CD pipeline. The lab will also introduce Git and GitHub. Git is a command-line tool for maintaining code and collaborating with other developers. The public GitHub website is the repository for most open source software, in addition to working examples of many exploits and detections as well. Most software organizations host their own GitHub or GitLab instances within their network.

The detection-rules project can be found at `https://github.com/elastic/detection-rules`. It contains the open source rule repository created by Elastic's detection team along with the functionality they have built to manage and maintain their repository. We will use the repository as a way to examine working examples of some of the concepts we discussed in this chapter.

Installing detection-rules from the command line

Here are the steps for installing the contents of the detection-rules repo via the command line:

1. The detection-rules repository requires `python 3.8` or higher installed in your environment. Check your Python version and upgrade or install as needed. You can check your Python version with the following command: `python --version`.

2. The detection-rules repository is hosted on GitHub. To use the package, we need to first fork it so that any changes we make are not inadvertently pushed back to Elastic's copy. First sign into `https://github.com/`. If you do not have an account, you will need to create one. Visit `https://github.com/elastic/detection-rules` and then click the **Fork** button at the upper right of the screen and fork a copy to your GitHub account, as shown in *Figure 8.6*.

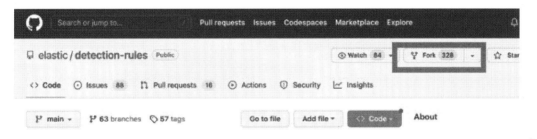

Figure 8.6 – Forking the detection-rules repository

3. To get the repository on our desktop, we need to clone it from the GitHub site. In your terminal, migrate to the parent directory where you would like to install the detection-rules repository and then type the following command, where `<ACCOUNT>` is your GitHub account hosting the forked repository. You can get this URL by clicking the green **Code** button in your forked version of the `detection_rules` repository:

```
git clone https://github.com/<ACCOUNT>/detection-rules.git
```

At this point, your fork of the repository should now be downloaded to your system.

> **If you got stuck...**
>
> If you do not have Git already installed within your environment or your credentials are not already installed at `github.com`, first install Git for your operating system (a quick web search will take you through the instructions). Once installed, create an account at `github.com` (it's free) and then upload your SSH tokens to `github.com`. This can be the most complicated step. To proceed, click on your user icon in the upper-right corner of the `github.com` site. From there, click **Settings**, and then on the left-hand panel click **SSH and GPG keys**. This page is where you can upload your SSH keys from your device to `github.com`. It also contains a guide for generating your keys and troubleshooting.

> **A note about GitHub repositories**
>
> Prior to reviewing what we downloaded, let's start by visiting the GitHub page for the repository at `https://github.com/elastic/detection-rules`. At the top of the page, we see icons for **Watch**, **Fork**, and **Star**. These statistics can be valuable in determining whether to use a GitHub project. A higher number can be indicative that more people trust and use the project. You can also look at how often and how recently the project was updated to see if development is still active. GitHub contains a tremendous amount of open source repositories, many of which are inactive or unmaintained and therefore should probably not be used as the basis for your production environment. If you click on the green **Code** button in the upper-right corner, you will get the URL we used to clone the Git repository to our computer.

Working with the detection-rules package

Within any Python project, we want to create our own virtual environment for the project. A virtual environment is used to keep the packages and versions of those packages consistent for that project so two projects do not conflict with each other. A virtual environment can be created with the command that follows in *step 1*. For this project, the detection-rules make file depends upon your environment being called env. We'll go through the steps for working with a virtual environment for this project here. You can also refer to the README.md **Getting Started** section for instructions:

1. Create the virtual environment by executing this command: `python -m venv env`.

2. Activate the virtual environment by executing the applicable command:

    *   On Windows: `.\env\Scripts\activate.bat`

    *   On Linux: `source env/bin/activate`

> **Important note**
>
> To deactivate the environment when you are done, type `deactivate`. Then reuse the preceding command to re-activate it for future use.

3. Install the requirements by executing this command: `pip3 install ".[env]"`.

4. Validate the install by executing this command: `python -m detection_rules --help`.

If the installation was successful, you should see an output similar to that in *Figure 8.7*.

```
(env) $ python -m detection_rules --help

DETECTION RULES

Usage: detection_rules [OPTIONS] COMMAND [ARGS]...

  Commands for detection-rules repository.

Options:
  -D, --debug / -N, --no-debug  Print full exception stacktrace on errors
  -h, --help                    Show this message and exit.

Commands:
  create-rule           Create a detection rule.
  dev                   Commands related to the Elastic Stack rules...
  es                    Commands for integrating with Elasticsearch.
  export-rules          Export rule(s) into an importable ndjson file.
  generate-rules-index  Generate enriched indexes of rules, based on a...
  import-rules          Import rules from json, toml, or Kibana exported...
  kibana                Commands for integrating with Kibana.
  mass-update           Update multiple rules based on eql results.
  normalize-data        Normalize Elasticsearch data timestamps and sort.
  rta                   Commands related to Red Team Automation (RTA)...
  rule-search           Use KQL or EQL to find matching rules.
  test                  Run unit tests over all of the rules.
  toml-lint             Cleanup files with some simple toml formatting.
  typosquat             Commands for generating typosquat detections.
  validate-all          Check if all rules validates against a schema.
  validate-rule         Check if a rule staged in rules dir validates...
  view-rule             View an internal rule or specified rule file.
```

Figure 8.7 – Detection rules package help

Reviewing the tool's functionality

Before diving into leveraging the detection_rules library, let's look at some cool features. The team at Elastic included a lot of capabilities, so take some time to explore by reading the CLI.md file on GitHub. The package mostly contains rule management, linting, validation, and deployment capabilities. Typosquat relates to a specific type of detection, while the dev option is a folder for a wide range of capabilities. Many of the other capabilities listed here are headers for sets of additional capabilities as well, so make sure to explore what is available:

- **Rule Management**:

  - create-rule

  - import-rules

  - rule-search

- mass-update

- export-rules

- generate-rules-index

- view-rule

- **Linting**:

  - toml-lint

  - normalize-data

- **Testing and Validation**:

  - rta (red team automation)

  - validate-all

  - validate-rule

  - test

- **Deployment**:

  - es

  - Kibana

Earlier in the chapter, we identified some capabilities that we wanted to perform, such as linting, testing, validating, and deploying our rules. We can map these steps in our pipeline to the capabilities within the detection_rules repository to illustrate how a team implements these steps. Based upon the implementation of the detection-rules library, we have moved the compile stage ahead of the linting stage in the pipeline shown in *Figure 8.8*.

Figure 8.8 – Pipeline with detection-rules implementation

To simulate our detection-engineering team we will assume the following configuration. Our detection engineering team is using the detection-rules packages capabilities to implement our internal pipeline. We have forked the package for our internal repository. Each team member has a local copy of the repository on their own computer. We have also implemented the Elasticsearch infrastructure as documented in *Chapter 3. Figure 8.9* shows how the GitHub repository should be forked for use.

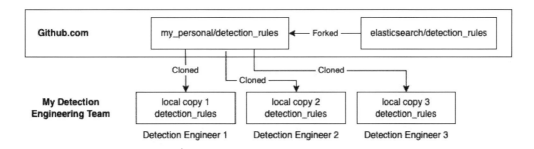

Figure 8.9 – Pipeline with detection-rules implementation

Let's use the `detection_rules` package to implement each of these steps:

1. We'll start by creating a new branch of our repository. This should always be completed when building new functionality:

```
git checkout -b  defense_evasion_iso_mounted_from_zip_temp_
directory
```

2. Next, we will import a rule using the `detection_rules import-rule` command. Since we already designed this detection in *Chapter 7* and we documented the detection at the start of this chapter, we can use this combined information to create the detection rule file listed here. The information listed within the file should directly match the documentation fields we identified earlier. Some of the field names have changed slightly to match the schema used by Elastic. The start of the rule document looks as follows:

```
[metadata]
creation_date = "2023/01/30"
maturity = "development"
updated_date = "2023/01/30"

[rule]
author = ["Jason Deyalsingh"]
description = """
This detection identifies an ISO mounted from a zip existing in
a temp directory, which is a procedure used by Qakbot
to perform MOTW bypass. Mark of the web tags exist on Windows
operating systems, to inform the user and system
when certain files were downloaded from the internet. This tag
attempts to block or otherwise subvert certain
potentially unsafe actions from being performed. Mark of the web
bypass techniques attempt to deliver files to the end
user without this tag set, allowing potentially unsafe actions
to be taken.
```

The rest of the contents of this file can be found in the book's GitHub repository here: `https://github.com/PacktPublishing/Practical-Threat-Detection-Engineering/blob/main/Chapter%208/Possible-MOTW-bypass-ISO.yaml`.

> **Note**
>
> Within the Git repository, we use a `.yaml` extension since it is a YAML file. The `detection_rules` project will expect the file to be renamed to a `.toml` file, as it is referenced in *step 3*.

3. Now that we have our rule, we can load it into the `detection_rules` repository. Copy the file into the `./rules/windows` folder. Since our rule has already been written, we will use the `import-rule` command. The `import-rule` command will still check for syntactical errors similar to a compiler. Execute the following command:

```
python -m detection_rules import-rules ./rules/windows/defense_
evasion_iso_mounted_from_zip_temp_directory.toml
```

If you are running a version of the `detection_rules` project similar to our own, you may get an error that ends like the one shown in *Figure 8.10*. This is because the `detection_rules` project checks the names and types of all events used within the rules and yet does not have full knowledge of all possible events. These checks are valuable, mimicking the syntax analysis of a compiler, to prevent detections being created with mistyped events. In order to resolve this error, we need to update a definition list for our rule to compile.

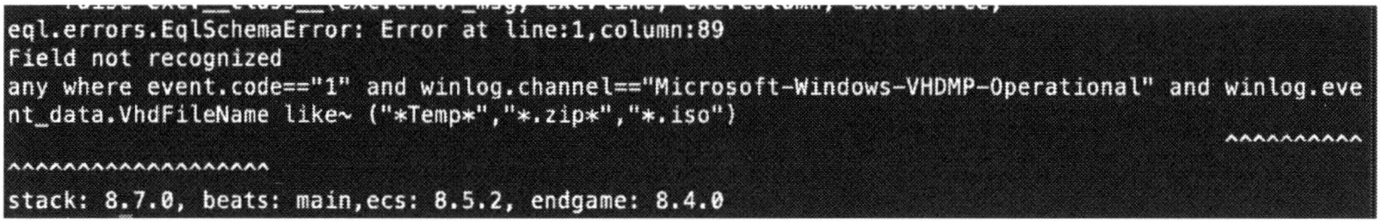

```
eql.errors.EqlSchemaError: Error at line:1,column:89
Field not recognized
any where event.code=="1" and winlog.channel=="Microsoft-Windows-VHDMP-Operational" and winlog.eve
nt_data.VhdFileName like~ ("*Temp*","*.zip*","*.iso")
                                                                                        ^^^^^^^^^^
^^^^^^^^^^^^^^^^^^^^
stack: 8.7.0, beats: main,ecs: 8.5.2, endgame: 8.4.0
```

Figure 8.10 – EqlSchemaError

4. Open the file called `non-ecs-schema.json` in the `detection_rules/etc` folder. In this file, we can see that the `winlogbeat winlog` event data properties do not include `VhdFileName` as an allowable event type. We can add the following line to the list of allowable events. After saving the file, the preceding command should now work.

Add the following line to `non-ecs.schema.json` under `winlogbeat-*` -> `winlog` -> `event_data`:

```
"VhdFileName": "keyword"
```

Successful execution of the `import-rules` command should result in an output similar to that in *Figure 8.11*.

```
(env) $ python -m detection_rules import-rules ./rules/windows/defense_evasion_iso_mounted_from_zi
p_temp_directory.toml

DETECTION RULES

[+] Building rule for /Users/gjkatz/Code/detection_engineering/elastic_detections/forked/detection
-rules/rules/iso_mounted_from_zip_temporary_directory.toml
```

Figure 8.11 – import-rules command output

Linting our rule

The next step after importing the rule is to run the linter against it. We can run the linter using the following command. Linting, as we discussed earlier, uses static analysis to identify syntax or stylistic issues with your rule:

```
python -m detection_rules toml-lint -f ./rules/windows/ defense_
evasion_iso_mounted_from_zip_temp_directory.toml
```

If successful, a message that says TOML file linting complete will be displayed.

Testing our rule

The detection-rules package has a variety of general tests it will perform against the rule, such as checking that the MITRE tactic and technique tags make sense, that the tactic is included in the tags for the alert, schema checks, and many others.

In addition to these general tests, specific unit tests checking the rule efficacy should also be developed. Earlier in the chapter, we discussed using test-driven development to first create the tests and then use them in the development of our rule. The rta folder contains red team automation scripts that can be used to generate test data for the associated rules. The red team scripts can then be run in a monitored environment to generate events for your SIEM or other detection engines. In *Chapter 9*, we will examine the use of testing to facilitate your detection engineering processes.

To execute the test scripts against all the rules, we can run the following command in the detection-rules folder:

```
python -m detection_rules test
```

The lists of tests are shown in the command output. If you want to see what a rule failure looks like, attempt changing the data in the file in an incorrect way. For example, remove Defense Evasion from the tags list. This will cause a quality check failure because the MITRE tactic is not included as a tag.

Publishing our rule

As we work on our rule, we add our files to a branch, commit them, and then push them to the repository. When our work on the branch is complete, we merge our changes into the main branch and push our results to the main branch. Traditionally, this would start our CI/CD process, which would kick off the pipeline on a container that would execute our tests, called a runner. If the previous stages of our pipeline passed, the pipeline would then let the `git push` command succeed and add our rule to the Git repository. If it failed, we could review the errors and resolve the associated issues. Since we are manually simulating our pipeline, the `git push` command does not kick off a pipeline and simply results in our new rule being added to our pipeline. The following commands will perform these steps:

1. Add our file to the current branch:

    ```
    git add ./rules/windows/defense_evasion_iso_mounted_from_zip_
    temp_directory.toml
    ```

2. Commit to the current branch:

    ```
    git commit -m "adding rule for defense evasion iso mounted from zip
    temp directory"
    ```

3. Merge the current branch with the main branch:

    ```
    a. git checkout main
    b. git fetch
    c. git pull
    d. git merge  defense_evasion_iso_mounted_from_zip_temp_
    directory
    e. git branch -d  defense_evasion_iso_mounted_from_zip_temp_
    directory
    ```

4. Push to the GitHub repository:

    ```
    git push
    ```

Now our new rule should be in the main branch of our GitHub repository.

Deploying our rule

The last stage of our simulated pipeline is to send our rule to the Elastic/Kibana instance. In a continuous deployment scenario, this would publish our rule to the production instance of our **security information and event management** (**SIEM**), after it had succeeded in the other stages of our pipeline. In this example, we will use the Elasticsearch cluster we created in *Chapter 3*.

To configure the detection-rules package to work with your cluster, you must first create a configuration file. The configuration file must be placed in the root directory of the project and is called `.detection-rules-cfg.json`. The `CLI.md` document provides information on the full set of configuration properties. For our usage, we only need to set the Kibana user, URL, and password. Replace the values in the following example with your actual username and password and update the URL if necessary:

.detection-rules-cfg.json:

```json
{
  "kibana_url": "http://localhost:5601",
  "kibana_user": "MY_USER_NAME",
  "kibana_password": "MY_PASSWORD"
}
```

Once the configuration file has been created, we can now call the following command to upload our rule to the Kibana instance:

```
python -m detection_rules kibana upload-rule --rule-file ./rules/
windows/defense_evasion_iso_mounted_from_zip_temp_directory
```

Our detection rule is now imported into our Elastic Stack instance.

Summary

In this chapter, we looked at how a detection pipeline can be used to automate and enforce your detection team's processes. We examined the steps of a standard detection engineering pipeline and looked at some more complex examples to see how a pipeline can be modified based on individual use cases.

The *Publishing a rule using Elastic's detection-rules project* lab was used to demonstrate how a team can build and leverage a set of capabilities to add structure and process to the creation of their detections. In this example, we performed the steps of our pipeline manually. These steps can be automated using a tool such as **Jenkins**, or a source repository site such as **GitHub** or **GitLab** can manage the pipeline as well.

The `detection_rules` package was built to support Elastic's internal detection team. While this package can be used and modified to support your own team's processes, you should choose the processes that align with your individual team. A common practice when building a CI/CD pipeline is to examine your current manual processes, identify what currently takes the longest in those processes and then force yourself to do it all the time. If testing is currently the bottleneck, set a goal to test every day. This approach forces you to automate your pain points and becomes the driver for how your pipeline and support infrastructure should evolve.

Now that we know how to deploy detections, in *Chapter 9* we will discuss how we can validate detections from different perspectives and evaluate some of the open source tools available to perform validation.

Part 3: Detection Validation

This part starts by looking at how we can validate the detections we create to ensure they are functioning as expected. It will introduce a couple of tools that can be used to perform validation and labs to work hands-on with those tools. The section will then end with an introduction to threat intelligence, specifically as it relates to detection engineering.

This section has the following chapters:

- *Chapter 9, Detection Validation*
- *Chapter 10, Leveraging Threat Intelligence*

9
Detection Validation

Cyber security defenses are designed to protect a company's information assets. This amalgamation of trained personnel, specialized technology, and underlying processes can be designed based on security best practices, threat modeling outputs, technical knowledge, available threat intelligence, and expert judgment. Once implemented, we need assurance that controls work as expected, under realistic conditions. Cyber security validation aims to create these conditions, that is, the techniques, tactics, and procedures used by threat actors, to measure the effectiveness of defensive control.

Cyber security validation has the goal of producing tangible measurements of how well a security program is performing. For detection engineering, well-executed validations give us the opportunity to find weaknesses or blind spots in our detection environment and remediate them before they can create an advantage for threat actors.

The process and techniques used to execute validation fall under the broader topic of security testing and assessment. This process comprises technical and non-technical steps, from documentation reviews to detonating command and control malware. Within the context of detection engineering, validation helps us understand which detections work well, what gaps exist in our current detections (where a procedure was executed and no detections were raised), and produces telemetry we can use to make any existing detections more precise or effective.

In this chapter, we'll discuss validating detections in order to assess a cyber security program. First, we'll provide an introduction to the validation process. We'll then demonstrate open source tools that can be used to perform the validation by simulating adversary activity as well as providing hands-on opportunities to test these tools within your own detection lab. Finally, we'll finish the chapter with guidance on how to use the results from validation to improve your program's effectiveness.

We will cover the following main topics in the chapter:

- Understanding the validation process
- Understanding purple team exercises
- Simulating adversary activity
- Using validation data

Technical requirements

The exercises in this chapter require the following:

- The Elastic Stack (as configured in *Chapter 3*)
- A Windows VM:
  - Minimum RAM: 4 GB
  - Minimum disk space: 80 GB
- A Linux VM:
  - Minimum RAM: 8 GB
  - Minimum disk space: 10 GB

> **An important note on the tools in this chapter**
>
> Most of the tools in this chapter are adversary emulation tools, meaning that they are designed to perform activities similar to those of a real attacker. As such, be mindful of the systems and networks on which you are running the tools as if not used properly, you could impact systems accidentally. They should also be used after a proper review of the documentation and at the user's own risk.

Understanding the validation process

The execution of cyber security validation is very similar to typical adversary simulation exercises. The emphasis, however, is on producing data that can be compared against a set of performance criteria defined for each defensive control. In broad terms, validation can be executed in three phases:

1. **Planning**: This is easily the most important phase. During this phase, the objectives of the validation exercise are defined, along with the scope, timelines, and stakeholders. The specific defensive capabilities targeted for validation and the criteria for determining their effectiveness are rigidly defined during this phase. Each validation needs to be mapped to a specific defensive control or controls, expected outcomes, and criteria for measuring the performance of the control(s). It is important at this time to also understand the possible limitations of each validation. For example, an organization may want to test T1048: Exfiltration over Alternative Protocol. In an ideal world, we would want to be able to test every possible way data can be moved out of the organization, using non-standard protocols. It goes without saying that this is difficult, if not impossible, to achieve. It can be more practical to test known techniques and accept the risk that the organization might not be able to detect yet-undiscovered T1048 procedures.

Even within the scope of known procedures, the organization may not have the capability to execute a technique they determine is relevant. At this point, they can either omit the validation entirely or design reasonable substitutions that capture the core functionality of the procedure.

It follows that this phase requires significant research of TTPs, to understand how best to approach validating the detections in scope. Threat intelligence plays an important role during this phase. For example, if the objective is to test the effectiveness of defensive controls against a specific threat group or campaign, threat intelligence maps those objectives to specific TTPs that will need to be executed to accurately simulate the threat group or campaign.

2. **Execution and data collection**: This phase is where the TTPs are executed against the target environment. Telemetry is gathered to show the performance of defensive controls in response to these TTPs.

3. **Analysis and reporting**: The output of the validation exercise is analyzed to identify which defensive controls performed well, which require further development, and what gaps exist across the defensive landscape. The results are formally documented, and the required improvements are tasked to the relevant teams for planning and implementation.

Validation can be designed for multiple levels of granularity. At the highest level, we can emulate all the **tactics, techniques, and procedures (TTPs)** used by a known threat actor, simulating a real-world attack by that threat actor. At the most granular level, we can design validations to test a very specific technical procedure used by threat actors as part of a larger operation. For detection engineering, we focus specifically on the response of the detection environment to the TTPs executed during the validation exercise.

Successful validations indicate that our detection environment raised alerts for the procedures being executed, with reasonable severity labels, and minimal false positives. If false positives are raised, alerts with inaccurate TTP labels are raised, or no alerts are raised at all following validation execution, then this indicates a deficiency in the detection environment.

Validations can be either automated or manually executed. With automated validations, a set of predefined scripts and programs are executed against an environment, with no manual intervention. These tests are useful for smaller environments or organizations, where there is limited access to red team resources. With automated validations, you trade agility and creativity for speed and scalability. When running manual validations, you have the ability to adapt and respond to defensive controls in real time, but the process takes considerably longer to both plan and execute.

The difference between detection testing and validation

While the execution of a test within the detection engineering process can at times resemble the execution of validation, the goals are slightly different.

The testing sub-process of the detection engineering life cycle is primarily concerned with ensuring a detection definition is properly implemented in code and accurately reflects the intent in production. This includes ensuring the rule returns the expected data, minimizes false positives, and is performant. The output of a successful test is a detection rule that is ready for implementation in production.

Validation, on the other hand, is specifically concerned with examining how the detection environment behaves in response to threat actor techniques. The output of validation is a tactic and technique-oriented report of how a subset of the detection environment responded to the techniques executed.

Additionally, validation does not need to be executed in-band with the detection engineering life cycle and can be used to validate a very broad set of adversarial tactics, or granular procedures, which may rely on the output of one or combinations of implemented detections.

Now that we understand the purpose of validation from a high level, we can look at how validations can be performed.

Understanding purple team exercises

Security functions can be broadly organized into two categories: the **blue team**, which focuses on defending an organization against cyber security threats, and the **red team**, which has the goal of emulating real-world adversaries. When the red and blue teams work together, collaboratively, to emulate an adversary, execute tactical defensive activity (where relevant), observe the performance of security controls, and execute responses in real time, this is referred to as a **purple team exercise**. While developed detections do get tested during a purple team exercise, the central focus of the exercise is not just the detection environment but rather the interactions between the red and blue teams. The exercises aim to help the blue team develop and improve response techniques while simultaneously helping the red team develop adversarial techniques.

Both teams work together to plan a simulated cyber-attack, comprising several tactics, within a predefined environment. The red team executes tactics transparently, observed by the blue team. The blue team reviews available telemetry to determine whether the red team activity was correctly handled by any automated defensive systems. At the same time, the blue team will execute tactical defensive responses as guided by their existing playbooks or cyber security incident response plans. This collaborative approach results in a rich, realistic, high-value experience. The red team receives immediate feedback on which techniques are less effective than others and can use that feedback to research and develop new adversary techniques. The blue team receives information and data about what specific techniques were executed by the red team, how technical and non-technical defensive components responded, where improvements can be made, and how to test the implementation of those improvements.

Let's look at how we can perform the role of the red team by simulating adversary activity.

Simulating adversary activity

For our detection lab, we may not have a red team readily available, but we still need to track how well our detections respond to realistic threat actor techniques. Fortunately, there are some free and publicly-available **breach and attack simulation** (**BAS**) resources we can use to emulate adversary behavior. We cover some noteworthy, freely available options in this section.

An important note on impairing security tools

Some validation tools and techniques can get blocked by different security controls, which is normally a good thing. However, this might prevent the validation exercise from being run as required. A preventative control on an endpoint can in some cases limit our ability to validate detective controls.

For example, consider the scenario where we need to validate detections for the creation of the log file associated with executing the `mimikatz misc::memssp` module. If we run `mimikatz`, but it immediately gets blocked and removed by Microsoft Defender, then we never create the telemetry needed to validate detections for the `misc::memssp` log file.

The common workaround for this issue is simply disabling controls as needed to create an ideal environment for the goals of your validation exercise. Impairing defenses is also a common technique used by threat actors to evade defenses. It can be valuable to understand how the different security controls behave once others are impaired.

Atomic Red Team

When it comes to adversary emulation, we recommend starting with **Atomic Red Team**. The Atomic Red Team repo is the easiest way to get started with emulating adversary activity for detection validation. Not technically a single, unified *tool*, Atomic Red Team is rather a collection of scripts that enable validation at the technique level. This collection is hosted on Red Canary's GitHub repository and is conveniently organized by MITRE ATT&CK technique. It's easy to see how using MITRE ATT&CK tags across detection and validation can make the outputs of validation more valuable. Validations executed for a specific collection of tactics, which produced ineffective or partial detection outputs, inform you which specific areas require further development, and which specific tactics you are most exposed to. You can view the repository at the following link: `https://github.com/redcanaryco/atomic-red-team`.

The requirements for working with Atomic Red Team are comparatively simple. You only need your detection environment, and a single test system to run tests on. To get started, clone the GitHub repository, or, alternatively, if you plan to test a specific technique, you can navigate directly to the relevant subfolder in the `atomics` directory, read the available technique documentation file, and execute the tests as instructed. Once complete, you can examine telemetry and any developed detections to determine whether they behaved as expected. If detections were raised, then the detection can be considered effective.

For example, we can look at a common persistence technique, Windows Registry Run key modification (**T1547.001: Boot or Logon Autostart Execution: Registry Run Keys / Startup Folder**).

Windows can be configured to automatically execute programs automatically when a user logs in. This has tremendous utility for a threat actor. One common problem threat actors need to overcome is maintaining remote access to a compromised system beyond network or power interruptions. Using this technique, the adversary can simply instruct the system to rebuild lost network connections when a user logs in. This technique can also be used to escalate privileges under the right conditions. The technical modification needed to make this procedure work is made in the Windows Registry.

Navigating to the relevant Atomic Red Team test (located here: `https://github.com/redcanaryco/atomic-red-team/blob/master/atomics/T1547.001/T1547.001.md`), we see that the writeup provides a detailed description of the technique and the specific registry modifications associated with it. Scroll down to the section labeled **Atomic Test #1** and review **Attack Commands**. The command provided uses the built-in `Reg` command to add a sub-key named `Atomic Red Team` in the current user hive, under the Run key `HKCU\SOFTWARE\Microsoft\Windows\CurrentVersion\Run`. For our test, we will make a modification to invoke the execution of the Windows calculator:

```
REG ADD "HKCU\SOFTWARE\Microsoft\Windows\CurrentVersion\Run" /V
"Atomic Red Team" /t REG_SZ /F /D "c:\windows\system32\calc.exe"
```

This should simply run the Windows calculator the next time the currently logged-in user performs a login. In this specific case, we know launching `calc.exe` automatically at login is not a malicious operation, however, nearly every other attribute involved in this activity is consistent with MITRE ATT&CK technique T1547.001. In a real-world execution of this technique, `calc.exe` would likely be replaced with some kind of nefarious executable or script that advances the adversary's objectives. This execution of a known malicious tactic, with benign payloads, gives us a way to safely test our detection of T1547.001. After launching this command, we can check to see whether appropriate alerts were generated by our detection systems.

CALDERA

CALDERA from MITRE (`https://caldera.mitre.org/`) provides an excellent interface for designing and executing adversary simulations. It enables the automated or manual execution of adversary simulations to help validate security controls.

CALDERA requires the installation of client software or *agents* on the systems that form part of the validation test. The agent software connects to the CALDERA server to receive instructions sent by the Caldera server. You can define a collection of tactics or abilities that get executed by the agents from the server in an *operation*.

There are multiple ways to install CALDERA, including deploying to a server or via Docker. In the CALDERA lab later in this chapter, we'll provision the CALDERA server via a Linux virtual machine, but the Docker method is an alternative you may choose to leverage instead since we also have

Docker deployed in our lab environment. The project's GitHub repo provides excellent coverage of the installation procedure (`https://github.com/mitre/caldera#installation`) and help for the more commonly seen error messages is detailed in the project's official documentation. (`https://caldera.readthedocs.io/en/latest/Troubleshooting.html`). After installation, you can reach the Caldera console using a web browser over port `8888`.

CALDERA's terminology is easy to understand, but important to review before getting started with it. The key concepts are summarized here:

- **Agents** run on endpoints and check for instructions from the CALDERA server at intervals.

- **Adversary profiles** are a collection of **abilities**, which are mapped to MITRE ATT&CK techniques. Adversary profiles let you design full validation tests comprising multiple techniques that emulate real-world threat actor behavior.

- The execution of abilities can collect **facts**, which can be used to design additional operation steps.

- **Operations** are a collection of atomic procedures or steps. When creating a new operation, you can define which adversary profiles are executed against which agent groups.

After installation, operations can be created for a number of pre-built adversary profiles or you can create your own adversary profile. During the execution of an operation, outputs are saved and made available in the interface. The interface also allows you to task the execution of manual ad hoc commands, enabling highly customized and dynamic validation exercises.

CALDERA lets you export operation reports that show the executed steps, the ATT&CK-tagged attack details, and the outputs of the operation steps. This data can be used to quickly identify which techniques were executed and which were detected.

With the knowledge of Atomic Red Team and CALDERA in mind, let's get some hands-on practice using these tools in our detection engineering lab.

Exercise – validating detections for a single technique using Atomic Red Team

In this section, we will execute some simple tests to review the effectiveness of implemented detections in the Elastic Stack. First, we need to enable some prebuilt detection rules and enable an additional Elastic agent integration. This will provide more complete coverage in our detection lab to more realistically simulate an enterprise environment.

Setup

We will use a single Windows workstation and Elastic Stack for these labs. We will also make use of **Endpoint and Cloud Security** integration since some of the prebuilt Elastic rules depend on it.

First, we need to enable Endpoint and Cloud Security integration for our fleet agents:

1. Navigate to **Integrations** from the main navigation menu or search for `integrations` from the main search bar.

2. Search for `Endpoint and Cloud Security Integration` to find the integration shown in *Figure 9.1* and select **Add Endpoint and Cloud Security.**

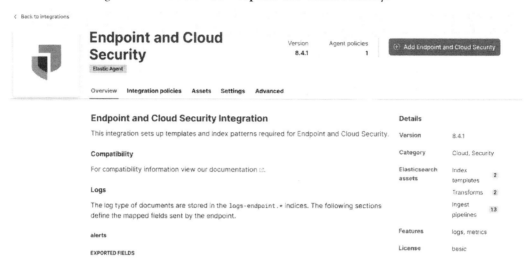

Figure 9.1 – Endpoint and Cloud Security integration

3. For step 1 of the add integration wizard, shown in *Figure 9.2*, provide a name and description for the integration. Leave the advanced settings as the default.

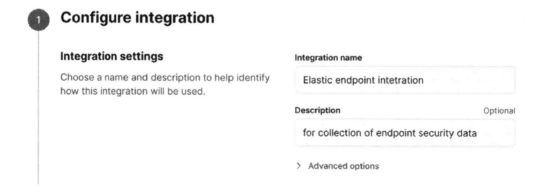

Figure 9.2 – Add integration wizard step 1

4. For step 2, shown in *Figure 9.3*, you can select **Existing hosts** to add the security integration to an existing policy, or **New hosts** to create a new agent policy. If you have completed the labs from the start of this book, you can use the existing **Windows Policy**.

Figure 9.3 – Add integration wizard step 2

5. If the Windows integration is not already added to the same policy, add that now following the same steps but by searching for `Windows integration` instead.

The Endpoint Security integration enables the collection of additional security events. With the basic license, you can enable basic malware protection and maintain custom application allow and block lists. The best way to interact with the data from the Endpoint and Cloud Security integration is by navigating to the Elastic Security app. From the sidebar menu, select **Explore** from the **Security** section. You'll see a screen similar to *Figure 9.4*.

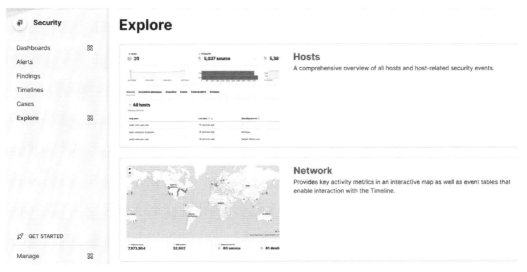

Figure 9.4 – Elastic Security app

Click on **Hosts**, then **Events** to see the view shown in *Figure 9.5*.

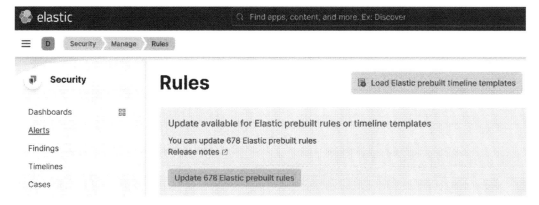

Figure 9.5 – Events view in the Elastic Security app

This will show a neat histogram of the event types being captured and processed by the Endpoint and Cloud Security integration.

The next step we need to take before getting into the Atomic Red Team part of the lab is enabling the Elastic prebuilt detection rules. From the Kibana Security app, click **Alerts**, then **Manage Rules**, and finally, if you see a message for updating Elastic prebuilt rules, similar to that in *Figure 9.6*, click **Update X Elastic prebuilt rules**. If this message does not appear, your rules are already up to date.

Figure 9.6 – Manage Kibana Security rules

For the final setup step, we'll enable a couple of rules. We'll focus on **OS Credential Dumping** techniques, specifically those that attempt to extract credential material from the LSASS process on Windows (**T1003.001**). You can read more about this technique on the MITRE ATT&CK technique page for **OS Credential Dumping: LSASS Memory**, here: `https://attack.mitre.org/techniques/T1003/001/`. From the search bar on the **Rules** page, enter `T1003.001` and press *Enter*. This will return the prebuilt elastic rules for detecting T1003.001. You'll notice that all of them are disabled. In the real world, you will likely be using a detection environment with a large number of detection rules enabled, tuned, and running. However, to keep our lab environment simple, we will start by enabling just a few. Enable the rule named **LSASS Memory Dump Creation** by toggling the control in the **Enabled** column.

Executing the validation via Atomic Red Team

Now that our environment is set up, we can look into executing the validation. For our lab, we'll be focused on validating the detections of the credential access technique T1003.001, using Red Canary's Atomic Red Team.

We can navigate over to the Atomic Red Team GitHub repository, look for the sub-folder T1003.001, and open the technique MD file (`https://github.com/redcanaryco/atomic-red-team/blob/master/atomics/T1003.001/T1003.001.md`). Review the description to understand how the technique is used by threat actors, and you'll eventually come across a set of links in the **Atomic Tests** section. Click on the link for **Atomic Test #1 - Dump LSASS.exe Memory using ProcDump**. The technique calls for the execution of the Sysinternals tool Procdump.

Log on to your test Windows workstation and download a copy of Procdump from Microsoft's site: `https://learn.microsoft.com/en-us/sysinternals/downloads/procdump`. You'll get a file named `Procdump.zip`. Extract the contents to a folder, then navigate to that folder from an elevated PowerShell prompt by searching for Windows PowerShell in the start menu, right-clicking, and selecting **Run as Administrator**. To change folders, or directories from the PowerShell prompt, use the `cd` command:

```
PS C:\Windows\system32> cd c:\users\devuser\Downloads\Procdump\
PS C:\users\devuser\Downloads\Procdump>
```

The next step is typically ill-advised but necessary for our tests. Recall in earlier sections that we mentioned it might be necessary to disable some defensive controls for the sake of testing others. Windows Defender does an excellent job of preventing LSASS memory dumps, as this technique is relatively well-known. For the relevant events to be visible to our Elastic environment, we need to temporarily disable Windows Defender real-time protection. The easiest way to get this done is by opening the Windows Security app, clicking on the **Virus & threat protection** tab, then turning **Real-time protection** off, as shown in *Figure 9.7*.

Figure 9.7 – Disable Windows Defender Real-time protection

Finally, we can run the `Attack` command specified in the procedure. From the elevated PowerShell prompt, enter the command as shown in the Atomic Red Team procedure, replacing the parameters as required. The result should be something similar to that shown in *Figure 9.8*.

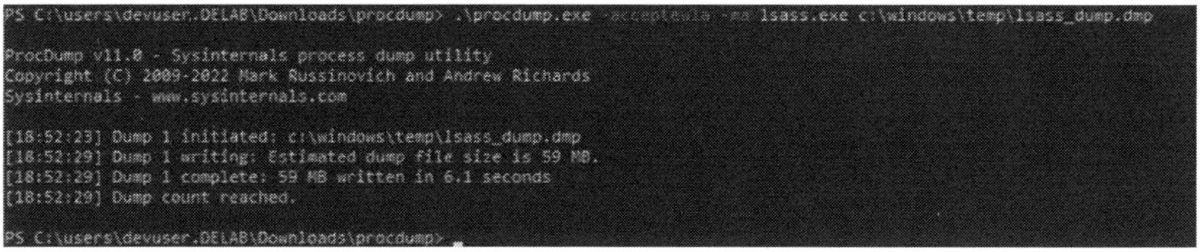

Figure 9.8 – Atomic Red Team test execution

Once the command executes successfully, we can go back to the Elastic Stack and check the **Alerts** section of the Elastic Security app.

Figure 9.9 – Alerts in the Elastic Security app

You should see a single alert similar to the view shown in *Figure 9.9*. This shows a single alert was raised for the activity we performed. Clicking the expand icon shows more details, as shown in *Figure 9.10*.

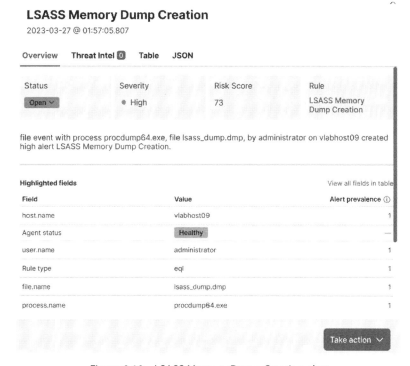

Figure 9.10 – LSASS Memory Dump Creation alert

Given that we received an alert that matches the technique that was executed, we can conclude this was a successful test. The detection environment raised an appropriate alert in response to the execution of technique T1003.001.

Additional exercises

During validation, it's important to test as many permutations as possible of a technique that will still achieve the technique objective. Attempt to rerun the technique with the following changes:

- Renamed versions of `procdump.exe`
- Change the output path and extension of the dump file

Check the alerts to see if the technique was detected after each run. Review the definition of the detection rule and see if there is a way to execute the technique without raising the alert.

For the next exercise, we will look at an alternative to Atomic Red Team that provides the capability to validate multiple techniques at once.

Exercise – validating detections for multiple techniques via CALDERA

For this exercise, we'll be adding an additional system to our lab environment and deploying CALDERA on the host to simulate adversary activity:

1. Before we begin working with CALDERA, we will enable additional detection rules that we want to validate. Navigate to **Security** | **Alerts** | **Rules** in the Elastic Stack. From the **Tags** drop-down menu, select **Windows** and **Discovery**. You can select all rules that match these criteria by clicking the checkbox next to the **Rule** column of the list, as shown in *Figure 9.11*.

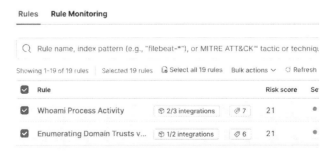

Figure 9.11 – Windows and Discovery rules

2. Next, enable all rules by clicking **Bulk actions**, then **Enable**. This will enable all available Elastic Windows rules tagged as relevant for discovery tactics.

3. For the next set of preparations, we'll provision our CALDERA server. We recommend provisioning a Linux virtual machine with 8 GB of RAM. The instructions for installing CALDERA can be found on the documentation site here: `https://caldera.readthedocs.io/en/latest/Installing-CALDERA.html`.

4. Once installed, you should be able to navigate to the server by browsing to the URL `http://[IP address of caldera server]:8888`. Log in using the default credentials (username: `admin`, password: `admin`) or the credentials you set during installation.

Deploying the CALDERA agent

To issue validation commands to our target system, we need to create a CALDERA agent and execute it on our target system. This will simulate the use of command and control tools used by threat actors to remotely control victim systems:

1. From CALDERA, in the **Campaigns** menu section, click **agents**, then **Deploy an agent**. We will use the default **Sandcat** agent.

2. Click **Windows** under **Platform**. You will be asked to fill in some additional options, as shown in *Figure 9.12*. For **app.contact.http**, replace the default IP address with the address of your CALDERA server. For **agents.implant_name**, you can leave the default value or replace it with your own value.

Figure 9.12 – CALDERA agent deployment

3. Copy the PowerShell commands listed, then save them to a file named `deploy.ps1`.

4. From the victim workstation, open the Windows Security app. As with the previous tests, we need to disable Microsoft Defender momentarily to conduct our tests. Click on **Virus & threat protection**, then under **Virus & threat protection settings**, click **Mange settings**. Ensure real-time detection is turned off.

5. Next, scroll down to **Exclusions** and add the path to our CALDERA executable. In our case, as seen in the deployment script, the Caldera executable will be downloaded to the path `C:\Users\Public\`. Click on **Add an Exclusion**, select **Folder**, then enter `C:\Users\Public`.

6. Once those changes have been made to Windows Defender, you can execute the contents of `deploy.ps1` – either by calling it directly from an elevated PowerShell prompt or by executing the commands individually from an elevated PowerShell prompt. If the agent was deployed successfully, you will see a new row for the agent appear on the Caldera **Agents** screen.

Starting a new operation

Once your agent is deployed successfully, perform the following steps:

1. Select **operations** from the navigation menu and then **Create Operation**.

2. Use any value for **Operation name**.

3. Select **Alice 2.0** for **Adversary**.

4. Select **basic** for **Fact source**.

5. Select **Start** and allow the operation to run.

After starting the operation, you will see a page similar to that in *Figure 9.13*.

Figure 9.13 – Operations in CALDERA

You'll notice quite a few discovery commands were automatically executed as part of this automated operation for the Alice 2.0 adversary. For our validation, we'll focus on these discovery commands.

In addition to the automated commands packaged with the Alice 2.0 adversary, we'll add one of our own. Click the **Manual Command** button at the top right of the **Operations** page. Ensure the powershell or psh executor is selected and enter the (invoke-webrequest ifconfig. me -usebasicparsing).content command, as shown in *Figure 9.14*.

Figure 9.14 – Manual commands in CALDERA

This command uses the ifconfig.me service to get the public IP address of your test system. If the command is run successfully, you should get a result similar to that shown in *Figure 9.15*.

Figure 9.15 – CALDERA Manual Command output

We can review the results of the operation using the **Debrief** plugin. Navigate to this view by clicking **Debrief** in the **Plugins** section of the navigation bar. You'll see a screen similar to that in *Figure 9.16*. This plugin shows details of selected operations, including the agents in use, steps executed, MITRE ATT&CK tactics and techniques, and any facts that were collected during the operation.

Figure 9.16 – CALDERA Debrief plugin

In the **Tactics & Techniques** section, shown in *Figure 9.17*, you will see the MITRE ATT&CK tactics and techniques executed as part of this operation. We'll focus on the techniques executed in the **discovery** tactic section.

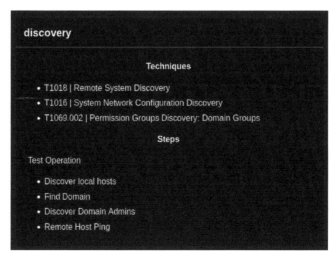

Figure 9.17 – Discovery techniques used in CALDERA operation

To highlight another feature of CALDERA, the debrief plugin provides a **Download PDF Report** button, which presents the same results in a convenient document format, similar to that shown in *Figure 9.18*.

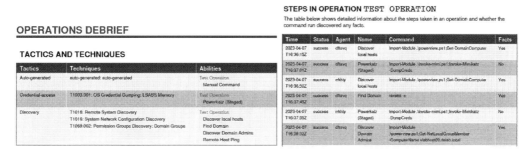

Figure 9.18 – CALDERA operation debrief PDF report

Reviewing detections in the Elastic Stack

Let's go over to the Elastic Stack and see whether the built-in detections for these techniques were triggered. Keep the time frames in which each technique was executed in mind. This will help us correlate the detection outputs with the validations being executed – which is important in production or generally busier environments.

Navigate to the Elastic Security app, then click on **Alerts**. To make results easier to compare and interpret, change the **Group by** value to `kibana.alert.rule.threat.technique.id`. This will cause the default graph to show the MITRE technique IDs instead of the default alert name. The following table, below the graph, can also be tweaked to show the technique IDs. To do this, first, click on **Fields** and search for `technique.id`. Select the checkbox next to the field, then click **Close**. If done correctly, you should have a new **Alerts** view that looks like the one in *Figure 9.19*.

Figure 9.19 – Modified Alerts view in Elastic Security

This view makes it easier to see which techniques were successfully detected as part of the validation exercise.

It's usually not enough to compare the technique IDs for the alerts generated to the technique IDs CALDERA reported as being executed. We need to look at the individual alerts and ensure they map to individual steps executed as part of the CALDERA operation. As an example, we can take a look at the manual command we executed as part of the operation. The report shows that the command was executed successfully, so ideally we should have an alert for the execution of that command, around the same time. In our case, our public IP discovery command was executed at 20:34:40 UTC. You will need to review your operations debrief for the timestamp relevant to your test case.

Searching for the properties related to that command execution, we should be able to find an event similar to the one in *Figure 9.20*. It triggered within several minutes of the time we executed the command, validating our detection coverage.

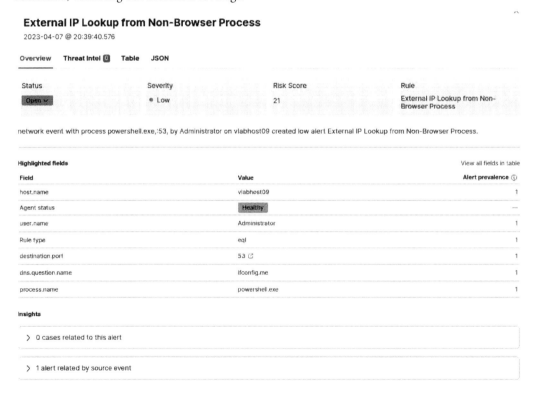

External IP Lookup from Non-Browser Process
2023-04-07 @ 20:39:40.576

Overview   Threat Intel   Table   JSON

Status	Severity	Risk Score	Rule
Open	● Low	21	External IP Lookup from Non-Browser Process

network event with process powershell.exe, :53, by Administrator on vlabhost09 created low alert External IP Lookup from Non-Browser Process.

Highlighted fields   View all fields in table

Field	Value	Alert prevalence ⓘ
host.name	vlabhost09	1
Agent status	Healthy	—
user.name	Administrator	1
Rule type	eql	1
destination.port	53	1
dns.question.name	ifconfig.me	1
process.name	powershell.exe	1

Insights

> 0 cases related to this alert

> 1 alert related by source event

Figure 9.20 – External IP Lookup from Non-Browser Process alert

To continue this exercise, repeat this check for all executed CALDERA steps and identify the detections that were raised for each step. Record the CALDERA step details and MITRE ATT&CK technique ID for all instances where an alert was not raised in response to the step execution. These are visibility gaps that need to be addressed.

Now that we've practiced a few methods of generating validation results, let's look at how such results can be used to improve our security posture.

Using validation results

After performing validations, we will walk away with some understanding of coverage. In the simplest form, validation results identify whether a detection is triggered for a given behavior. If we run a command to set persistence via a Registry Run key during validation, and we expect a detection to be triggered by that activity, we can record the result as either failed or successful by reviewing our triggered detections. Validation results, however, can also operate on more of a scale. For example, maybe a detection triggered but it was not the specific rule we expected. Or maybe we have variations of Registry Run key persistence and some were detected but others weren't, in which case we might have partial coverage. Therefore, validation results are not always black-and-white, but they will provide some level of guidance as to what happens when a chosen test is executed, which can be leveraged to improve our detection engineering program.

With the validation results in hand, we must decide how to leverage the findings in order to improve our detection engineering program. In *Chapter 2*, when discussing the requirements discovery stage, we mentioned how continuous activities can become a source of detection requirements. If our validation results highlight a gap in coverage, then it may result in the creation of a detection requirement. Before immediately taking a failed validation result and turning it into a detection requirement though, we must understand why the validation failed.

When reviewing validation results, begin by extracting the results that are potentially going to require the creation of a detection requirement. This means narrowing down the results to those that specifically failed. Furthermore, we care about validations where the simulation ran successfully but there was no detection, so remove any validations that failed because the simulation itself didn't execute as expected. Once we know what simulations ran successfully but were not detected, we have a list of potential detection requirements.

The next stage of analysis involves understanding the visibility we had of activity related to a validation. When developing detections, we must have something to detect against, so we need to understand the telemetry and data sources available to us with regard to a specific activity. In some cases, our architecture may not support a given detection. For example, if a validation failed in detecting a large outbound file transfer over **File Transfer Protocol** (**FTP**), but we do not have any network logging implemented that records data transfer sizes of FTP flows, then it is not really a detection gap as much as it is a limitation of our current security architecture. At this point, a decision would need to be made about whether the value of the detection is worth also implementing the additional logging requirements, whether a workaround exists, or whether the risk should be accepted. Either way, it is important to understand whether the visibility required to develop a detection exists before assuming a detection gap should immediately result in a detection requirement.

Assuming the visibility is present, the final question to ask is whether the behavior should have been detected given our existing tool set. By this, we mean, did the validation fail because there was no detection in place or because an existing detection failed? For example, let's say we run a validation for T1053 (Scheduled Task/Job) and it fails but we know that we have a detection rule developed for scheduled tasks. In this case, we've not uncovered a need for a new detection, but rather a shortcoming of an existing detection. This could range from an error in the syntax of the rule that was not observed via testing, or a sign the rule is too narrow and missed certain types of scheduled task activity. Either way, we do not want to report this as a need for a new detection, but instead should properly identify the issue with the existing rule and use that as the basis for a detection requirement for an update to an existing detection rather than the creation of a new one.

It is important to understand when reviewing validation results that there is never going to be such a thing as 100% detection coverage. Technologies evolve and so do threat actors. As we begin to become adept at detecting techniques, threat actors will find new ways to evade those detections. It truly is a game of whack-a-mole. That is why we have methods of triaging detection requirements. We want to focus our efforts on the detections that will have the biggest impact on our defenses. As such, we must also approach deciding how validation results should feed into detection requirements with a similar mindset. We are not looking to take every failed validation and provide coverage; we are looking to use it as additional guidance for our future development efforts.

Measuring detection coverage

In this section, we will review how to quantify your detection coverage using validation. The purpose of validation is to prove that your detections will identify the adversary. It is not to prove how well you can detect the validation tool. The topic gets a little meta, so apologies in advance. We're going to attempt to keep it grounded and focused on how we can practically define and understand the detection coverage for a technique to make sure your validations are providing metrics that accurately quantify the expected performance of your detections.

To start, we need to refer to our *Chapter 1* definitions. In *Chapter 1*, we talked about the durability of a detection, which identifies how long we expect a detection to be effective. If a detection is identifying an indicator on the lower echelons of the pyramid of pain, or anywhere there is an almost infinite number of variations that the adversary can change to execute the attack, the durability is limited to the ops-tempo of the adversary changing that part of the attack. As an example, if your detection is limited to an IP address or domain, there are almost unlimited variations of the IPs or domains used by the adversary. The durability is thereby associated with how often the adversary changes this infrastructure. Similarly, if we look at the open source tool Remcom, mentioned in *Chapter 7*, we notice that the tool creates the `RemComSvc_Logs.log` log file. This may seem like a good indicator. It is fairly unique in name and is a constant artifact of the tool. Unfortunately, since the file is created by an open source tool, the adversary can easily change the filename (or not produce a log file entirely).

The durability of the detection is limited only by the laziness of the adversary. Our goal, therefore, is to create detections that are based upon a set of features (indicators) that have a definable set of variations and that our detection encompasses that definition.

Ideally, we want to identify not just a feature with a defined set of variability but the feature with the least amount of variability. If we were to think about this on an X/Y graph (visualized in *Figure 9.21*), we have a set of indicators that can be used to identify a procedure on one axis, and on the other axis, the variability of each indicator. The indicator with the least amount of variability is the choke point for that procedure. It is the thing that the adversary can't get around doing and yet has a well-defined way for us to identify the artifact or action as being associated with the malicious activity. Our goal, therefore, is to write a rule around that indicator, or indicators, to accurately detect malicious activity.

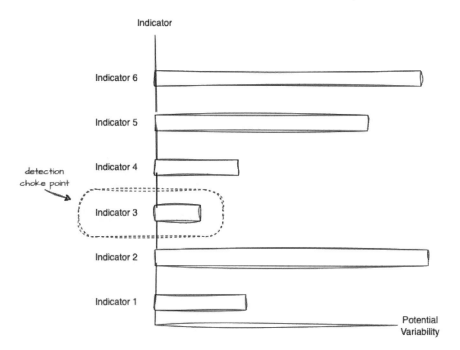

Figure 9.21 – Indicators and potential variability

As we have discussed earlier in the book, a procedure is a set of steps that the adversary takes to implement a technique. We can capture telemetry about that procedure at varying levels of fidelity. This is similar to describing a user's interaction with a website. We could capture a video of the user clicking on buttons. We could capture the button clicks as events, or the network traffic between the website server and the web browser. We could look at the API calls made between the web browser and the server or look at the functions called within the web browser itself. Depending on what procedures we were looking at tracking, different types of telemetry would be useful in tracking that activity. The same is true for the telemetry and indicators used to identify malicious procedures.

This means the choke point may not be consistent across the procedures used to accomplish a technique. During the detection development's discovery phase, we identify the multiple procedures and their choke points that could be used to achieve the technique. This information defines our **detection space** – how the adversary can vary their attack across those choke point parameters and how close our detections can be defined to include that variation without being so broad as to include an unacceptable rate of false positives. *Figure 9.22* demonstrates detection space and how detections can result in differing levels of coverage of an attack procedure with varying false positive rates.

Non-malicious activity

Attack variance of a procedure's indicator

Detection 1

Detection 2

Detection 3

A one-dimensional view of an attack space and the detections
written around it. This view adds a dimension with each
indicator used as an "and" condition within the detection.

Detection 1: No false-positives, but misses true-positives
Detection 2: Includes false-positives but will not miss true-positives
Detection 3: Includes false-positives not possible by adversary, and encompasses only some true-positives

Figure 9.22 – Detection space

In order for our validation tests to provide accurate coverage metrics of a procedure, they must consider what we are detecting. The variance of the tests should occur at the same level as the detection indicators. Misalignment can result in validation tests showing greater detection coverage than is in place. As an extreme example, visualized in *Figure 9.23*, consider a tool that can implement three separate procedures to perform the same attack. A single detection could be written to detect the tool The underlying implementation of the procedures could vary greatly, and yet the validation tests would show complete coverage.

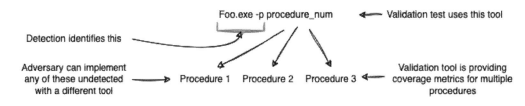

Figure 9.23 – Validating tools versus procedures

As a real-world example, consider a SOC that actually performed this approach to skew the validation results of a red team. The SOC successfully identified the red team by researching the red team's C2 prior to the test and creating a detection for that C2. The red team was thwarted at every turn. The SOC detected whatever was thrown at it. If we look at the validation results, the SOC's detection capability against the techniques attempted by the red team was perfect. They detected everything.

The SOC correctly identified a high-fidelity indicator of the red team, a C2 which they were not updating. From a black-box validation test perspective, the red team could attempt any procedure they wished and the SOC's detections would be successful in identifying the attack. Their actual detection coverage, though, was completely unknown, despite these results. This is because the variability of change performed by the red team was at the technique, procedure, and tool level. The detection logic performed by the SOC was at the network C2 level. While the SOC passed the red team test with flying colors, the results showed nothing about their ability to detect an actual adversarial attack.

We could possibly claim that only the C2 technique was discovered and not the individual procedures executed on the infrastructure. While technically true, the point can be re-emphasized by including a hypothetical network traffic decoder providing a list of commands executed by the red team. The impact is the same, just with greater fidelity in detecting the red team's actions.

We can use our detections and the attack space to identify what we need to validate. Our validation tests should ideally encompass the entire attack space of a technique. The attack space can be defined by the procedures that can be executed to achieve that technique. The variance in a procedure can be defined by how much the values of the set of indicators used by the detection can change while still achieving the objective of the technique. Therefore, we only need a single validation test using a procedure not covered by our detections to identify that procedure-level gap in coverage, while we need a set of validation tests that vary across the allowable values of the indicator(s) to confirm our detection will identify all variations of an individual procedure covered by our detection rules.

While a single rule can be written to detect multiple procedures (or vice versa), we will equate one detection to one procedure to simplify our explanations. The approach, though, holds true under either circumstance.

Pseudocode example of one rule detecting multiple procedures of a technique

```
If detection_of_procedureA OR detection_of_procedureB OR detection_
of_procedureC ALERT ON TechniqueXYZ.
```

The definitions in *Table 9.1* allow us to identify four types of procedure coverage that can exist when validating a technique:

State	Test result	Test variance
Fully detected Procedures that are fully identified by our detections	All tests for the procedure must pass	Tests vary across all bounds of valid values for detection indicators that would achieve the technique's objective
Partially detected Procedures partially identified by our detections	A subset of tests pass	Tests vary across all bounds of valid values for detection indicators that would achieve the technique's objective
Missed coverage Known procedures not covered by our detections	All tests fail	A single test of a procedure would identify failure
Zero days Unknown procedures not covered by our detections	N/A	No known test exists. Not possible to test.

Table 9.1 – Types of procedure coverage

Figure 9.24 visualizes coverage across the attack space and detection space broken up by procedures.

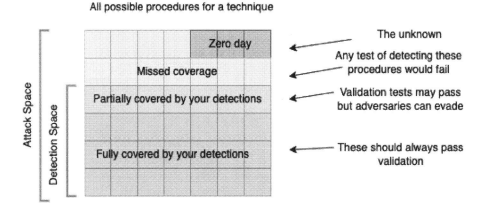

Figure 9.24 – Attack and detection space of multiple procedures

By definition, if a detection fails to identify a validation test, the test must either be testing a procedure that is uncovered by your detections or testing a variation of the procedure that your detection, incorrectly, does not cover. This means that third-party (black-box) validation will identify missed coverage for any procedure they test but we do not have a detection for it. There is no guarantee third-party validation would identify partial coverage (unless the validation suite is varying their tests along the same parameters at which your detections are working).

Validation can therefore be approached with the following processes:

1. Validate whether detections exist for at least one variation of a procedure:

   - **Unit Tests**: Map the procedures identified during the discovery phase to existing validation tests or create new validation tests for each procedure.

   - **Third-Party Validation**: Leverage third-party validation to either implement any of the above unit tests or to identify procedures not identified by research. Third-party validation tests that do not result in a successful detection would be indicative of either partial detection coverage for a procedure or missed coverage.

2. Validate whether procedures for a detection are fully covered:

   - **Edge Cases**: Test the edge cases of procedures by altering the value of the indicator artifacts across a representative set of allowable values that would still achieve the adversary's goals. If the technique can be achieved without resulting in that artifact being created or changed, that is, by definition, a different procedure and should be captured by its own detection.

   - **Peer Review**: If it is not practical to write validation tests across the allowable values, a peer review system can be used by documenting, based on research, how the adversary could alter their attack and having another detection engineer check that the detection would encompass the possible adversary evasions.

This process can result in two types of metrics:

- **Test or validation coverage metrics**: These metrics are defined by how many techniques have unit tests for each procedure identified and how many procedures have edge case tests implemented. Third-party validation tools may be useful in providing unit test coverage for procedures.

- **Test or validation pass-rate metrics**: These metrics are defined by how many unit tests and edge case tests our detections successfully detected for each technique.

There are some limitations to this approach that can impact a detection engineering team's ability to fully implement the above processes. As noted at the start of this section, the goal of these processes is to help quantify your detection coverage versus necessarily resulting in complete coverage for a technique. Here are some common roadblocks that teams may encounter:

- **Requires mature processes and resources**: Implementing a validation process like the one mentioned previously requires a large enough team to support both detection creation and validation. If a team is simply attempting to put in place a base level of detection, it would be impractical for them to have the resources to fully investigate a technique and iterate through a detection and validation workflow. Even with a reasonably large detection engineering team, it is still necessary to choose where to focus resources. Every technique cannot be fully investigated and validated.

- **False positive acceptance**: Fully encompassing a procedure may result in an unacceptable number of false positives, especially if implementing behavioral detections that overlap with acceptable actions from network administrators or other users within your environment. Therefore, while it may be possible to fully validate that all variations of a technique are detected, the detections may result in unacceptable noisiness.

- **Identifiable choke points**: There is an implicit assumption that a technique has a set of choke points that can be identified to constrain how an attack can be implemented. There is no guarantee this is the case. It may take a significant amount of time and skill during the investigation phase to perform this analysis. In identifying a definable scope for the choke point(s), we may increase the number of procedures to an unacceptable number.

- **A limited set of procedures**: The approach assumes that the ways to execute the technique can be captured in a "reasonable" set of procedures. Similar to the issue with choke points, if the detection engineer is unable to group the variations of a technique into a limited scope, they will be unable to create validation rules to encompass those procedures.

- **Available telemetry**: The approach assumes that once the procedures and choke points are identified, there is sufficient telemetry to provide the necessary visibility for writing detections to identify the choke points.

The information in this section should provide a methodology for taking the results of validation attempts, interpreting the results, and using them to improve your overall security.

Summary

In this chapter, we provided an overview of validation as it relates to assessing the maturity of a detection engineering program. We then introduced a series of open source tools that can be leveraged by organizations without purple teams to perform validation tests easily and effectively. The exercises in the chapter leveraged some of these tools to simulate adversary activity in order to validate detections. Finally, we concluded the chapter by explaining how the results of validation tests can be leveraged to improve your detection posture.

In the next chapter, we will take a look at the topic of threat intelligence. We'll discuss the different types of threat intelligence and the roles they can play in detection engineering.

Further reading

While we focused on Atomic Red Team and CALDERA during our discussion of **breach and attack simulation** (**BAS**) tools, there are many commercial and open source solutions out there that can be used as alternatives. Let's highlight two popular open source options:

- **Infection Monkey**:

  Infection Monkey is an open source platform that can be used for launching realistic attacks against a specified set of target endpoints: `https://www.akamai.com/infectionmonkey`

- **Network Flight Simulator (flightsim)**:

  AlphaSOC's **Network Flight Simulator (flightsim)**, focuses instead on generating malicious-looking network traffic, specifically for testing detections built for network telemetry: `https://github.com/alphasoc/flightsim`

10

Leveraging Threat Intelligence

When discussing detection requirement sources in *Chapter 2*, we introduced the topic of **threat intelligence** as it relates to detection engineering. In this chapter, we will take a deeper dive into the topic and, specifically, the role it plays within detection engineering. First, we'll provide a very brief overview of the types of threat intelligence we will be looking at. After the brief introduction to the topic, we'll focus on its role in the *Requirements Discovery*, *Triage*, and *Investigate* phases of the detection engineering life cycle. The final topic in this chapter is threat assessments and how they can be used as a source of detection requirements. These concepts will be illustrated through the use of a variety of examples of leveraging real threat intelligence to develop detections.

In this chapter, we will cover the following main topics:

- Threat intelligence overview
- Threat intelligence in the detection engineering lifecycle
- Threat intelligence for detection engineering in practice
- Threat assessments

Technical requirements

Since going into further depth on threat intelligence is beyond the scope of this book, we won't go heavily into the topic except as it relates to detection engineering. We encourage you to read more into the topic from dedicated threat intelligence learning resources if you want to gain a deeper understanding. We've provided some additional resources at the end of this chapter.

Threat intelligence overview

Before we look at its role in detection engineering, we must understand what threat intelligence is. Cyber-threat intelligence is data collected and analyzed in order to understand the context related to emerging or existing threats. It can help us understand a threat actor's motives; targets; **tactics,**

techniques, and procedures (**TTPs**); and more. This in turn can help us understand how we can detect such threats. At the simplest level, threat intelligence may be provided in the form of indicators. For example, URLHaus by AbuseDB includes lists of malicious URLs that can be accessed by API: `https://urlhaus.abuse.ch/downloads/text/`. There are many open source feeds that will provide a list of known malicious indicators without context. Even at this level, we have the potential to use our intel to develop detections, even if it's just a simple detection for the presence of a value from the list. The major downside to using indicators from threat intel for detection is that often threat intel is published after the attack has occurred. This is much less effective at detecting real-time attacks and becomes stale quickly, as threat actors modify their tools and infrastructure to evade detection. Threat intel, however, can extend to include much more useful data. Along with indicators, we also can find intelligence that provides us with detailed context and guidance that will result in more robust detections. In order to understand what types of threat intel we have available to us, let's first understand the two key sources of intel: open source and internal (or proprietary).

Open source intelligence

When we talk about threat intel, many people immediately envision open source reporting, and justifiably so. Most organizations are not large enough to have a dedicated threat intelligence team to produce proprietary intel and, thus, rely on open source reporting to provide actionable information to be used when setting up detection. **Open source intelligence** (**OSINT**) is distributed in a variety of formats containing varying amounts of detail. Some common sources include the following:

- Indicator feeds

- Scanners and sandboxing platforms (such as VirusTotal)

- Social media, blog posts, and whitepapers

The quality and type of data you can get from OSINT are going to vary greatly between sources. It is important that from a quality perspective, you are leveraging trusted sources, such as blog posts from established companies or well-known and widely used intel feeds. Indiscriminately pulling intelligence from any source increases the risk of introducing *bad* forms of detection into your environment.

Many organizations identify numerous threat feeds and pipe them into their environment for indicator-based detection without determining the fidelity and context of the content. It's important to identify the feeds likely to provide indicators with a high likelihood of being malicious. Additionally, the context of the feeds needs to be analyzed in depth. For example, there are feeds that provide a list of spam IP addresses, which will likely produce a large quantity of low-severity results in your environment. How you leverage the threat feeds can also affect the false positive rate. For example, if you use a list of IP addresses and try to alert on the presence of that IP address in any situation, such as firewall block events, the value of detections is reduced. If you instead focus your implementation on activity that is active on the network (allowed connections instead of all connections), the activity becomes more valuable without overwhelming the analyst. All of this is to say, ensure that you are evaluating threat feeds in depth and understand how you can leverage them in a way to avoid a high false positive rate, which can overwhelm analysts.

The type of data is also going to be dependent on the source. From the list of common sources just given, for example, you are likely to receive less context from the sources at the top than at the bottom. As mentioned before, threat intel feeds provide a list of indicators, usually without significant context. They may simply be a generic feed of known malicious but unrelated indicators, or the list may contain related indicators, such as a feed of spam **IPs or Emotet payload hashes**. In the latter case, the context will likely be indicated in the feed title or description while the content of the feed itself is still a simple list of indicators.

The second source we mention is scanners and sandboxing platforms. These tools go beyond intel feeds and involve some sort of automated analysis, which will ultimately return further context. Once again, even within this source category, we will see variations based on the capabilities of the tool. For more mature platforms, such as VirusTotal, there are many integrations that generate a large amount of context. Later in this chapter, we will look at how VirusTotal can be leveraged during the *Investigate* phase to improve detections.

Lastly are social media, blog posts, and whitepapers. Social media varies in value and is based on the ability to filter through the noise to find information worth leveraging. This involves finding accounts that publish valuable content, such as those associated with reputable organizations and threat researchers. Most social media platforms have a concept such as *tags* or *word lists*. Which you can leverage to find relevant posts based on a topic rather than a specific author. For example, if you are concerned about ransomware attacks, search based on the hashtag or keyword **ransomware** or, even more narrowly, a specific ransomware family, such as **Maze ransomware**. The results, if tuned properly, should provide insights from industry organizations and researchers. Many researchers share indicators of compromise and in-the-wild TTPs. Finding the right accounts and keywords to follow can leave a treasure trove of intelligence.

Whitepapers and blog posts from established sources can provide a wealth of information. Many vendors publish whitepapers or blog posts based on attacks actively observed in the wild and based on their expert analysis of the activity. The benefit of these is that they typically provide much more context than the previous sources. In particular, we can often use blog posts and whitepapers to identify TTPs instead of just indicators of compromise. As you may recall, TTPs are at the top of the pyramid of pain, as it is challenging for threat actors to change TTPs, so detections of this type are harder for attackers to bypass.

Internal threat intelligence

Internal threat intelligence is going to heavily depend on an organization's security processes and capabilities. In larger organizations, you may have a dedicated threat intel team. Typically these teams have various responsibilities related to using intelligence to secure a company's posture. They may be responsible for digesting OSINT to identify what is relevant to the organization; in which case, detection engineers may not need to perform intel research for detection requirements, as the intel team fills that role for them.

In addition to processing OSINT, threat intel teams will often attempt to form structured intelligence, whether developing reports or gathering indicators of compromise, related to internal incidents. This internal intelligence may come from threat hunting if the tools and capabilities exist, or from the **security operations center** (**SOC**) and **incident response** (**IR**) teams, who can provide data from incidents for the threat intelligence team to research, substantiate with context, and disseminate information on.

In smaller organizations, there may not be a dedicated threat intelligence team. However, there is still internal threat intelligence available from either the SOC or the IR team or available through your own threat-hunting methods. In this case, though, the responsibility of uncovering this data and ensuring it's being collected for use may fall on the detection engineering team. An organization needs to develop procedures that ensure that the communication and data sharing needed to leverage internal threat intelligence for detection engineering are implemented.

Gathering threat intelligence

Prior to leveraging threat intelligence for detection engineering, we have to develop the processes through which the detection engineering team will receive threat intelligence. This depends on the responsibilities of teams in your organization and the intelligence sources being leveraged. If you have a threat intel team, then you should establish a process by which the intelligence they produce is fed to the detection engineering team. If you don't have a threat intel team but have a SOC, then you need to determine what type of data you would like to receive from that team and determine the process for receiving it. If you are not relying on any internal teams and are solely gathering OSINT within your own team, you need to determine what sources you will leverage, who is responsible for processing intelligence, what findings should lead into detection requirements, and how they should be documented. The processes you develop can include documentation, communication, and automation-related aspects of data collection, depending on your organization's capabilities and use cases. However the intelligence is gathered, it should be done in a way that is standardized and easily digestible by the time the requirements end up with the detection engineering team. With an understanding of what threat intelligence is, we can look at how it applies to us in the context of detection engineering.

Threat intelligence in the detection engineering life cycle

Threat intelligence can play a role in multiple phases of the detection engineering life cycle. In this section, we are going to look at how intelligence can be leveraged in the first three phases of the life cycle: *Requirements Discovery*, *Triage*, and *Investigate*.

Requirements Discovery

The first stage of the detection engineering life cycle is *Requirements Discovery* and it's the phase in which various sources provide us guidance for what detections need to be developed. Either through the DE team's own research or a threat intel team's reporting, intelligence can become a source for detection requirements. For example, if a blog post comes out about a threat actor targeting organizations in your industry, it might become a requirement to ensure coverage for detecting the TTPs used by that threat actor. Or from an internal threat intel perspective, if threat hunters observe patterns of undetected malicious activity, their findings should be leveraged to improve detections.

The results of threat assessments are another key source for detection requirements. Later in this chapter, we'll discuss threat assessments further, specifically how we can take the results and turn them into detection requirements.

Triage

When it comes to leveraging threat intel in the *Triage* phase, we are focused on using it to prioritize our detection requirements. In *Chapter 2*, we discussed several criteria for prioritizing our requirements. In this section, we're going to look at how we can leverage threat intelligence when determining organizational alignment and the risk of active exploits.

Organizational alignment

As a reminder, *Chapter 2* gave the following perspective on organizational alignment:

"If the requested detection falls within the overlap of external threats and what is being internally protected, it has organizational alignment."

Threat intelligence is what allows us to identify external threats. When doing research into a threat, we want to understand how relevant it is to our specific industry, organization, infrastructure, users, and data. Let's say, for example, we are deciding whether to prioritize a detection requirement for FIN6 activity. Research via OSINT would reveal that FIN6 targets hospitality and retail organizations with point-of-sales malware. If our organization is a software company that does not leverage point-of-sales systems, we would want to de-prioritize that detection requirement since it is not likely to target our organization. In another example, if we receive a detection requirement for the Bundlore adware, OSINT would tell us that it is written to target macOS. If our organization primarily uses macOS machines, then we would prioritize this over a Windows-focused detection.

Active exploits

In *Chapter 2*, we provided the following list of questions to consider when determining whether an active exploit should play a role in the triage of a detection requirement:

- Is my organization affected by this exploit?

- What is the impact of this exploit?

- Does enough information exist for adversaries to implement the exploit or for a detection to be created against it?

- How easy is it for an adversary to implement the exploit?

- Is the exploit being currently used in the wild, or by adversaries that target your organization?

- How quickly will the affected applications provide an update to patch this exploit?

Threat intelligence will help us answer many of these questions. First, if a **Common Vulnerabilities and Exposures** (**CVE**) ID has been assigned, we can look at the **National Vulnerability Database** (**NVD**) to get details on the vulnerability, such as the impact that successful exploitation will have. Social media is a good place to look for posts related to new zero-days as researchers will often post any findings related to **proof-of-concept** (**PoC**) exploit code. With high-visibility vulnerabilities, it's not uncommon to see companies publish content discussing the technical details of an exploit, which can provide insight into the likelihood an attacker could implement an exploit of their own. Furthermore, for widely exploited vulnerabilities, we will often see open source reporting from various security vendors detailing observations. As can be seen, various types of open source reporting (informational databases, social media, and blogs) can be used in conjunction to help determine whether a detection requirement related to a vulnerability is of high priority to the organization.

As can be seen, there are many ways to leverage threat intelligence for triaging detection requirements, regardless of what criteria you are trying to validate.

Investigate

For many detection requirements, threat intelligence will be used heavily during the *Investigate* phase. This is the phase in which we gather all of the information needed to write an efficient detection rule. In order to do this, we need to carefully understand what conditions should trigger the detection and what exclusions should be made to reduce false positives. Often, sufficient details will not be provided as part of the detection requirement. In those cases, threat intel can provide the details necessary to build a robust detection.

In the examples in the following sections, we'll see how threat intelligence can be leveraged for creating detection requirements. The examples will also demonstrate its value in the other phases such as triage and investigation. The resources we use in these examples can be used across the phases to expand our understanding of a threat and either broaden or narrow our detection criteria as needed.

Threat intelligence for detection engineering in practice

This section contains two examples demonstrating how we can use OSINT from different types of sources to develop a detection. The first will take a blog post published by a reputable vendor and turn the free-from text into detection criteria. The second example walks through leveraging VirusTotal, an online sandbox, to take a static indicator and obtain contextual information for more robust detection.

Example – leveraging threat intel blog posts for detection engineering

In this example, we will take a blog post about an attack campaign and see how we can use it to develop a detection. We performed an exercise in *Chapter 6* similar to this but focused on indicators. Now, we are going to look at all levels of the Pyramid of Pain in an attempt to create more robust detections.

For this exercise, we will use a report from Trend Micro about a threat actor delivering a backdoor via a watering hole attack: `https://www.trendmicro.com/en_us/research/23/b/earth-kitsune-delivers-new-whiskerspy-backdoor.html`.

The flow chart at the start of the blog post gives us an outline of all the places for which we could detect the attack. The key events in this attack chain are as follows:

1. The user visits a compromised website.
2. The compromised website delivers an installer via a malicious script.
3. The installer executes two loaders.
4. The loaders execute the final stage backdoor.

For each of these steps, we can identify different correlation criteria (the *Investigate* phase) and create detection logic (the *Develop* phase). We can combine the detection logic of multiple phases or, for broader detections, create individual rules for each stage. For example, we could create a rule that looks for a user visiting a site, followed by an installer download, followed by two files being created, followed by the payload being executed. That will detect the exact chain of events shown in the blog post. The benefit of this is there is a lower likelihood of false positives, but it also means that if an attacker modifies their attack chain, the detection will no longer work. Alternatively, we can create a detection code for each of the four stages. This will detect the activity even if the attack chain is modified, and it has a chance of detecting the activity earlier before the final payload is executed; however, this method also increases the risk of false positives since it will result in much broader detection logic. For the purpose of this example, we are going to create the detection logic separately. During the *Test* phase, we can identify the likelihood of false positives for each rule and combine rules if needed.

> **Optional exercise**
>
> If you want to use this example as an additional exercise, pause here. Review the blog post linked to earlier and for each of the stages, write down possible methods of detection, as well as the data sources that can be leveraged for visibility.

The attack begins with a targeted user visiting the compromised website. Unfortunately, we are not given enough context to be able to distinguish this activity from a user visiting legitimate websites. For this reason, we will ignore creating detection logic for this first step.

After the user visits the site, they are presented with a popup, which leads to an injected script that will download a malicious installer. *Table 10.1* provides a summary of the associated facts from the blog post related to this stage, possible detection logic, and relevant data sources.

Report Detail	Detection Logic	Data Sources
`popup.js` redirects to `Codec-AVC1.msi`	Network connection to the URL ending with `popup.js` followed by the network connection to the URL ending with `Codec-AVC1.msi`	Next-generation firewall logs
`Codec-AVC1.msi` is downloaded to the system	Creation of a file named `Codec-AVC1.msi` on the system, most likely in the `Downloads` folder .Network connection to the URL ending with `Codec-AVC1.msi`	Endpoint logs AV/EDR alerts Next-generation firewall logs

Table 10.1 – Installer delivery detection development

If we look back at the Pyramid of Pain, the detection log here relies on network/host artifacts rather than TTPs or tools, which are closer to the top of the pyramid as they are hard to change. At this stage, however, this is the approach available to us since URL redirection and file downloads are too broad to detect on without more narrowed criteria. However, this means that if the threat actor changes the filenames they use (`Codec-AVC1.msi` and `popup.js`), the detection will no longer work. This is why we will continue to create detections for each phase so that if this detection fails, we have additional chances to catch the threat actor.

The next stage is the execution of the installer to drop two loaders on the system. *Table 10.2* provides the same details as before but this time focused on the subset of activity related to the installer's execution.

Report Detail	Detection Logic	Data Sources
A malicious installer calls the `Invoke-WebRequest` PowerShell command four times to download additional files	Execution of `powershell -c "Invoke-WebRequest <url> -OutFile"` PowerShell spawning from MSI	PowerShell script block logging (if enabled) – `EventCode 4104` in the `Windows-PowerShell/Operational` event log, see the `Message` field Sysmon logs (if enabled) – Event ID 1 in the `Sysmon/Operational` event log, see the `Image` and `Parent Image` fields
Download binary is saved to a OneDrive folder for persistence	`vcruntime140.dll` created in the `\microsoft\onedrive` path	Endpoint logs AV/EDR alerts

Table 10.2 – Installer execution detection development

PowerShell Script Block logging is disabled by default, so that additional prerequisites must be met prior to implementing such a detection. Sysmon is also not installed by default and must be configured prior to its use for detection. Additionally, the PowerShell activity is relatively broad as `Invoke-WebRequest` as well as PowerShell spawning from MSI can both occur in legitimate use cases. You'd need to evaluate how common such activity is in your environment as it might cause too high a false positive rate. The OneDrive folder and binary are less broad but, once again, rely on specific host artifacts.

The final stage to evaluate is the backdoor installation and execution by the loader. *Table 10.3* presents the assessment of this activity.

Report Detail	Detection Logic	Data Sources
The loader connects to a hardcoded URL to download, decode, and execute the main payload	Network connection to a URL ending with `help.jpg`	Next-generation firewall logs
The backdoor establishes C2 communication	Network connections to known related C2 servers	Next-generation firewall logs Sysmon Event ID 3

Table 10.3 – Installer execution detection development

Similar to the first stage, we can look at network connections to URLs hosting payloads with unique names. The last piece of detection logic returns to the use of indicators. As we've mentioned multiple times, while not as resilient as detections for TTPs, detections for indicators still serve their purpose. Trend Micro provides a list of indicators of compromise at the end of the article. This list can be used for detecting known bad hashes and domains at various points of visibility.

Unfortunately, this attack involves a lot of behaviors that would be observed in legitimate cases, so we must find the balance between creating a detection that will lead to high false positives and a detection that will become stale quickly with attacker modifications. Part of finding the balance relies on an understanding of your environment and testing. If you determine that it is unlikely anyone or any applications in your environment will run the `Invoke-WebRequest` PowerShell command, then detecting all usage of that module might provide value. If you test the detection and you find out that there is a legitimate use of that PowerShell command in your organization, it might need to be tuned. This could be done by either setting stricter criteria (specific parameters or parent processes) or creating exclusions for the known good activity (if it is limited enough not to cause too much overhead).

Let's summarize the steps you would take to extract detection opportunities from a blog post:

1. Extract a list of indicators of compromise (hashes, IPs, etc.).
2. Extract a list of each behavior mentioned in the article.

3. For each behavior in the list, do the following:

- Identify relevant context (associated commands, file paths, etc.)

- Define the associated detection logic (something unique that you can alert on with high fidelity)

- Determine the relevant data sources that will capture the behavior

Whenever you're reading threat reports, approach them with a detection engineering mindset, identifying how such behaviors would appear in logs and what criteria would be unique enough to not cause false positives.

Example – leveraging VirusTotal for detection engineering

As mentioned at the beginning of this chapter, another source of OSINT is public scanners and sandboxes. These platforms provide tools for analyzing files, URLs, domains, and IP addresses. Most often, in exchange for the free use of these tools, any findings are shared with the public, allowing for a treasure trove of information. One of the most popular examples of this is VirusTotal. VirusTotal allows you to analyze files and URLs, or search for information on hashes, domains, and IP addresses. When analyzing files, the samples are run through multiple sandboxes, and the results of both static and dynamic analysis are provided. These results are then stored in its database and can be found by searching for the file hash. This is valuable when you are provided with a hash but not the file and want to see whether there is any publicly available information about it. To demonstrate its value, let's look at an example.

In the previous example, a list of indicators was provided, including the hashes of the backdoor. Let's say we received those hashes but the article did not provide us with enough context to write an effective detection, so we want to have a more thorough analysis of the payload. In this case, we'll look at the `3D4107C738B46F75C5B1B88EF06F82A5779DDD830527C9BECC951080A5491F13` hash, which Trend Micro says is tied to the WhiskerSpy backdoor. Searching for this hash from the main page will lead us to the file's overview page here: `https://www.virustotal.com/gui/file/3d4107c738b46f75c5b1b88ef06f82a5779ddd830527c9becc951080a5491f13`. Visit this link to reference the views that will be discussed shortly.

Detection details

Within the **Detection** page of the hash we are examining, the following sections are present:

- **Detection rate** – The number of security vendors that have detections for this file.

- **Tags** – Various automatically applied tags based on static and dynamic analysis.

- **Submission time** – The date and time that the file was originally submitted for analysis.

- **Navigation** – Various tabs providing different types of information related to the file.

- **Threat category/family** – Identified malware category and families, if applicable. In this case, VirusTotal reports that it is a Trojan named WhiskerSpy, which aligns with Trend Micro's analysis.

- **Security vendor detections** – Specific detection names assigned by security vendors.

This provides a good high overview to help determine whether a file is malicious, and if so, what kind of threat it is, but from a detection perspective, we are more interested in the details, relations, and behavior tabs.

File details

The Details tab is primarily made up of static analysis information, such as various hashes, the file type, and the file size. As a brief overview, the following sections are provided on this page:

- **Basic properties** – File properties such as hashes, type, and size

- **History** – A file creation timestamp along with VirusTotal-related timestamps

- **Names** – Any identified filenames associated with the hash through file metadata or submission names

- **Portable Executable Information** – For executable files, details about the compilers, headers, sections, imports, and exports

This will be most helpful from a detection engineering perspective if you have systems that only support a specific type of hash. For example, Trend Micro only provided the SHA 256 hash, so if you have systems that only report the MD5 hash, this is a method of getting that hash.

Relations

The **Relations** tab provides details of related indicators based on static and behavioral analysis. For network relations, some examples of potential indicators are as follows:

- Contacted URLs

- Contacted domains

- Contact IP addresses

For file relations, some examples of potential indicators are as follows:

- Execution parents

- Bundled files

- Dropped files

- PE resource children

This information can help with expanding your static indicator-based detections. In our example, we see that VirusTotal's analysis identified that an IP address and domain were contacted in the course of the malware execution, as well as an execution parent. We can now detect these observables too if we find them to be high-fidelity, and we can also pivot to the analysis of those indicators of VirusTotal to gain even more context.

Behavior

Lastly, we have the **Behavior** tab, which provides dynamic analysis results. This page provides a wealth of information that is particularly useful from a detection engineering perspective. At the top of the page, we see a list of sandboxes that the samples were run in and an overview of the resulting findings. Below that, an activity summary outlines the highlights of what information is provided in the rest of the report. The first section maps the sandbox analysis to MITRE ATT&CK Tactics and Techniques. Broken up by tactic, it provides the technique observed, along with the behavior or property that resulted in the identification of that technique, and a severity symbol.

The bottom part of the page provides the behavioral findings from the sandboxes broken up by category. We can see network, registry, process, and service activity. All of these can provide additional detection opportunities. The Trend Micro report did not go into detail about the process tree or registry actions, so this is an opportunity to create more narrowed detections based on such properties. It is important to do research into any behaviors you want to detect to ensure that they are in fact unique instances of behavior associated with malicious activity and not just system activity captured during sandbox execution.

As can be seen throughout the previous example, public scanners and sandboxes such as VirusTotal can be leveraged to take a simple hash, the lowest level in the Pyramid of Pain, and start building TTP-based detections, at the top of the Pyramid of Pain. These can be valuable tools for the *Investigate* phase of the detection engineering life cycle. In the *Resources and further reading* section, we will provide links to resources that provide lists of popular online scanners and sandboxes.

Threat assessments

As mentioned in the *Threat intelligence in the detection engineering life cycle* section of this chapter, threat assessments are a source of valuable detection requirements. Threat assessments define a process for evaluating threats to an organization and its information systems and describing those threats, providing a report detailing organization-specific risks. Organizations often leverage threat assessments to identify areas for improvement of detection and prevention coverage. Sometimes, this can be the identification of vulnerabilities or misconfigurations that should be changed to prevent certain threats. It can also include information about the types of threats and attack vectors that are the greatest risk to your organization. This is where most of the value, for detection engineers, comes from, as the identification of these risks allows us to determine what coverage is most applicable to our organization.

Since performing threat assessments and details of reports are outside the scope of this book, if you would like to learn more about what assessments contain and how they are performed, see the following resources:

- `https://www.cisa.gov/sites/default/files/video/22_1201_safecom_ guide_to_cybersecurity_risk_assessment_508-r1.pdf`

- `https://www.sans.org/blog/tips-for-creating-a-strong- cybersecurity-assessment-report/`

To understand how threat assessment findings can result in detection requirements, we are going to look at a few examples of threat assessment findings and how we can use them to develop relevant detections. If you've performed a technique coverage validation using the methods discussed in *Chapter 8*, it is a good idea to have the results present when processing threat assessments and developing detection requirements, as you can figure out quickly which detections may already exist that meet the requirements.

Example – leveraging threat assessments for detection engineering

Let's look at an example of how findings from a threat assessment can lead to detection requirements and how we can leverage threat intel to gather all the necessary information to create a detection. A threat assessment may include a variety of types of findings. For the sake of this example, we are going to look at three possible findings that may be seen in a threat assessment. We'll look at each one and how we can leverage the information to generate a detection strategy:

- *Finding 1*: The organization may become a target of Winnti Group, which is known to target gaming companies.

- *Finding 2*: Ransomware attacks are becoming increasingly popular and targeting various industries and geographies. The organization should be prepared for these attack attempts.

- *Finding 3*: The organization stores files that contain sensitive data, which may become a valuable target for threat actors and present a major risk to the organization.

For each of these findings, we will map them to associated techniques in order to develop a better detection requirement.

Threat group-based finding

Starting with *Finding 1*, we are provided with the intelligence that there is a threat group targeting organizations in our industry. The threat group's name, Winnti Group, is our starting point for investigating how we could detect any associated activity. In *Chapter 1*, we introduced MITRE ATT&CK, primarily focusing on Techniques and Tactics, but we also mentioned that MITRE has a knowledge base of threat actors. Not all threat actors are included, but for those that are, it provides a great starting point for mapping the name of a threat group to detection opportunities. Winnti Group falls under group ID G0044 in the MITRE ATT&CK knowledge base. The information page for the group can be found here: https://attack.mitre.org/groups/G0044/. From a detection engineering perspective, the three sections of most interest to us are **Techniques Used**, **Software**, and **References**. Let's start with the **Techniques Used** section, as shown in *Figure 10.1*.

Techniques Used

ATT&CK® Navigator Layers ▾

Domain	ID		Name	Use
Enterprise	T1583	.001	Acquire Infrastructure: Domains	Winnti Group has registered domains for C2 that mimicked sites of their intended targets.[1]
Enterprise	T1083		File and Directory Discovery	Winnti Group has used a program named ff.exe to search for specific documents on compromised hosts.[1]
Enterprise	T1105		Ingress Tool Transfer	Winnti Group has downloaded an auxiliary program named ff.exe to infected machines.[1]
Enterprise	T1057		Process Discovery	Winnti Group looked for a specific process running on infected servers.[1]
Enterprise	T1014		Rootkit	Winnti Group used a rootkit to modify typical server functionality.[1]
Enterprise	T1553	.002	Subvert Trust Controls: Code Signing	Winnti Group used stolen certificates to sign its malware.[1]

Figure 10.1 – Winnti Group – Techniques Used

This is a list of known techniques implemented by the threat actor based on public reporting. The first columns have the ID and name of the technique, which are hyperlinked to the associated ATT&CK technique pages. The last column contains context specific to how the technique is leveraged by the threat actor. This can help in creating more narrowed detections for the techniques if desired. For example, for *T1083*, we might not want to create a broad detection that detects any attempts to search for files, as that might result in a high number of false positives. The details provided, however, tell us that Winnti Group uses a program named ff.exe to do this, so if we look for file and directory discovery by a program named ff.exe, we can greatly reduce the number of false positives while still detecting this threat actor. The [1] number seen at the end of this column points to the link in the **References** section (which we'll look at later in this section) from which the technique was extracted.

Below the **Techniques Used** section, we have the **Software** section (see *Figure 10.2*).

Software

ID	Name	References	Techniques
S0501	PipeMon	[6]	Abuse Elevation Control Mechanism: Bypass User Account Control, Access Token Manipulation: Create Process with Token, Access Token Manipulation: Parent PID Spoofing, Boot or Logon Autostart Execution: Print Processors, Create or Modify System Process: Windows Service, Deobfuscate/Decode Files or Information, Encrypted Channel: Symmetric Cryptography, Fallback Channels, Ingress Tool Transfer, Masquerading: Match Legitimate Name or Location, Modify Registry, Native API, Non-Application Layer Protocol, Obfuscated Files or Information, Process Discovery, Process Injection: Dynamic-link Library Injection, Shared Modules, Software Discovery: Security Software Discovery, Subvert Trust Controls: Code Signing, System Information Discovery, System Network Configuration Discovery, System Time Discovery
S0013	PlugX	[1]	Application Layer Protocol: DNS, Application Layer Protocol: Web Protocols, Boot or Logon Autostart Execution: Registry Run Keys / Startup Folder, Command and Scripting Interpreter: Windows Command Shell, Create or Modify System Process: Windows Service, Deobfuscate/Decode Files or Information, Encrypted Channel: Symmetric Cryptography, File and Directory Discovery, Hide Artifacts: Hidden Files and Directories, Hijack Execution Flow: DLL Search Order Hijacking, Hijack Execution Flow: DLL Side-Loading, Ingress Tool Transfer, Input Capture: Keylogging, Masquerading: Match Legitimate Name or Location, Masquerading: Masquerade Task or Service, Modify Registry, Multiband Communication, Native API, Network Share Discovery, Non-Application Layer Protocol, Obfuscated Files or Information, Process Discovery, Query Registry, Screen Capture, System Network Connections Discovery, Trusted Developer Utilities Proxy Execution: MSBuild, Virtualization/Sandbox Evasion: System Checks, Web Service: Dead Drop Resolver
S0141	Winnti for Windows	[1][2]	Abuse Elevation Control Mechanism: Bypass User Account Control, Application Layer Protocol: Web Protocols, Boot or Logon Autostart Execution: Registry Run Keys / Startup Folder, Create or Modify System Process: Windows Service, Deobfuscate/Decode Files or Information, Encrypted Channel: Symmetric Cryptography, Execution Guardrails: Environmental Keying, File and Directory Discovery, Indicator Removal: File Deletion, Indicator Removal: Timestomp, Ingress Tool Transfer, Masquerading: Match Legitimate Name or Location, Native API, Non-Application Layer Protocol, Obfuscated Files or Information, Process Discovery, Proxy: External Proxy, Proxy: Internal Proxy, System Binary Proxy Execution: Rundll32, System Information Discovery, System Services: Service Execution

Figure 10.2 – Winnti Group – Software

This section provides information regarding the software leveraged by the threat actor. Similar to the group knowledge base, MITRE ATT&CK also has a software knowledge base that provides data for both malicious and legitimate software seen in use by threat actors. The first column lists the MITRE-assigned ID for the software and the second column is the name of the software. The third column points to the links within the **References** section from which the context was gathered. The last column is a list of the techniques the software is capable of performing.

To discover more detection opportunities, we can look at the associated Software pages and see the details of the technique used. For example, if we were to visit the software page for Winnti for Windows (`https://attack.mitre.org/software/S0141/`), we would see that for the technique *T1547*, it says **Winnti for Windows can add a service named wind0ws to the Registry to achieve persistence after reboot**. We can leverage that knowledge to detect any services named `wind0ws` (a unique and unusual string) being added to the Registry.

The last section on the Winnti Group page is the **References** section. This section provides links to articles about the threat actor from various cyber security organizations and researchers. These links are valuable to detection engineers, as the source reports will likely contain more detail than MITRE provides in its overviews. For example, the first link points to a Kaspersky blog post and whitepaper that provide an in-depth analysis of the malware and network infrastructure used by the attacker. It also provides dozens of hashes, domains, and other indicators that could be leveraged for detection. While MITRE ATT&CK can act as a starting point and provide high-level information, we talked earlier in this chapter about the value that can be found in whitepapers and blog posts for detection engineering, so it is wise to dive into the related reports when researching a threat actor via ATT&CK groups.

Using MITRE ATT&CK's knowledge bases and the associated references, we can build a list of TTPs, tools, and indicators tied to the attacker. We can then take validation results, as discussed in *Chapter 8*, and determine which of the techniques leveraged by this threat actor and their software we already have coverage for and which we should prioritize creating detections for. For the detections that aren't yet covered, we can use the techniques shown in *Chapter 6* to develop detections. In that chapter, we demonstrated developing detections for TTPs, tools, and indicators, all of which are relevant to use for this use case. Any detections that need to be created should become requirements and go through the detection engineering life cycle.

Threat type-based finding

Moving onto *Finding 2* from our example, we are warned about the increasing number of ransomware attacks targeting a variety of organizations. This is a much broader assessment than focusing on a specific threat actor or malware family. We won't go into depth here on specific detections to be created, but we will show some methods of using OSINT to find possible detection opportunities. Approaching a broad requirement such as this is going to require leveraging your personal expertise along with online resources to find detection criteria. As we've talked about with the Pyramid of Pain, ideally, we will create detections for TTPs rather than tools or indicators. This is especially preferable in this case due to the number of ransomware families and operators in existence. Attempting to create broad coverage for ransomware by analyzing every single ransomware family is unrealistic. Instead, we want to identify common TTPs used by many ransomware actors and create detections for them.

With the wealth of information publicly published by security vendors related to almost every topic in cyber security, performing a search via your favorite search engine is a great way to uncover potential sources of information. In this case, we want to understand what TTPs are commonly associated with ransomware attacks, so `Ransomware TTPs` would be an appropriate search query to start with. Our results when performing this search led to articles from Kaspersky, Scythe, and other vendors providing lists of the most common TTPs implemented by ransomware actors. Conveniently, many of the articles map their observations to MITRE ATT&CK techniques. As mentioned in the previous section, once we do the research that leads to a list of relevant techniques, we can use the strategies from *Chapter 6* to build detections by technique.

Also relevant to this specific example technique, the ultimate goal of ransomware is typically to encrypt data. MITRE ATT&CK technique *T1486* (Data Encrypted for Impact) details this exact final objective:

`https://attack.mitre.org/techniques/T1486/`. The information and references on this page would also prove a valuable starting point for understanding ransomware and further investigating the different groups and software related to this technique.

This example shows that building detections of a category of threats first requires identifying the TTPs relevant to that threat. A list of relevant techniques can be built based on a combination of security expertise and the wealth of articles and other resources consistently being published as OSINT. Once this list is established, previously mentioned methods for building TTPs based on techniques can be implemented to design a detection. In terms of prioritizing the list of TTPs, we can use the *Triage* phase criteria for identifying their priority while also taking into consideration which of the techniques have the most overlap between threat actors and malware families. For example, your list might contain *T1555.003* (Credentials from Password Stores: Credentials from Web Browsers) as well as *T1490* (Inhibit System Recovery). When determining which detection requirement should be prioritized, ideally, your research would reveal that while only some ransomware actors perform credential theft from browsers, most ransomware families perform some sort of system recovery prevention. Since this requirement came from the need to detect ransomware attacks in general and not a specific ransomware family, *T1490* would be the wiser technique to tackle first as it will defend a larger percentage of ransomware attacks than a detection for *T1555.003* will.

Threat objective-based finding

Finding 3 is focused on the fact the organization has sensitive files that would likely be of interest to threat actors and are at risk of exfiltration. This maps to the behavior that we want to detect based on the threat actor's objective. Their goal is to exfiltrate sensitive data from our network, whether it be for espionage or financial gain. With that goal in mind, we can think about the key tactics and techniques involved in such an attack. Starting at the higher, tactic level, we can determine which tactics will aid us most in identifying data theft. As a reminder, these are the tactics that MITRE uses to categorize techniques for enterprise-focused attacks:

- Initial Access

- Execution

- Persistence

- Privilege Escalation

- Defense Evasion

- Credential Access

- Discovery

- Lateral Movement

- Collection

- Exfiltration

- Command and Control

For data theft specifically, the attacker must perform a few key activities. They must discover the data, collect the data, and then exfiltrate the data. This conveniently aligns with MITRE ATT&CK's Discovery, Collection, and Exfiltration tactics. Now that we know what tactics we are interested in, we can review the techniques for each one and determine which are relevant to an attacker attempting to steal sensitive data from the network.

First, we will look at the **Discovery** tactics page for a list of associated techniques: `https://attack.mitre.org/tactics/TA0007/`. Since the finding is focused on files, we can narrow down to a couple of specific techniques that are related to files, the primary one being *T1083* (File and Directory Discovery). The only other possibly relevant technique within this tactic is *T1619* (Cloud Storage Object Discovery), but as indicated by the **Platforms** attribute of the technique, this is only relevant if you have a cloud environment. We repeat this process with the **Collection** (`https://attack.mitre.org/tactics/TA0009/`) and **Exfiltration** (`https://attack.mitre.org/tactics/TA0010/`) tactics. The following is a list of the techniques associated with each tactic that would most likely be used by an attacker attempting to steal files:

- **Collection**:

  - T1560 - Archive Collected Data

  - T1119 - Automated Collection

  - T1530 - Data from Cloud Storage

  - T1213 - Data from Information Repositories

  - T1005 - Data from Local System

  - T1039 - Data from Network Shared Drive

  - T1074 - Data Staged

  - T1114 - Email Collection

- **Exfiltration**:

  - T1020 - Automated Exfiltration

  - T1048 - Exfiltration Over Alternative Protocol

  - T1041 - Exfiltration Over C2 Channel

  - T1052 - Exfiltration Over Physical Medium

  - T1567 - Exfiltration Over Web Service

  - T1029 - Scheduled Transfer

  - T1537 - Transfer Data to Cloud Account

Not all of these techniques will be leveraged in every data theft attempt; different actors will use different subsets of techniques. Furthermore, some of these techniques may not be relevant to your organization or there may be additional techniques you feel are in scope. At this point, you would need to use any additional context provided in the threat assessment (such as the type or location of the files that present the greatest risk) and your knowledge of your organization to create a more specific list.

In all three examples, we follow a very similar process of taking a threat assessment finding and brainstorming detections. Let's summarize these examples in a series of steps:

1. Understand what the assessment finding means to you as a detection engineer.

   Identify what threat actor or type of attacks and behaviors this finding is discussing.

2. Identify sources of intelligence to map our starting point (a threat type, attacker, or risk) to techniques, tools, or indicators:

   - MITRE ATT&CK has a wealth of information, which will provide a great starting point. Look at the group, software, or technique pages associated with the identified starting point.

   - Searching for blog posts or whitepapers discussing the threat you are investigating is another useful method. For example, if the finding is related to APT1, search blogs such as CrowdStrike, TrendMicro, Palo Alto, and more for articles detailing the threat actor's behavior.

3. Gather detectable data from those sources.

   This means creating a list of indicators for indicator-based detections or behaviors for more mature TTP-based detections.

4. Create detection requirements out of the detectable behaviors from *step 3*.

   Include any resources or information gathered from your investigation so that the source of the detection criteria can be referenced if needed.

5. From the final list of detection requirements, perform a triage (as discussed in *Chapter 5* in the *Triaging detection requirements* section) to determine which requirements should be prioritized.

6. Develop detections based on the processes discussed in *Chapter 6*.

In brief, we take the threat assessment, identify the associated techniques and behaviors for a given finding, and then apply the detection engineering life cycle, starting with *Requirements discovery*, to develop associated detections. Be sure to document the resources leveraged to identify techniques and behaviors as this information will also prove useful in the Triage and Investigate phases, as discussed in the *Threat intelligence in the detection engineering life cycle* section of this chapter.

With the information in the above sections, you should understand how to leverage threat intelligence to both create detection requirements and enhance existing detection requirements. Before closing out the chapter, the next section provides some resources related to further learning about and leveraging threat intelligence.

Resources and further reading

The following resources provide lists of the sources discussed in this chapter, as well as further informational material related to threat intelligence and MITRE ATT&CK.

Threat intelligence sources and concepts

`https://github.com/hslatman/awesome-threat-intelligence`

This GitHub repository contains a variety of types of resources related to threat intel including sources, such as threat intel feeds, formats, frameworks, platforms, tools, research, standards, and books.

Online scanners and sandboxes

`https://github.com/rshipp/awesome-malware-analysis#online-scanners-and-sandboxes`

The `Online Scanners and Sandboxes` section of this GitHub repository provides a comprehensive listing of tools similar to VirusTotal that can be leveraged for the methods discussed in this chapter.

MITRE ATT&CK

Here are the sources that you can refer to for MITRE ATT&CK:

- `https://attack.mitre.org/resources/getting-started/`
- `https://attack.mitre.org/resources/`

These pages from MITRE provide research papers, presentations, and other resources that will provide in-depth information on all aspects of the MITRE ATT&CK framework.

Summary

In this chapter, we went into greater depth on the concept of threat intelligence and, specifically, its role in detection engineering. First, we introduced the types of threat intelligence at a very high level. We then looked at how we can leverage this threat intelligence during the *Requirements Discovery*, *Triage*, and *Investigate* phases of the detection engineering life cycle, using examples to solidify the concepts. Finally, we touched on threat assessments and how a threat assessment combined with threat intelligence can lead to important detection requirements.

In the next chapter, we will discuss performance management. This chapter will look at leveraging metrics to both identify the current state of your detection engineering program and road-map improvements to your program.

Part 4:
Metrics and Management

In *Part 4*, we look at the management side of detection engineering. This includes understanding how our current set of detection performs and being able to communicate that effectively. We'll discuss various metrics that can be used to calculate the effectiveness and efficiency of a detection engineering program and how we can leverage those findings to improve our detections.

This section has the following chapter:

- *Chapter 11, Performance Management*

11
Performance Management

In previous chapters, we have explored the detection engineering life cycle, from creating a test lab and building your first detection to testing and validating your detections. In this chapter, we will discuss a seemingly simple yet difficult-to-answer question: how good are we doing? We will look at this from multiple perspectives: the maturity of the detection engineering program and its associated productivity or efficiency, how well we historically detected the adversary, and how well we can expect to detect the adversary in the future.

We will cover the following main topics in this chapter:

- Introduction to performance management
- Assessing the maturity of your detection program
- Measuring the effectiveness of a detection engineering program
- Measuring the efficiency of a detection engineering program
- Calculating a detection's efficacy

Introduction to performance management

We are using the term *performance management* in this chapter to describe the various knowledge and techniques we can use to identify how to most effectively improve the performance of our detection engineering program. In an ideal world, we'd detect all bad behavior and not flag any legitimate activity. There is, however, no magic solution that allows for that. As such, we need to know how and where our detection program and our detections are falling short.

This chapter will break down different aspects that we can assess to get a better idea of areas of improvement. We'll be able to identify where issues exist that are causing our detection program or detection rules to underperform. With that knowledge in hand, we can slowly take steps to prioritize changes that will lead to improved performance and, over time, increase the maturity of our program.

We'll start this chapter by giving you a way to assess the current maturity level of your program to understand where you are and where you want to go. Then we'll move on to looking at analysis techniques for determining the performance of your detections both in their entirety and as individual rules. At the end of that section, we'll guide you to further reading on topics such as project management and metrics that are out of the scope of this book but can assist in operationalizing lessons learned from performance management.

Assessing the maturity of your detection program

Understanding the maturity of their detection engineering program allows leaders to set realistic goals for the organization and identify where to focus next on their journey. In earlier chapters, we introduced some basic concepts of detection engineering that are necessary for any detection engineering program to master and discussed advanced processes and metrics that will not be used by organizations until later in their maturity. Any article or book describing the maturity of a program requires obligatory maturity levels aligned to **Capability Maturity Model Integration (CMMI)**, and we will not disappoint here. We will identify when to begin applying these more advanced concepts through the maturity model, which is designed to help organizations track their journey and identify where to focus next. The maturity model we have established is visualized in *Figure 11.1*.

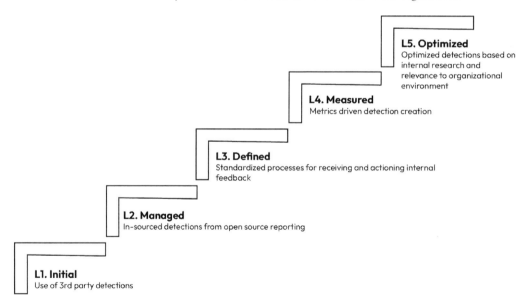

Figure 11.1 – Detection engineering maturity model

The criteria for each level in the model align with the following:

- **L1: Using third-party detections only**: The organization mainly relies upon detections provided by vendors such as their SIEM, EDR, cloud, or NDR appliance. The organization may tune these detections and has processes in place to triage and review the associated alerts.

- **L2: Creating detections from open source reporting**: Organizations at level 2 have begun creating their own detections, mainly driven by open source reporting of adversary behavior.

- **L3: Creating/updating detections from internal feedback**: The organization has processes for analysts' feedback and requests for updates or new detections. A team of analysts has the responsibility of researching the requests and creating the detections.

- **L4: Metrics-driven detection creation**: Optimizing detection creation with metrics to understand the efficiency and efficacy of the detection program. Despite this alignment with CMMI level 4, there are metrics that we will discuss within this chapter that can only be implemented once teams are performing their own internal research.

- **L5: Creating detections from internal research**: At this level, teams are performing their own active research into how techniques can be performed and identifying the optimal ways to detect techniques and identify their relevance to the organization's environment.

As your detection engineering team progress into levels 4 and 5 of the maturity model, additional processes can be adapted to track the efficiency and effectiveness of the organization. Efficiency can be evaluated in terms of the productivity of the detection engineering team and of the analysts triaging and reviewing the alerts created by the associated detections. Efficiency metrics are used to track the amount of time or personnel required to create detections or review associated alerts. We can borrow from software development metrics, such as agile point velocity, to calculate the efficiency of the organization. Similar to software development metrics, these can be easily manipulated and therefore should only be used internally by the team for planning and trending purposes and not by upper management for evaluating the organization's performance. A high velocity creating large numbers of detections with poor coverage and durability has less value than a much smaller number of detections with high coverage and durability.

Measuring the efficiency of a detection engineering program

The first metric related to efficiency to be discussed, **velocity**, is **productivity over time. Productivity** can be defined as the number of detections but in an agile methodology should be measured in terms of story points. Story points are a unit of measure that is defined by each team as a consistent way of identifying how much work is required. Using points provides the added benefit of allowing team members to consider the complexity and uniqueness of the work required to create the detection.

Point estimation requires teams to first normalize the value of a story point by reviewing some sample detections together and creating a consensus view of the points required to complete the work. Once there is a common agreement on point values, team members can estimate the amount of work required to complete a task, such as the creation of a new detection or the update of an existing one. The velocity of the team can therefore be defined as the number of points worked over a period of time (agile typically uses two-week sprints). Since points are self-defined, the number itself has limited value, but when compared against the backlog, it is a valuable forecasting tool. The trending of the velocity (change in velocity over time) can be used to track changes in efficiency or to identify bottlenecks and issues. Additional information about agile methodologies and metrics has been provided in the *Further reading* section of the chapter.

Equally important to the detection team's efficiency is the impact it has on the efficiency of other teams within the SOC. The quality of the detection and its documentation can greatly affect the performance of the SOC analysts required to triage and review the associated alerts. The most basic metric we can capture for SOC analyst efficiency is simple **alert counts**. How many alerts from this detection resulted in something an analyst needed to review? Notice the caveat. We are not measuring every alert created by a detection. A second layer of processing provided by a SIEM or XDR may reduce the number of alerts created by the security device down to a lower number that an analyst must spend time on. Since we are looking at the impact on the analyst, we should use this final number when computing the metric.

The alert count over time is the **time claimed per detection**. How much time does it take an analyst on average to review an alert fired from that detection? This metric can be used to identify whether the detection is producing the correct evidence to easily disposition the alert, or whether it is properly documented so the analyst understands why it is firing and how to respond. Too low of a value, in conjunction with a high false positive rate, could indicate that analysts are not reviewing the detection and simply marking it as a false positive each time it appears. We can identify circumstances where this is partially true by looking at variance. A high variance in time claimed could indicate that some analysts are reviewing the alert, while others are not. It could also indicate that some analysts inherently know how to investigate that alert, but poor documentation or other factors have made investigating that alert tedious for less knowledgeable analysts. Lastly, you can look at the **change in time claimed** in the short time after an update until the detection was deployed. This value will provide the efficiency impact of the update. *Table 11.1* provides an overview of these metrics:

Metric	Definition	Value
Alert Count	Number of alerts requiring analyst review created by the detection	Identify noisy detections.
Average Time Claimed Per Detection	The average amount of time it takes an analyst for disposing alerts created from a detection	High values can indicate missing evidence or documentation. Low values can indicate analysts are not reviewing the alerts.

Variability in Time Claimed Per Detection	The standard deviation of the time claimed per detection	Can indicate that not all analysts are reviewing the alerts.
Change in Time Claimed Per Detection	Change in average time claimed per detection, measured shortly after the deployment of an update or other factor change	Identify the change in efficiency in triaging alerts created by the detection.

Table 11.1 – SOC efficiency metrics for detecting engineering

These metrics allow an organization to identify bottlenecks in their workflows or how their products, the detections, are affecting other teams and measure the impact of changes meant to address these issues. The metrics are inward looking. The SOC's purpose, though, is outward facing. Its impact on the company it supports is measured by how well it can identify or stop an attack. The next set of detection engineering metrics is designed to focus on this goal.

Measuring the effectiveness of a detection engineering program

While efficiency is a measure of productiveness, effectiveness is a measure of success. How well is the detection engineering team actually helping to achieve the SOC's goals, which should have a direct correlation to the value the organization provides? Quantifying the value of a cyber security program is always difficult. The cost of a cyber-attack cannot be quantified until after it has occurred and the damage has been assessed. It is therefore difficult to quantify how much stopping an attack has saved the organization. Should the value of a cyber security organization be judged based on the number of attacks performed by adversaries? Should an attack attempt to steal a random user's credit card number be counted the same as an advanced adversary attempting to steal the company's intellectual property or hold it for ransom? Stopping thousands of indiscriminate phishing attacks may not matter as much to the company's bottom line as stopping one determined adversary.

Rather than attempting to calculate the financial costs of successful attacks against an organization or the more difficult task of calculating the potential cost of a prevented attack, we will evaluate effectiveness in terms of how difficult it is for an adversary to evade our detection. We will first review one of the most popular metrics in SOC effectiveness and understand its limitations. Then, we will build upon the validation coverage metrics introduced in *Chapter 8* to evaluate how well the detection engineering program has supported the SOC in preventing future cyber-attacks against the organization.

Within this section, we will look at effectiveness from multiple perspectives:

- **Historical detection effectiveness**: How effective was the organization in detecting previous historical attacks? This is primarily shown through the mean time to detect.

- **Detection coverage**: How effective is the organization's detections in identifying different attack techniques?

- **Detection drift**: Automatically identifying false negatives to determine how much our detections are becoming less effective.

- **Detection volatility**: How long are detections effective once they are deployed or updated?

The historical effectiveness of a SOC is a look at how well the organization was protected against cyber-attacks. Traditionally, this is identified by looking at the **MTTD**, which is defined as the mean time for the organization to detect an attack performed by an adversary. The metric has the benefit of being easy to calculate. Take the duration of each attack (detection time minus start time) for each attack and then take the average of those values. The metric is popular for good reason. The goal of the SOC is to prevent an intrusion, and when one occurs, we need to quantify how quickly it identified that attack. MTTD is an excellent way to depict that understanding. It is also easy to compute and is well understood in the industry:

$$MTTD = \frac{\sum_{0}^{n}(detection\ time_i - start\ time_i)}{n}$$

Where n is the number of attacks and i is the attack instance.

Despite its popularity, MTTD suffers from being a historical evaluation of effectiveness. You can only calculate this metric *after* the adversary has performed an attack and it assumes the SOC has identified the attack in the first place. If the adversary is fully successful, then the attack is not included in the MTTD metric. MTTD only includes attacks you have stopped and does not include attacks that you never detect. This doesn't mean that mean-time-to-detect is not a valuable metric. It is. But if you are attempting to provide metrics on the value of the work your team is doing to prevent the next attack, MTTD does not describe that. It describes historical facts, not future ones.

Historical performance is only valuable within the context of understanding the adversary. The adversary is lazy. They will use the same attack as long as it is successful. This means that either the attack was successful on your network, and they believe it will be successful again (with some minimal variation), or that the attack will be successful on someone else's network and they'll bother those people and leave you alone. The attacker, though, will alter their procedures if they find it to be unsuccessful within those parameters, which the preceding metric does not reflect. It says nothing about how your SOC will perform against significantly new (relative to your organization) types of attacks. The metric only defines how well the SOC performed in yesterday's attacks.

MTTD is also defined by adversaries. Adversaries define the variation in the tests used for the computation and there is no guarantee that their tests are complete. Instead, the opposite is true. The test performed by the adversary is one attack for the technique that was detected. Forensic analysis will identify additional techniques that the adversary performed successfully prior to detection. The analysis can also be used to extrapolate further in the kill chain using the processes defined in Lockheed's *Intelligence Driven Defense* paper. This analysis, though, only identifies the attack procedures from one attack, as illustrated in *Figure 11.2*.

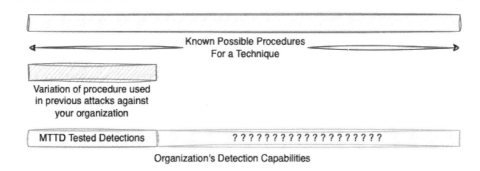

Figure 11.2 – MTTD detection testing

This distinction is a key issue limiting MTTD's use as a metric for effectiveness for detection engineering. The metric is basically the equivalent of a **User Acceptance Test** (**UAT**) performed on a software system. The users play around, and the developers see whether anything breaks. Some feedback is provided on the usability or performance of the system, but a development team would never use a UAT as their primary test performance metric. Instead, software systems have test coverage and pass rate metrics defined by testing teams identifying edge cases. Developers build unit tests to check nothing breaks as updates are made to the code. Automated static and dynamic analysis of the system is used to test the system for security vulnerabilities. Detection engineering effectiveness metrics should similarly reflect the coverage and pass rates to detect or mitigate the full range of potential attacks rather than only those seen in previous attacks.

Prioritizing detection efforts

To define and track true effectiveness metrics for detection engineering, we need to set some limitations on what we track at what fidelity. There are over a dozen MITRE ATT&CK matrices for various environments, each with techniques and sub-techniques numbering into the hundreds that can then be executed using a range of procedures. It is therefore impractical to track effectiveness metrics on each of these attack techniques and sub-techniques. Any organization needs to prioritize where to focus their energy and these focus areas also define the fidelity at which our metrics are tracked. MITRE has released some tools to support this effort, including the MITRE Top ATT&CK Techniques (https://top-attack-techniques.mitre-engenuity.org/), which will help propose the most impactful techniques a team should focus on detecting based upon a short survey about the organization. Organizations can also use both internal and external threat intelligence as well as knowledge about their organization's infrastructure and assets to prioritize their detection engineering efforts. This analysis should result in grouping techniques into one of three categories:

- **Top 10 or 20 high-impact techniques**: Techniques the organization has identified as high-value to which they should dedicate a concentrated effort in detecting. These are techniques for which we either have completed or plan to complete an in-depth investigation into the attack procedures, resulting in high-coverage detections.

- **Medium or high impact**: Important techniques that we want to track but have accepted the risk that we will not be performing in-depth analysis. For these techniques, we will create detections based on open source reporting and leverage third-party detections, but they are not part of our backlog to perform an in-depth analysis of the techniques.

- **Low impact or low fidelity/visibility**: Low impact, not applicable, or rarely used techniques (reconnaissance is low impact)

Let's review each of these, starting with the least critical and working our way upward. Low-impact or low-fidelity/visibility techniques are techniques that the organization has accepted as having minimal detection. This may also include techniques that are not applicable based on the organization, such as **Industrial Control System** (**ICS**) specific techniques in a Windows-only environment. Alerts from these techniques will most likely be informational rather than reviewed by an analyst. Medium- to low-maturity SOCs may ignore default alerting or put no effort into creating detections for these techniques. For example, we may have tools that detect scanning of our network but only use this information for forensic analysis. In these circumstances, coverage metrics do not make sense. We have accepted the risk of not having visibility. Instead, we only want to capture efficiency metrics. This allows us to identify whether SOC analysts are still triaging these alerts and how much valuable time is being spent on them. Even though we are not building detections for these techniques, identifying and categorizing them is still valuable so they are not included in our medium- and high-impact technique metrics.

Medium- to high-impact techniques are those that the organization has identified as valuable but has not identified for in-depth analysis. In these circumstances, we may be reliant upon detections included within third-party tools or open source detections. The majority of techniques most likely will fall within this category. In these circumstances, we may create some low-fidelity coverage metrics such as the number of detections per technique, or efficacy metrics such as false-positive rates.

High-impact techniques are techniques the SOC has identified as commonly used by adversaries that target their organization's infrastructure and thus are marked for in-depth analysis. These are techniques that the SOC is building custom detections for and should track metrics that answer the difficult question *How good are we doing?* Tiering techniques allow a detection engineering team to prioritize their resources and capture metrics that reflect those prioritizations. *Figure 11.3* shows an example of which metric types could be captured per tier.

Metric	Low Impact	Medium / High	High Impact
Efficiency	X	X	X
Precision and Recall		X	X
Low fidelity coverage		X	X
Automated validation		X	X
High fidelity coverage			X

Efficacy spans the rows: Low fidelity coverage, Automated validation, High fidelity coverage.

Figure 11.3 – Metrics by criticality

Precision, noisiness, and recall

Efficiency metrics were covered at the start of this chapter. Precision and recall metrics have been mentioned throughout the book as well. In this section, we will review the data and equations required to actually calculate these values. When we discuss these metrics, we need to distinguish between the following:

- Did the detection create an alert for what it was supposed to detect?
- Did the detection create an alert for something malicious?

Consider a detection rule identifying multiple incorrect logins from a new location. If the rule incorrectly checked whether the location was new, it would fail to detect what it was supposed to. Even if the rule was written correctly though, such activity may or may not be indicative of malicious activity. Calculating precision and recall metrics requires first defining false positive, true positive, true negative, and false negative in relation to detection engineering:

- **True positive**: An alert fired for actual malicious activity
- **False positive**: An alert fired for non-malicious activity
- **True negative**: An alert did not fire for non-malicious activity
- **False negative**: An alert did not fire for malicious activity

These four data points are useful for calculating many of the metrics we discuss in this chapter. Unfortunately, you may need to look across multiple data sources to identify this information. Analysts can disposition alerts as true or false positives within the native security device or a centralized event and alert system, such as a SIEM. The organization may also have a ticket management, SOAR, or case management system specifically used for managing the team's processes. Even if such a system exists, you should check that the internal processes of the SOC align with your expectations. Some SOCs may only create a ticket for alerts they choose to investigate while others may choose not to ingest all alerts within a centralized system even if one exists. These metrics support the overall SOC management so it may be possible to convince leadership to alter processes in support of more consistent metric gathering.

False negatives are more difficult to identify. Toward the end of the chapter, we will look at a metric called detection drift, which helps automatically identify false negatives for a set of detections related to similar activity, such as a specific technique. An organization can also identify false negatives manually by forensically analyzing an attack to identify earlier stages or by reviewing artifacts that identify future techniques of an attack. This information can be compared against the rules designed to detect these portions of an attack. For example, an analyst could execute malware in a sandbox that was found in a phishing attack to determine whether the C2 protocol would have been detected. A false negative would be identified if detections designed to alert on that activity did not fire during the test.

Figure 11.4 visualizes these concepts in a quadrant format.

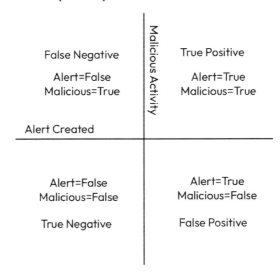

Figure 11.4 – Alert determinations

These definitions allow us to define the equation for the statistical accuracy of our detection program, although we cannot easily calculate it. In statistics, accuracy is defined as the number of correct predictions / total number of predictions:

$$Accuracy = \frac{Number\ of\ Correct\ Detections\ Decisions}{Total\ Number\ of\ Possible\ Detections\ Choices} = \frac{TP + TN}{TP + TN + FP + FN}$$

It is not practically possible to calculate the total accuracy of a detection program. For example, we cannot easily calculate true negatives (i.e., the number of times that we did not fire an alert for non-malicious activity). We can, though, calculate a detection's **precision**. Precision refers to the second question listed previously, *What proportion of alerts created for a detection was for something actually malicious?*

Precision is the true positive rate for our detections, which is defined as follows:

$$True\ Positive\ Rate = Precision = \frac{TP}{TP + FP}$$

The opposite of this is noisiness, or the false positive rate, which answers the question, *What proportion of alerts created for this detection was not malicious?*

$$False\ Positive\ Rate = Noisiness = \frac{FP}{TP + FP}$$

Recall answers the question, *What proportion of malicious activity was detected by the detection that it was supposed to detect?*

$$Recall = \frac{TP}{TP + FN}$$

Referring to *Figure 11.4*, we can see that false negatives are defined as malicious activity that did not fire an alert. Like MTTD, this is a historical view of the problem. We can identify false negatives through forensic analysis if an attack was detected at a different stage or if we layer detections for the same activity, such as network and endpoint devices using separate telemetry to identify the same thing. Usually, as we attempt to improve our recall, that is, detect more variations of an attack, we will also increase the false positive rate, resulting in more alerts for our SOC analysts to review.

Plotting detection performance

ROC (short for **receiver operating characteristic**) curves are a common data analytics technique that can be a useful construct in evaluating changes in your detection approach for a procedure or technique. At its core, a ROC curve plots the true positive to false positive values for different thresholds in machine learning or other types of analytics. In our case, we can use them to plot how changes we make affect a detection's performance. A standard ROC curve looks something like the one in *Figure 11.5*. On the *x* axis, we plot the false positive values, and on the *y* axis, the true positive values. As we change the threshold of the analytic, more stuff will be caught, increasing the true positives, but usually the noisiness increases as well, increasing the false positives.

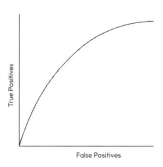

Figure 11.5 – Standard ROC curve

Adapting ROC curves to our use case, we can evaluate multiple variations of detection or overlapping detections of the same activity to identify whether the changes provide sufficient performance improvements to justify additional work by the SOC analysts to triage false positives. Consider an example where we have four approaches to detection. Each approach adds conditions to catch additional variations of the attack that we wish to detect (i.e., increasing the threshold):

- **Approach 1 (A1)**: Condition 1

- Approach 2 (A2): Condition 1, condition 2

- Approach 3 (A3): Condition 1, condition 2, and condition 3

- Approach 4 (A4): Condition 1, condition 2, condition 3, and condition 4

During our testing phase, we would like to determine which of these approaches should be deployed within our environment. We retrieve the true positives and false positives after each test. Any tests against data identified specifically for this detection would be categorized as a true positive detection. Tests against our known good dataset, either previously curated or from live environment tests that resulted in a false detection, would be tagged as false positives. By plotting their true positive and false positive values, as shown in *Figure 11.6*, we can create a ROC curve to help our analysis.

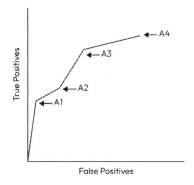

Figure 11.6 – Evaluating detection approaches using a ROC curve

Looking at the graph, we can see that our initial detection had few false positives but also was insufficient in detecting a decent portion of the malicious activity. Adding in rules for conditions 2 and 3 greatly improved our true positive rate while increasing the false positive rate as well. The fourth approach provided a minimal increase in detection while greatly increasing the noise. As detection engineers, we might decide that approach 4 did not have sufficient value over approach 3 to justify the false positives created.

Now that we've looked at how to assess how the detection program is operating as a whole, let's step back down to the detection level so we can understand how certain detections may be affecting our performance at the program level.

Calculating a detection's efficacy

Mean time to detect, discussed earlier in this chapter, provides a historical view of the effectiveness against attacks performed against the organization. We will group additional efficacy metrics into three areas: low-fidelity coverage, automated validations, and high-fidelity coverage. When we refer to coverage, we are talking about a measure of how much of the potential attack space can be detected. The attack space is defined by what you are trying to measure. It could be a single technique or multiple MITRE ATT&CK matrixes. We'll start by looking at some low-fidelity methods of determining coverage.

Low-fidelity coverage metrics

A common low-fidelity coverage visualization is mapping your detections to a MITRE ATT&CK matrix, as shown in *Figure 11.7*. Each technique is colored according to the number of detections that have been created for it. This visualization is easy to produce, and many tools will automatically provide some form of the matrix. The number of detections, though, is a poor representation of coverage. One well-crafted detection may have higher coverage of the technique than 10 detections and 10 detections of individual procedures may provide little value if the adversary can choose from hundreds of variations. If a leader has trust in the quality of the detections created by their organization, the visualization does have value, especially when paired with intelligence.

Figure 11.7 – MITRE ATT&CK matrix example

Comparing your detection attack matrix to other matrixes can help prioritize new detection creation, support gap analysis, and identify which techniques should be included in your coverage calculations.

Comparing organization attack surfaces and visibility

At the start of any detection coverage process, we can identify which techniques are applicable based on the organization's network. For example, if the organization does not host external websites, techniques attacking those surfaces would not be applicable to the organization. Patching or removing vulnerable infrastructure are also ways to mitigate potential threats and reduce the need for detection in those areas. In addition, we can map the visibility available to the organization to the techniques that can leverage that visibility. Gaps in what cannot be detected can help prioritize adding additional sources of telemetry but also accurately represent what is possible to identify.

Comparing threat intelligence

Many threat intelligence providers will document techniques used by an adversary, as well as objectives, industries, and geographical interests the adversary commonly targets. This intelligence can be represented within a MITRE ATT&CK matrix. By identifying which adversaries commonly target your organization and mapping their techniques to MITRE ATT&ACK, you can overlay the information against your detection ATT&CK matrix to identify potential gaps. If a technique is leveraged by adversaries but is not within your detection coverage, this can signify a gap in detection that can be addressed by the team. The opposite does not hold true. Techniques leveraged by an adversary but with detection coverage may not signify that you are protected. A more careful examination of the adversary's procedures and how your organization detects them would be necessary to truly validate coverage.

Automated validation

Commercial or open source validation tools provide a quick method to identify gaps in detection. The ability to quickly test hundreds of attack procedures against your detections allows an organization to rapidly identify coverage gaps without requiring a large amount of effort. *Chapter 9* introduced these capabilities, so we will not go into detail here. It is important to remember that validation tools do not confirm that a technique or procedure is fully detected. It may be possible to alter a procedure used by the validation tool to evade the associated detection.

High-fidelity coverage metrics

The last metric group we'll look at includes high-fidelity coverage metrics. The goal of high-fidelity coverage metrics is to quantify how well the organization detects specific techniques. Some of these metrics are more labor-intensive, making them difficult to adopt broadly across a detection engineering program.

Validation coverage

In *Chapter 8*, we discussed the first of these metrics with high-fidelity validation coverage. Validation coverage, especially when implemented using the approaches in *Chapter 8*, is one of the best ways to measure effectiveness. It is defined based upon the work performed by the detection engineering team and it directly correlates to the team's ability to detect the adversary for the validated techniques. This approach requires an in-depth analysis of known procedures for a technique and validation tests that are based on how the detections were implemented.

As a quick refresher, the approach works by grouping procedures that implement a technique into four categories: fully covered, partially covered, missed coverage, and zero days. This is visually represented in *Figure 11.8*. Specific test requirements are used to identify each category and migrate a procedure's detection from one category to another.

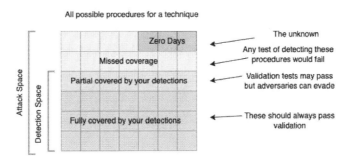

Figure 11.8 – Categories of detection validation results

Our goal is obviously to maximize the detections categorized as fully covered and have no procedures identified as missed coverage. Unfortunately, this may not always be practical, resulting in some procedures being partially covered or missed, and there is always the possibility of zero days. It takes significant effort to thoroughly analyze variations in how a technique can be executed, and even then, new procedures are identified over time as adversaries change their behaviors. It may be possible that the analysis was complete when it was performed, but since that time new information has become available. How often should an organization revisit its analysis and how can it identify when its detections are starting to be less effective? The next two metrics are used to identify when that coverage has changed and how quickly it is changing.

Tracking detection drift

Detection drift occurs when a set of detections, designed to identify an adversary or TTP, begin to be less effective as the adversary adapts their procedures. These missed alerts are false negatives of detections that did not fire when they should have. Identifying when this happens and by how much allows an organization to track the quality of their detections related to a specific adversary or TTP, where those detections are now failing, and patch the holes in their detection strategy. The approach allows an organization to create metrics that track this drift and proactively patch their detections as adversaries begin to evade them.

To track detection drift, we need a way to identify that the adversary has evaded a subset of our detections. Defense in depth is a common industry term and practice where multiple layers of detections or other defenses (such as restricting access control, reducing the attack surface, patch management, etc.) force the adversary to evade multiple layers of defenses to achieve their objective. By employing multiple detection strategies, we raise the cost of an attack. An adversary must change all parts of their tooling and infrastructure, or risk being identified. This was first widely documented in *Lockheed Martin's Intelligence Driven Defense* paper, which outlined the **Cyber Kill Chain** but also demonstrated how to use the kill chain to forensically analyze an attack, identifying earlier stages of the kill chain and artifacts that could be used to identify later stages of activity, as shown in *Figure 11.9*. By creating or updating detections, a SOC could continue to detect an adversary who had only partially changed its tools and infrastructure.

Figure 11.9 – Cyber Kill Chain analysis to identify missed activity

The **kill chain analysis** can be used to evaluate the defensive performance in moving horizontally across the MITRE ATT&CK matrix. We can also evaluate our drift vertically across multiple layers of detections for the same technique. A single technique could be detected by multiple detections at one or more stages, as shown in the pyramid of pain. For example, we may have network signatures identifying the C2 protocol of a malware family, file signatures identifying the tooling, and behavioral rules to identify the activity performed with those tools.

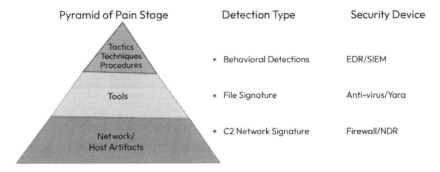

Figure 11.10 – Pyramid of pain and detection types

Whether analyzing the procedures used by an adversary across the phases of a kill chain or creating multiple detections for the same technique, it is important to remember that this analysis has occurred at a point in time. As an adversary attempts to evolve their procedures to evade defenders, not all detections continue to be effective. Ideally, we'd like a way to track not just what TTP a rule is detecting, but also how many alerts should fire together. This would track the continued effectiveness of our detections and prioritize future work for the detection engineering team. Detection drift is the difference between detections that should have detected the activity and those that did detect the activity:

$$
\begin{aligned}
\textit{Detection Drift} \\
&= SUM(\textit{detections that should have detected adversary activity}) \\
&- SUM(\textit{detections that did detect adversary activity})
\end{aligned}
$$

This is not as simple as it seems. Despite creating multiple detections based on our understanding of the adversary or technique, we would not expect all detections to hit each time. For example, if we identified two tools that are used by adversaries when performing a particular technique, we could write yara signatures to identify those tools in the future. We would only expect one of these tools to be used in an attack and thus only one signature to hit if the adversary deployed this technique. If the adversary used a new tool though, which did not hit against either signature, we would have a gap in coverage and our detections will have drifted from current adversary methods. This coverage gap might be difficult to detect. Suppose, for example, the adversary's new tool continued to use a shared library employed by tool number 2, which we also had built a detection for. The SOC analyst would still receive an alert for the shared library but might not recognize that a second expected detection at the tool level did not occur, requiring an update by the detection engineer.

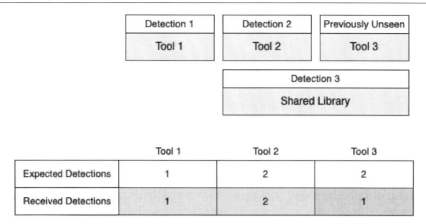

Figure 11.11 – Detection drift for mulitple attacker tools

In the example shown in *Figure 11.11*, detection 1 should only alert on its own, while detections 2 and 3 should always alert together. Detection 3 alerting without detection 2 shows a detection drift.

These variations can be broken into three categories, visualized in *Figure 11.12*: either a group has its own detection for that category, a detection spans across multiple groups, or no detection exists for a subset of groups. A group can be defined based on your needs. Each procedure for a technique can be its own group, or a common or necessary attack path taken by an adversary identified using the kill chain analysis. A group is just a representation of the set of detections that should fire together where you want to track detection drift.

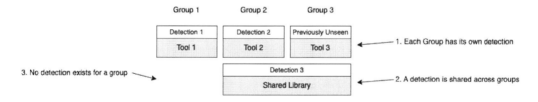

Figure 11.12 – Variations in detection coverage

During the Investigate phase of the detection engineering life cycle, we can map capabilities to their associated groups. An **abstraction map**, introduced in the SpecterOps *Capability Abstraction* blog, is a tool that can be used to track these relationships and will help demonstrate how we can track detection drift. The blog is linked in the *Further reading* section and is an excellent way to understand abstraction maps. We will provide a short explanation of the concept as follows, but the blog reviews a detailed example if you are interested.

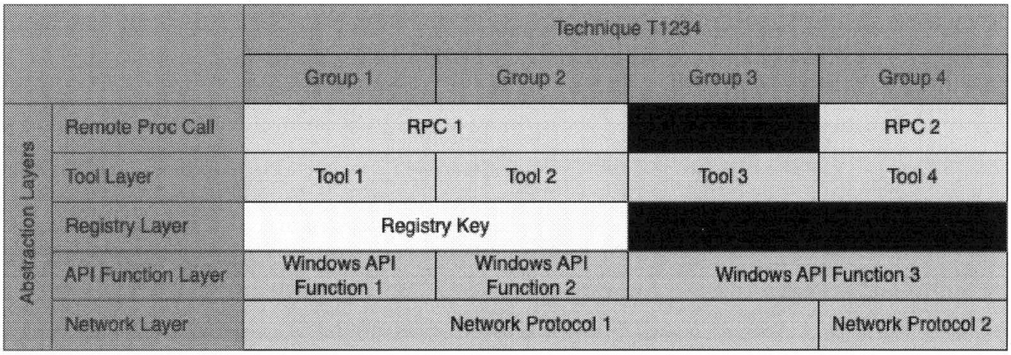

		Technique T1234			
		Group 1	Group 2	Group 3	Group 4
Abstraction Layers	Remote Proc Call	RPC 1			RPC 2
	Tool Layer	Tool 1	Tool 2	Tool 3	Tool 4
	Registry Layer	Registry Key			
	API Function Layer	Windows API Function 1	Windows API Function 2	Windows API Function 3	
	Network Layer	Network Protocol 1			Network Protocol 2

Figure 11.13 – Abstraction map with five layers

The abstraction map, an example of which is shown in *Figure 11.13*, works by breaking the capability into a subset of groups and peeling back the capability to identify different layers of abstraction. As each layer is investigated, the associated artifacts are captured and mapped across the groups that they apply to. These artifacts can then be used to create the associated detections. An artifact detail can be missing because it is not applicable or because the investigation did not uncover that detail or was incomplete. A generalized version of the abstraction map is shown in *Figure 11.14*.

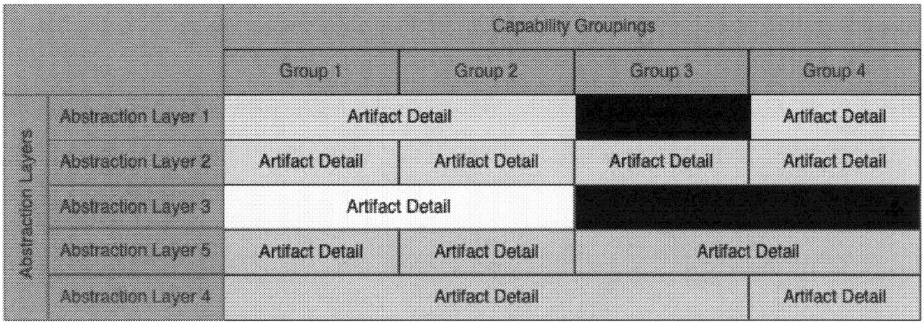

		Capability Groupings			
		Group 1	Group 2	Group 3	Group 4
Abstraction Layers	Abstraction Layer 1	Artifact Detail			Artifact Detail
	Abstraction Layer 2	Artifact Detail	Artifact Detail	Artifact Detail	Artifact Detail
	Abstraction Layer 3	Artifact Detail			
	Abstraction Layer 5	Artifact Detail	Artifact Detail	Artifact Detail	
	Abstraction Layer 4	Artifact Detail			Artifact Detail

Figure 11.14 – A generalized abstraction map

An abstraction map can be useful in the investigation phase of the detection engineering life cycle. To identify detection drift, that is, false negatives, we are using it to easily determine the minimum number of detections that should fire under different circumstances. In the preceding example, if a detection was created for each artifact detail, the abstraction map can be broken into 12 detections with anywhere from three to five detections alerting based upon the attacker's approach. Not only that but for the same detection, such as Network Protocol 1, in some circumstances, there are four other detections that would alert and in other cases, only two other detections would alert.

To calculate the detection drift, we can add a tag to each of these detections with the **Minimum Detections** (**MDs**) that should occur with that detection for the associated capability grouping (in this example, the capability grouping is Technique T1234). When any new alerting occurs related to one or more of these detections, we can use these tags to calculate the detection drift. An example of an abstraction map with tags applied is shown in *Figure 11.15*.

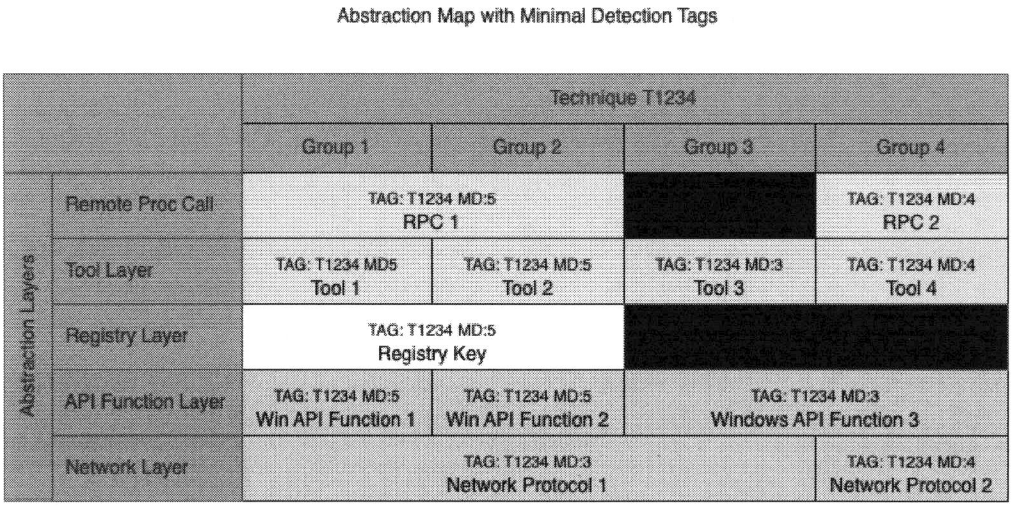

Abstraction Map with Minimal Detection Tags

		Technique T1234			
		Group 1	Group 2	Group 3	Group 4
Abstraction Layers	Remote Proc Call	TAG: T1234 MD:5 RPC 1			TAG: T1234 MD:4 RPC 2
	Tool Layer	TAG: T1234 MD5 Tool 1	TAG: T1234 MD:5 Tool 2	TAG: T1234 MD:3 Tool 3	TAG: T1234 MD:4 Tool 4
	Registry Layer	TAG: T1234 MD:5 Registry Key			
	API Function Layer	TAG: T1234 MD:5 Win API Function 1	TAG: T1234 MD:5 Win API Function 2	TAG: T1234 MD:3 Windows API Function 3	
	Network Layer	TAG: T1234 MD:3 Network Protocol 1			TAG: T1234 MD:4 Network Protocol 2

Figure 11.15 - MD tagging example

To calculate the MD drift, we take the *maximum* of the MD tags for the associated alerts. The formula for this is shown in *Figure 11.16*.

$$Minimum\ Detection\ Drift = Max(MD_1, MD_2, MD_n) - n$$
$$Where: n = number\ of\ alerts$$

Figure 11.16 – MD drift formula

These tags can be added as part of the details of an alert when it fires. The capability grouping name is used to identify alerts that should be included within the same calculation. Let's look at some examples.

Example 1

For our first example, we will look at the set of detections identified in the *Group 1* column in *Figure 11.15*. Group 1 has artifacts identified for each of the abstraction layers.

Example 1 without drift

This first example assumes that all detections are triggered at all abstraction layers for Group 1:

Detection	Tag
RPC 1	T1234 MD:5
Tool 1	T1234 MD:5
Registry Key	T1234 MD:5
Win API Function 1	T1234 MD:5
Network Protocol 1	T1234 MD:3

Table 11.2 – Group 1 without detection drift

Using the MD count in *Table 11.2*, we can calculate detection drift with the previously defined formula for MD drift:

$$Minimum\ Detection\ Drift = Max(5, 5, 5, 5, 3) - 5 = 0$$

In this most basic example, there are a maximum of five potential detections and all five occurred, resulting in zero detection drift.

Example 1 with drift

To observe what detection drift looks like, let's assume that the RPC 1 and Win API Function 1 detections did not fire, resulting in the modified table shown in *Table 11.3*:

Detection	Tag
Tool 1	T1234 MD:5
Registry Key	T1234 MD:5
Network Protocol 1	T1234 MD:3

Table 11.3 – Group 1 with detection drift

Using the MD count in *Table 11.3*, we can calculate detection drift with the previously defined formula for MD drift:

$$Minimum\ Detection\ Drift = Max(5,5,3) - 3 = 2$$

Re-performing the calculation identifies that a minimum of two detections did not result in alerts, revealing how detection drift shows potential gaps in detection.

Example 2

In example 2, we will use *Group 4* from *Figure 11.15*, which contains a gap in coverage in the registry layer.

Example 2 without drift

Table 11.4 shows the detections that did fire and the associated tags in Group 4 without coverage for the registry layer:

Detection	Tag
RPC 2	T1234 MD:4
Tool 4	T1234 MD:4
Win API Function 3	T1234 MD:3
Network Protocol 2	T1234 MD:4

Table 11.4 – Group 4 without detection drift

Using the MD count in *Table 11.4*, we can calculate detection drift using the previously defined formula:

$$Minimum\ Detection\ Drift\ =\ Max(4,\ 4,\ 3,\ 4)\ -\ 4 = 0$$

Once again, we observe no detection drift, meaning that our detections cover all possible layers of abstraction of the capability group. Next, let's see what happens if one of the previous detections doesn't fire.

Example 2 with drift

Table 11.5 assumes that the same Group 4 capabilities are being analyzed, but this time the Network Protocol 2 detection does not trigger:

Detection	Tag
Tool 4	T1234 MD:4
Win API Function 3	T1234 MD:3

Table 11.5 – Group 4 with detection drift

Using the MD count in *Table 11.5*, we can calculate detection drift with the previously defined formula for MD drift:

$$Minimum\ Detection\ Drift\ =\ Max(4,3)\ -\ 2 = 2$$

In this second example, we don't know whether two detections failed or there were more, but we do know that something changed in the adversary behavior that caused at least a subset of our detections that should have hit to not fire.

In summary, this section demonstrates how the concept of detection drift can highlight how and where changes in adversary behavior can affect the coverage of your detections.

Adapting to account for an automated response

One complexity of this approach is that many detection devices now have the ability to also respond to an attack in addition to detecting it. In these circumstances, detections occurring after the response occurs need to be accounted for.

This is similar to the modified approach that would support kill chain analysis. In both circumstances, detections that occur after the attack are expected to be stopped and would not be included within the MD count.

In *Figure 11.17*, we assume that an EDR would stop the attack prior to seeing network activity. Notice the updated MD values for detections occurring prior to the EDR response and that the value remains unchanged for the network protocol detection.

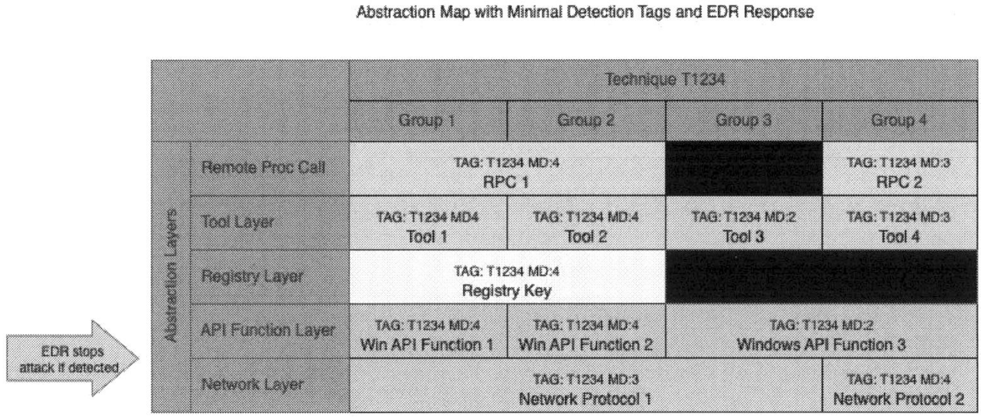

Abstraction Map with Minimal Detection Tags and EDR Response

Figure 11.17 – Abstraction map with EDR response

Tracking detection drift is one approach for identifying when an organization's detections are becoming less effective. These calculations provide the ability for an organization to repair its defenses by automatically identifying changes in adversary behavior that are no longer detected. There are several limitations in implementing detection drift that should be recognized:

- Many detection engineers will include multiple artifacts within the same detection rule. If those artifacts have different MD scores, it becomes difficult to automatically output the MD value from within the alert.

- Mapping detections to an abstraction map or similar matrix is a time-consuming effort. This limits the ability to calculate detection drift on high-impact techniques or attackers where such analysis is justified.

- Not all alerts are sent to the SOC in the same instant, therefore this calculation cannot be performed accurately in real time. Instead, it must be performed once all alerts have arrived. This can be accomplished either as a scheduled or on-demand query against the alert data.

- A security device may send multiple alerts for the same detection. When building your query, make sure that the detection IDs are distinct.

- The calculation does not distinguish between detections that are easy for the adversary to adjust around (such as a hash) and detections that are more difficult to avoid. If the detections are based upon artifacts lower in the pyramid of pain that are easy for the adversary to change, detection drift may occur too commonly to action, and you may decide to purposefully ignore those artifacts from the calculation.

Now that we know how to track detection drift, let's move on to our second high-fidelity coverage metric: **volatility**.

Calculating volatility

Our final metric for high-fidelity coverage addresses the last point in the list of limitations of detection drift, calculating a detection's volatility. Volatility measures how much the detection needs to change over time to accommodate the evolution of the adversary's attacks. The lower the volatility, the more stable your detections are. Detections with high volatility may indicate that additional research should be applied to identify better methods that detect the activity. The historical volatility is constant over time – for example, the detection is usually effective for about six months – so we could be on the lookout for changes in the adversary's procedures both from our internal telemetry and external threat intelligence. The volatility of a detection can also help identify when our confidence in its effectiveness may have decreased, resulting in prioritizing a hunt to identify similar activity. The most common use of this metric is to evaluate how the volatility is changing over time, or the volatility trend. As a detection engineering program matures, the volatility of its detections should decrease, indicating that the detections are more stable. If the detections created by the team have high volatility, it may indicate that the team is *chasing the adversary* or building signatures that are easy for the adversary to evade, requiring a large number of updates.

This metric should also only be calculated if an attack is caught or missed by a detection. It is not calculated if the detection never fired or never had the opportunity to fire. An interesting byproduct of this property is that detections with high numbers of data points in their volatility calculation are also associated with the tools, infrastructure, techniques, procedures, and so on that are frequently used by the adversary. Therefore, detections with high volatility may be good targets for additional research since there is a lower confidence they will detect the next attack and a higher confidence that the adversary will exploit what they are intended to detect.

Volatility suffers from some of the same constraints mentioned previously for MTTD. It is a metric based on the adversary's attacks. This limitation, though, aligns with what we are trying to measure. Our goal is to understand how changes made by the adversary impact the effectiveness of our defenses.

As mentioned previously, the first step to calculating volatility is identifying the scope of detections you are calculating the volatility for. Volatility can be calculated for an individual detection or for a set of detections that may be used to identify variations of the same technique. It can also be calculated for each detection across the entire detection repository. A valuable use case is calculating the volatility of a particular abstraction layer in an abstraction map or the pyramid of pain. This answers the question, "What is the volatility of detections based upon this abstraction layer?" High volatility for that abstraction layer means the adversary changes their attack at that abstraction layer and therefore the associated detections are not flexible enough to account for those changes. Simple examples would be lower echelons of the pyramid of pain, such as adversaries constantly changing a malware's hash, making it an ineffective mechanism for detection over a long time period.

The second variable to identify is the period for which we are calculating the volatility. We can calculate the volatility for a period of time, such as days or weeks. We can also calculate the volatility over a period of campaigns. This can be an interesting distinction. Many adversaries will retool or change their infrastructure between campaigns. Since different adversaries conduct campaigns at their own op tempo, it may seem that one detection is more volatile than another when in reality, both detections only last for a scope of a campaign, but the length of a campaign differs between the adversaries caught by those detections. In *Figure 11.18*, detection 1 would be calculated as having lower volatility than detection 2 when using days as the period for the calculation. If we use campaigns as the period, detection 2 is shown to be more stable. This indicates that in the long run, detection 2 continues to be effective as the adversary retools, while detection 1 has limited value once the campaign is complete.

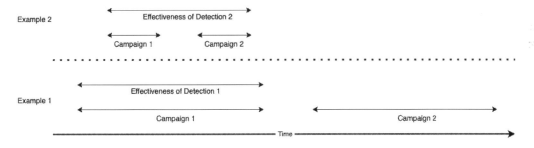

Figure 11.18 – Effectiveness of detections over time

Once we have identified the level of fidelity/scope and we know how we wish to identify the period (days, campaigns, etc.), we can capture the data necessary to calculate volatility. These data points are as follows:

- **Number of detection updates over the period of time**
- **Number of new detections over the period of time**
- **Days between False Negative (FN) and update (optional)**

For each detection within our defined scope, count the number of updates deployed for that detection over the defined time period. If you are using detection as code processes, you can capture these metrics as part of your CI/CD pipeline. If you are calculating the volatility of a technique's detections, capture the number of updates or new detections associated with the entire technique rather than each individual detection.

Calculating the volatility for a set of detections is actually very easy. It is simply the sum of the number of updates or new detections created over that time period. This is because if there was no volatility in our detections, then zero updates would be required. Therefore, the average amount of change from the ideal situation is the sum of the changes for the scope of activity:

$$Change = Volatility = \sum Updates + \sum New\ Detections$$

If we wish to be conservative in our calculations, we can also add the days between a false negative and an update to the overall update count for that detection. This change makes the assumption that for every day there was no update, there was a potential change by the adversary. While this is an overcorrection, it will result in detections that were not updated after failing as having a high volatility instead of having a low volatility simply because their issues were unattended.

It can be valuable to also calculate the volatility of our detection volatility. For example, say you are calculating the volatility for the set of detections identifying activity related to technique T1234. When you calculate the volatility for that group of detections, it is high. This would seem to indicate that a detection engineer should spend some effort better understanding T1234 so the adversary cannot evade the detections as easily. Standard volatility calculations, though, will identify how much "scatter" there is in our data. If the volatility of the number of updates is low, this would indicate that our detections for technique T1234 are not stable and we should invest in identifying better ways to identify the malicious activity. If the volatility is high, this could indicate that some of our detections require frequent updates to be effective, while others do not. Therefore, we may wish to turn off the unstable detections requiring frequent updates since we have more stable ways to detect the activity. We could visually look at the scatter of data points to make this determination manually, but if we wish to identify this condition across a large number of groups (such as every technique), it is easier to automatically calculate the average number of updates and the volatility of that average for each group.

We start with the average number of updates (the mean) across the set of detections. In our example, the set is all the detections for technique T1234. Next, we calculate the variance across the detections with the following equation:

$$Variance = \frac{\sum_{i=1}^{n}(DetectionUpdates_i - mean)^2}{n}$$

Where n is the number of detections, **DetectionUpdates** is the number of updates for each detection, and the mean is the average number of updates across all of the detections, which is the first volatility equation provided previously.

Last, we calculate the standard deviation, by taking the square root of the variance. The higher the standard deviation, the more volatile the value of detection volatility is:

$$Volatility_{of\ detection\ volatility} = Standard\ Deviation = \sqrt{Variance}$$

The following quadrant shows how we can use the volatility of a set of detections and the volatility of that value to identify actions to take in an organization. Quadrant 1 identifies either stable detections that do not require frequent updates or activity that was not seen by the organization (you can identify which by the number of data points). The second quadrant identifies a high number of updates but there is significant scatter in the data. This shows an inconsistency in the number of updates required per detection in the group. This may indicate that some of the detections may not be worth maintaining if what they are detecting overlaps with other detections within the group. If the detections identify different activities (such as different procedures for implementing the same technique), the volatility in the data may be indicative of a subset of the detections being exercised more than others. Lastly, quadrant 3 identifies detection sets with a high number of updates across the group, indicating that more effort should be focused on improving detection in this area.

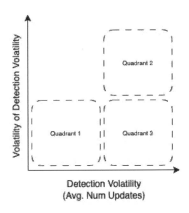

Assume data points are plotted for each set of detections
(ex: the set of detections for each technique)

Figure 11.19 – Plotting aspects of detection volatility

The hardest part of tracking volatility is identifying when a false negative has occurred, which is used to alert the team that an update to a detection must be performed. False negatives, as defined earlier, are when a detection should have created an alert but did not. These can be uncovered through forensic analysis after an attack. A more consistent approach can be implemented by leveraging the detection drift tagging to enable the calculation of volatility for an abstraction layer. If our detection drift calculations identify no drift, then no update is needed. If our detection drift calculations identify that a drift has occurred, we can map the alerts that did fire back to their associated abstraction layer within the abstraction map and narrow our scope of which detection did not create an alert.

Volatility can also be used for creating new detections. Ideally, we would like to identify choke points in the adversary's attack that cannot be evaded and thus are excellent choices to detect malicious activity. This is not always possible. In many cases, the potential variations in the attack cannot be fully accounted for in our detections. In these circumstances, we would like to identify indicators with the least volatility to build our detections around. During our investigation, we will uncover multiple attacks, either within our own alerting, threat intelligence, or other external sources. This information can be represented within an abstraction map. The abstraction map, though, does not consider when each of these variations occurred. Calculating the volatility of data within each abstraction layer will identify which indicators vary the least over time and thus are best suited for creating detections.

When looking at volatility, be careful to first have a solid detection baseline. Volatility is only shown when updates to a detection are performed. If an organization is missing detecting large portions of adversary activity, then the only activity they are detecting may also be the focus of updates. The activity they are entirely missing would obviously not show up in the volatility calculations and could cause the organization to continuously focus on improving a subset of detections. Therefore, volatility should only be one input used in determining the prioritization of effort.

Summary

This chapter provided metrics for calculating both the efficiency and effectiveness of an organization. We started by reviewing a CMMI model to track the maturity of our organization and then identified agile process metrics to track the efficiency of the organization. MTTD was introduced as a common organization-wide effectiveness metric. Some limitations of MTTD were identified, which should be understood when using this metric. Next, we categorized our detections into three tiers, allowing us to identify metrics for each tier that reflect their importance to the organization. Low-fidelity coverage using the MITRE ATT&CK matrix and high-fidelity coverage metrics through validation, detection drift, and volatility were examined as ways to calculate coverage and track how coverage changes over time. In the final chapter, *Chapter 12*, we'll wrap up by discussing what a career in detection engineering looks like, how you can progress your skill set, and the future of the field.

Further reading

Here are some resources to deepen your understanding of some of the concepts in this chapter:

- **Agile metrics:**

  - `https://agilemanifesto.org/`

  - `https://www.atlassian.com/agile/project-management/metrics`

  - `https://www.atlassian.com/agile/project-management/estimation`

  - `https://www.wrike.com/agile-guide/story-points-estimation/`

- **Capability abstraction:**

  `https://medium.com/specter-ops-posts/capability-abstraction-fbeaeeb26384`

- **MITRE Top ATT&CK Techniques:**

  `https://top-attack-techniques.mitre-engenuity.org/`

- **Metrics definitions:**

  `https://developers.google.com/machine-learning/crash-course`

- **Volatility:**

  Empirical Intelligence Valuation Through Indicator Volatility Analysis, Michael Cloppert. 2012 DoD Cybercrime Conference

Part 5: Detection Engineering as a Career

In the final part, we will close the book by discussing detection engineering as a career. We'll provide guidance for finding jobs in detection engineering, along with how to continue to improve your skill sets and boost your resume. We'll also touch on our insights regarding the future of detection engineering. Finally, we will provide options for contributing to the community.

This section has the following chapter:

- *Chapter 12, Career Guidance for Detection Engineers*

12

Career Guidance for Detection Engineers

As this book comes to a close, if you're not yet working as a detection engineer, you may be interested in pursuing such a job. This chapter will aim to help answer some questions you may have and provide some guidance to assist in getting your first detection engineering position.

The chapter will cover the following main topics:

- Getting a job in detection engineering
- Detection engineering as a job
- The future of detection engineering
- Getting involved

The first section is focused on what to look for in job postings, training and certification opportunities, and further ways to develop your detection engineering skills. We'll then discuss what a day in the life of a detection engineer looks like in terms of job responsibilities. Next, we'll make some predictions on how detection engineering will evolve over the coming years. Finally, we'll wrap up with ideas on how you can contribute to the field of detection engineering.

Getting a job in detection engineering

In this section, we discuss some information on preparing for and finding jobs in detection engineering, starting with what to look for in job postings.

Job postings

The role of a detection engineer is a relatively new one compared to many security and tech positions. As such, there's not necessarily a standardized job title or description that you'll find for roles related to detection engineering. For that reason, we must be able to understand the roles and responsibilities of a detection engineer to identify relevant job postings. In the most ideal scenario, the job position will be titled something that clearly indicates it's a detection engineering role, such as **Threat Detection Engineer**. In some cases, however, you'll find detection engineering roles categorized under the broader job title of **Security Engineer**. This is where an understanding of what a detection engineer does is required. Security engineering can cover a wide variety of positions related to the development of security-related content or code. Looking at all security engineering positions will likely lead you to postings for jobs more focused on the development of secure infrastructure rather than the development of detections. The following is a list of examples of job responsibilities you might see for a detection engineering-focused role based on actual job postings from companies hiring for such positions:

- Build security detections and detection frameworks

- Conduct tuning activities to mitigate false positive or noisy alerts

- Use big data and real-time streaming technologies to build and refine threat detections

- Investigate anomalous and suspicious behavior for new detection opportunities

- Conduct alert validation and triage within SIEM and EDR platforms

- Research, build, and maintain detection capabilities for the latest threats across SIEM correlations and security tool signatures

- Research and innovate net new mitigation, detection, and response capabilities given input from industry trends, customer feedback, and personal research

Another way to differentiate detection engineering positions from other security engineering roles is based on the qualifications/requirements section of the job posting. Many security engineering roles will be focused on programming and development abilities with security skills playing a background role, but for detection engineers, there should be more of a focus on the security side of things with the development skills being secondary. The postings targeted for detection engineering will often look for knowledge of frameworks (such as MITRE ATT&CK), experience with SIEM and other detection-related technologies, and an understanding of security concepts.

In summary, when looking at job postings, you don't want to narrow yourself to just job titles with *Detection Engineer* in the name as some companies leverage a broader *Security Engineer* role. To determine whether the role aligns with what you are looking for, review the job responsibilities and requirements to determine whether the position they are describing matches that of a detection engineer.

Developing skills

Part of the requirements for finding a job in detection engineering is to have and demonstrate the skills necessary to fulfill such a role. In this section, we are going to discuss how to increase your chances of landing a position in detection engineering. We'll approach it in three parts:

1. Training and certifications

2. Relevant skill sets and learning recommendations

3. Getting involved

All three of these areas will help increase your skill set as a detection engineer as well as building your resume for increased visibility when applying for job postings.

Training and certifications

Due to the relative newness of detection engineering as a career, the certifications and training available specific to such a role are limited. Therefore, when it comes to specific training and certification requirements associated with job positions, at the time of writing, there are not any detection engineering-specific requirements for such roles. There are, however, a few options available for those interested in getting additional training. The price of this training varies, with some being on the expensive side, so if your employer provides a training budget, this is a great opportunity to leverage it. If you do not have the ability to pay for these formal training and certification options at this time, the next section provides additional ways to develop your skill set via free resources.

MITRE themselves offer training through their MITRE ATT&CK Defender program, focused on threat hunting and detection engineering using the ATT&CK framework. This training leads to the ATT&CK Threat Hunting Detection Engineering certification, one of several certifications the program offers related to applying the ATT&CK framework to security operations. More information on this certification can be found here: `https://mad-certified.mitre-engenuity.org/collection/9edbe772-c054-4004-bf4c-f5e7b09d2640`.

Earlier in this book, we mentioned **Sigma**, an open standard language for writing detection queries. *Applied Network Defense* offers a course, *Detection Engineering with Sigma*, that teaches you how to write Sigma rules based on real-world examples of malicious activity in logs. For details on this training, see `https://www.networkdefense.io/library/detection-engineering-with-sigma-58157/310172/about/`.

Finally, *GIAC* offers the **GIAC Certified Detection Analyst (GCDA)** certification, details of which can be found here: `https://www.giac.org/certifications/certified-detection-analyst-gcda/`. The affiliated training for this certification is offered by SANS through their course SEC555: SIEM with Tactical Analytics: `https://www.sans.org/cyber-security-courses/siem-with-tactical-analytics/`. It is worth noting that while the name of the certification indicates it is detection-focused, the content of the course is much broader and has a large focus on SIEM maintenance and other SIEM operation topics, so the training is not solely focused on detection engineering. We choose to mention it, however, due to the lack of formal training dedicated to detection engineering.

As authors of this book, we have taken the MITRE training and certification and found immense value in the content. With regard to the Applied Network Defense and SANS training, we have not personally taken either of these courses, but both are reputable training providers in the industry. It will not be surprising to see more training and certifications enter the market over the coming years as the demand for dedicated detection engineers expands. As the options expand, we will see whether any certifications arise as the standard employers expect from their prospective employees, but for the time being there is no detection engineering-specific certification or training that is expected across DE job postings. That being said, any training or certifications related to the skillset you do obtain are worth highlighting on your resume as they may be the thing that sets you apart from other candidates. Regardless, more knowledge from a reputable training provider is valuable in itself.

Outside of formal training and certifications, there is an abundance of blog posts, podcasts, and YouTube videos available for free to continue your detection engineering education that can easily be found with a quick internet search. Additionally, conferences often offer workshops, including those focused on detection engineering. If not workshops, detection engineering is becoming a popular topic for conference talks as well, often focused on specific sub-topics. Check out local and online conferences or conferences you already planned on attending for any relevant content worth checking out.

Relevant skill sets and learning recommendations

Outside of formal training and conferences, there are many self-learning options available to current and future detection engineers.

Detailed information about cyber adversaries used to be limited. Prior to the Mandiant APT-1 report, quality open source reporting about nation-state activities or specific threat actors was mostly unavailable. Threat intelligence about adversaries was closely held secret by organizations. IOCs identifying adversary infrastructure, such as IP addresses or domains, provided significant value that allowed SOCs to stop attacks. Today, this information has limited use as adversaries can stand up and break down infrastructure with little to no cost. These changes have forced detection engineers to focus on more complex signatures and indicators of behavior. Analysts and organizations have opened up to sharing this information on the internet through blogs, social media, or other mediums. Many top security device providers share detection signatures they have created in open source repositories.

These changes provide significant opportunities for new detection engineers to learn from experienced professionals and build their skills. The techniques taught in this book should be practiced beyond the exercises within the chapters. As an aspiring detection engineer, you can identify detection signatures within open source repositories and attempt to recreate them from associated open source intelligence. Identify and follow popular blogs or analysts' social media accounts and take the information they provide as a starting point to investigate new adversary activity and build your own detections. Publish those detections to open source repositories or social media to build your portfolio. These activities will help improve your skills but also provide employers with examples of your capabilities.

Cyber defense and cyber offense are two sides of the same coin. If you want to understand how to truly stop an adversary from performing an attack, it is necessary to understand how that attack is performed and not just identify what telemetry about an attack is captured through your current visibility. This is accomplished by studying the platforms you are protecting. If you are building detections for a Windows environment, study how the internals of the operating system function, and how common adversarial tasks can be performed such as creating a process or getting a handle on a process. Attempt to dive deep into a single technique and learn everything about how it is performed. This includes not just how an adversary executes it today but how the operating system or software leveraged in the attack works internally as well. This may require increasing your skills to include reverse engineering and exploit creation. While some courses are available in reverse engineering for detection creation, most are focused on malware analysis or red teaming. These are still applicable. The processes and tools used are similar, just the objective has changed.

One source to look at to begin further exploring detection engineering is the Awesome Detection Engineering GitHub repository: `https://github.com/infosecB/awesome-detection-engineering`. This repository contains both tools and resources related to detection engineering in a variety of formats. First, it provides a list of frameworks and concepts, such as MITRE ATT&CK and Pyramid of Pain, which were discussed in the book, as well as some we did not discuss specifically. On the open source signature side of things discussed at the start of this sub-section, there is a list of sources from various vendors in various formats that can be used to better understand what signatures look like for different threats. Many of these repositories can be contributed to by the public also. Next, to learn more about the data sources that we can leverage for detection, as well as ways to manage these logs, there is a section on logging, monitoring, and data sources. The repository ends with general resources and blog posts on various topics related to detection engineering.

Another great resource, mentioned in the Awesome Detection Engineering repository, is Zack Allen's Detection Engineering Weekly: `https://www.detectionengineering.net/`. This newsletter is a high-quality weekly digest of recent blog posts and tweets related to detection engineering, blog posts on new threat research, and open source tools that readers might be interested in checking out. This provides a continuous, up-to-date feed of new material related to the field. We highly recommend subscribing and using the content to continue learning as the field is constantly evolving.

Additional skills not directly tied to detection engineering but useful for the responsibilities included in such a role are the following:

- Network, endpoint, and cloud security
- Scripting and/or programming skills
- Basic understanding of CI/CD frameworks and tools
- Reverse engineering

Spending time understanding and developing skills in these various areas of expertise will expand your detection engineering capabilities, increase your chances of getting a job, and overall evolve your expertise in the industry. All of these areas are widely developed concepts with extensive online resources only a Google search away.

Getting involved

Throughout the book, we've referenced open source projects related directly or adjacently to detection engineering, and many of these efforts are only as good as the community that contributes to them. As such, we highly advocate using our skill sets as detection engineers to give back to the community as able. Additionally, any contributions to the projects we discuss can be added to your resume in order to demonstrate your skills and make yourself more appealing to potential employers. In this section, we'll look back at some of the projects we mentioned as well as some other ideas of how you can use your newly developed detection engineering skills to get involved in the community.

As mentioned, open source projects rely on contributions from the users of their projects in order to grow. This is especially true for projects such as Sigma. The more Sigma rules that exist, the more coverage for threats that exist for those leveraging the project. While the creators and maintainers of the repository are consistently publishing new rules, they are limited by their own time. If you are practicing the detection engineering skills you learned in this book and building out detections, consider submitting them in a pull request to the Sigma repository. As part of an organization, you might face challenges trying to share internally developed content to a public space, but if the rules don't contain sensitive information, consider appealing to management about the value of giving back to the community by releasing your rules. Sigma is just one example of a project that you can contribute to. There are other rule standards that you could release rules for that the community would benefit from, such as YARA and Snort/Suricata. If you have more in-depth development skills, there are open source tools such as the Elastic Stack that can be contributed to.

MITRE ATT&CK was repeatedly mentioned over the course of the book. Since ATT&CK is based on real-world threats, they rely on reporting from organizations on the front lines to inform their data model. They are constantly looking for information on new **techniques, tactics, and procedures** (**TTPs**), threat intelligence, data source information, and more. At the time of writing, their FAQ page specifically mentions they are looking for contributions related to Linux and macOS. For any accepted contributions, MITRE provides attribution to the contributor, which makes for great resume fodder too. For more information about how to contribute, check out their guidance at the following link: `https://attack.mitre.org/resources/contribute/`.

Lastly, there are plenty of opportunities to pass on the knowledge you've obtained to the public. Regardless of your favorite method of spreading knowledge, there are opportunities for you. If you prefer writing, blog posts are a great way to share information on a given topic. Blogging platforms, such as Medium, provide a free avenue to quickly and easily publish content. If you prefer teaching in person, look for conferences with calls for papers or training to submit talks and workshops to. Even if you don't create content, conferences are a great opportunity to network with others in the industry, which can lead to collaboration and idea generation that can benefit everyone.

Regardless of how you approach it, there are many different options to give back to the community. Detection engineering relies on an understanding of what we need to detect, and a single organization cannot have visibility of all threats, especially proactively. This requires us to create a culture of collaboration and sharing though, because most people won't be as motivated to put effort into generating content and sharing information unless they are also receiving the same from their peers. Furthermore, any public contributions you make should be added to your resume to show the work you've done as well as to show that you value that community connection.

Now that you now understand how to get into a detection engineering role, let's look at what your day-to-day job may look like once you're in such a position.

Detection engineering as a job

In a previous section, we mentioned some examples of responsibilities listed in job postings for detection engineers, which gave a high-level idea of the types of work you'd be performing as a detection engineer. Before we look in more detail at the roles and responsibilities of a detection engineer, we're first going to discuss some related job roles and how they differ, as well as how those jobs can be used to show your experience in detection engineering when applying for jobs. While there are many sub-specialties in cyber security, we're going to focus on a few roles that are most closely related to detection engineering in terms of the skills used:

- **Security Operations Center** (**SOC**) analyst

- Incident responder

- Threat hunter

- Threat intelligence analyst/threat researcher

All of these roles, while much different from a full-time engineering position, involve responsibilities that will either directly align with or help with understanding some of the responsibilities of detection engineering.

Starting with SOC analysts, this role is common for those new to the industry as a stepping stone to other sub-specialties, including detection engineering. The SOC analyst role is much broader than detection engineering and typically involves a mixture of monitoring and triage or response. Working in a SOC, you will likely be responsible for day-to-day security monitoring using either dedicated security tools or reviewing logs. The ability to review security alerts and triage them to understand whether they are true or false positives is valuable when it comes to detection engineering. In detection engineering, this skill set can be used to review the performance of created detections and fine-tune them to reduce false positives. Depending on the tooling used in the SOC you work in, you may have the responsibility of creating detections for your organization's platforms or tuning a SIEM. These skills should be highlighted when applying for detection engineering roles as it shows an understanding of how to take data from an environment, provide meaning to it, and use the interpretation to improve the organization's security posture.

Incident responders are brought in to handle security threats that require an increased level of expertise over SOC analysts or where the organization does not have a SOC to handle incidents. Incident responders are less proactive and more reactive, but their involvement in active attacks provides experience that can be drawn upon as a detection engineer. Incident responders understand how to look at a variety of data sources during an attack and put together a story of how the attacker carried out their activities. Similar to SOC analysts with monitoring experience, this maps to detection engineering in the sense that it shows an understanding of being able to form a meaningful interpretation of activity from large amounts of data. Incident response is more of an erratic job position in terms of its schedule and tasking, so if you're an incident responder looking to apply your analytical skills in more of a proactive rather than reactive position, consider detection engineering as a possibility.

Threat hunters require a very similar mindset and approach to detection engineers. Just like detection engineers, they must understand a specific threat and how to identify activity related to that threat. The primary difference between the two is that threat hunters look for the activity occurring in the environment already rather than developing a mechanism to protect the environment if it occurs. The findings from threat hunters, however, can be used to develop detections to mitigate future risks.

Threat intelligence analysts primarily focus on more of a research role than the technical and implementation side of things. It is a very relevant position to detection engineering though, as we discussed in *Chapter 10*. The skills a threat intelligence analyst can bring to a detection engineering role are immensely valuable, as being able to research a threat in depth results in the understanding required to, in turn, know how to detect that activity. There is also value in the ability to understand what threats are most relevant to an organization based on industry, geography, and the current threat landscape.

If you're in one of the aforementioned roles and looking to pivot to detection engineering, these skills are highly adaptable to the responsibilities of a detection engineer. The same is true in reverse. If you are in detection engineering and looking for a new challenge, many of the preceding roles will have similar aspects to your current role.

Detection engineering roles and responsibilities

In general, you'll be performing the work we've described throughout this book, the tasks associated with each stage of the detection engineering life cycle, as well as continuous activities. This section will briefly summarize the associated responsibilities you might encounter in such job positions, although it'll vary depending on the size of the team and your specific assignments.

At the start of the detection engineering life cycle, we have requirements discovery. This responsibility is partially going to depend on the organization you're in. If you have a **security operation center** (**SOC**), threat intel team, and/or red team, then you might be able to rely on those sources of requirements. Your primary role here might then come down to communication with those teams, as cross-team collaboration is vital in such an organizational structure. If the organization doesn't have other teams like that or if the other teams do not have processes to provide your team with detection requirements, however, it may fall on the detection engineers to actively seek out detection opportunities and create the requirements themselves.

Throughout the *Triage* and *Investigate* phases, detection engineers essentially act as researchers. Whether it's through direct testing, data analysis, or searching the internet, detection engineers must be able to take a requirement and perform research to fully understand the behavior attempting to be detected. After these phases, the *Develop*, *Test*, and *Deploy* phases start to require the *engineering* side of detection engineering more heavily. This may involve some programming and/or DevOps depending on the tooling being used by the organization.

Finally, on the continuous activity side of things, detection engineers must perform data analysis and generate metrics to understand the performance of detections. To perform this data analysis, it is useful to have an understanding of how to work with large sets of data, potentially in varying formats, and understand how to glean insights from it in order to produce actionable feedback. Along with using these metrics for improving detections, the performance analysis resulting from continuous activities is important for communicating with management and stakeholders. Stakeholders will want to understand the return on investment they are receiving from the detection engineering team. As such, being able to communicate performance with (often) non-technical personnel is an important skill in this job role.

As can be seen in the brief summary, detection engineers have various responsibilities each requiring diverse skills. The skills involved in detection engineering range from research to development, to communication and collaboration. The diversity in such a position also makes it a very interesting role!

All that being said, this field is new and rapidly evolving, so we also should discuss what we expect to see in the coming years.

The future of detection engineering

Detection-as-code is focused on applying engineering and software development processes and technology to detection creation. Therefore, we should continue to see maturity in processes and the adoption of tools and technology most prominently from the software engineering, data engineering, and machine learning fields. There are many external factors that will continue to influence and perpetuate the need for detection engineering. In addition, there are issues that consistently hinder detection creation and some new X-factors that we will need to see if they last through their hype. In the following sections, we have identified many of those areas and how they will affect detection engineering going forward. Writing predictions for the future is a dangerous task, so while we call these predictions, they are mostly trends in the field that we believe will continue the need for detection engineering.

Attack surfaces

The scope of what a company is expected to protect and how it can protect it has expanded over time. Originally, defenders could expect that their organization's assets were in an internal network boundary. As work from home, cellphones, and other personal devices became part of the company ecosystem, those assumptions disappeared. In addition, cloud services, point-of-sale devices, and other types of infrastructure continued to expand as well. This evolution will obviously not slow down and will not stop. Each of these are new attack surfaces, which will have new vulnerabilities, new visibility, and other complications, will require detection engineers to create custom detections that will identify associated adversary activity. This increase in niche attack surfaces will only reinforce the need for organizations to have their own detection engineering teams.

Visibility

In *Chapter 4*, we introduced detection data sources, which are the bedrock upon which our detections are built. The data sources and events they provide are continuously evolving. Some of these additions are from direct requirements by detection engineers to help identify malicious activities. Others may be specific to your organization, provided by logs or events created by your custom software. New telemetry equals new opportunities for detection.

Security device capabilities

For many years, **security information and event management** (**SIEM**) has been the universal log management and detection capability. SIEM's ability to adapt to new log sources and allow the analyst to write detections against those sources has made it flexible to support new use cases. This flexibility can also make it more difficult to use than some newer security devices, such as **Endpoint Detection and Response** (**EDR**). EDR agents run on the endpoint, have access to more telemetry, can detect adversary endpoint activity better, with fewer false positives, and can provide more in-depth explanations of the attack. For these reasons, EDRs have exploded in popularity as the primary detection tool for many SOCs. Security devices will continue to specialize in new attack surfaces, such as the cloud, users, and other areas where a specialized focus can enable improved fidelity.

Extended detection and response systems (**XDRs**) are seen as an extension of EDRs by starting with a high-fidelity alert (such as an EDR alert) and correlating data from the same attack. This second-layer processing will continue to grow in the future. Today, many detection engineers write descriptions that provide details for the SOC analyst on how to triage the alert and determine whether it is a true or false positive. Second-layer processing, such as XDR, will help facilitate these actions by automatically performing many of the actions that SOC analysts have to do manually today. As these second-layer processing capabilities improve, it will enable new detections to be written that have a higher false positive rate but can capture more adversarial activity. Since the second-layer processing can triage these alerts and combine them with other low-confidence signals, nosier detections can be written without overwhelming the SOC.

Machine learning

Machine learning has traditionally focused on detection models such as antivirus, anomaly detection, and triaging results. We purposefully did not cover the creation of models within this book because the approaches are significantly different than rule creation. If you'd like to learn more about machine learning models, there is plenty of material online readily available on the topic, such as this article: `https://www.coursera.org/articles/machine-learning-models`. While most security devices now include some level of machine learning and many now allow analysts to deploy their own models, there are limitations. Machine learning requires large datasets to build an accurate model, and many of these models require supervised learning. This means the data must be categorized for the algorithm to train the model. In addition, data scientists must identify the correct characteristics within the data, called features, as part of the training process. Data scientists are usually reliant upon domain experts, such as detection engineers, to identify important features, categorize data and review results. While some security devices can use machine learning to identify new adversarial procedures and rapidly deploy updates, most require significant effort and large development times. Custom detection rules can be more rapidly created and deployed in response to new threats even if they will eventually be replaced by a machine learning model that will provide more complete coverage.

The introduction of **large language models** (**LLMs**) is rapidly redefining the capabilities of machine learning and how it can be used to support cyber security use cases. While many of these models have initially focused on chatbot use cases, the technology is rapidly advancing and will likely expand into other spaces. The chatbot technology will help document and summarize attacks from across multiple alerts and events. Its ability to support analysts in the writing of new rules by speeding up the investigation, development, and test phases will continue to accelerate. Additionally, LLMs may support the SOC in identifying and performing the steps to investigate and respond to alerts.

Sharing of attack methodology

Most information about attack behaviors and how to identify them is currently shared in blogs, on Twitter, or in other unstructured text and images despite attempts to create and adopt structured data-sharing formats, such as **Structured Threat Information Expression** (**STIX**). There are economic reasons for this that cannot be ignored. Companies want people to go to their websites so they can sell their products. People want a following on social media to raise their profile and job prospects. (We are not casting aspersions – at least they have only a minor affliction; we're writing a book for goodness' sake.) Without a similar economic benefit, it will be difficult to encourage more machine-ingestible forms of intelligence even if the technology issues are solved. We can, though, encourage more actionable forms of data to be shared by identifying and encouraging best practices. To do this, we either need to push the industry toward adopting STIX or a similar structured data distribution method or find a better way of parsing unstructured data. The first approach requires that industry tools implement support for the standards and that intelligence distributors provide their data in a common structure. This approach often takes time and extensive encouragement. If the customers push this as a point of interest in the solutions they are looking for or the resources they are seeking out, it may fulfill the economic benefit mentioned earlier. Alternatively, advances in machine learning may also help parse unstructured data and transform it, although if this technology becomes so good that individuals are no longer reading blogs or posts, the incentives to share data may decrease. At its core, this is a game theory problem. If you are a game theorist detection engineer, we need your help here.

The adversary

Incentives and economic benefits will also continue to drive adversaries to create new attack techniques and procedures and identify new attack surfaces and ways to exploit their victims. Cyber-attacks are a multi-billion-dollar illicit industry. The economic benefits to criminals and nation-states will continue to drive innovation in cyber offense capabilities, resulting in similar investment and innovation to defend against these attacks.

The human

Computer graphics pioneer Robert Cook is quoted as saying, "*Programming today is a race between software engineers striving to build bigger and better idiot-proof programs and the universe trying to produce bigger and better idiots. So far, the universe is winning.*" This quote applies well to the cyber security field too. As long as users can be convinced to open a file, click on a link, or perform some other action necessary for an attack to succeed, they will continue to remain the most exploitable attack surface. "Humans," in this equation, should not be limited to the end user. Software developers will continue to create new applications, build upon unsecured open source libraries, and misconfigure infrastructure, providing new opportunities for adversaries to exploit.

Summary

In this final chapter, we moved away from the details of detection engineering processes and pivoted our focus to detection engineering as a career. If you're reading this book and not already in detection engineering, this chapter was intended to help guide you on your journey to a position in this field. We hope that the information provided here, as well as the skills learned throughout the book help increase your chances of landing such a role. If you're already in a detection engineering role, hopefully, this chapter and the rest of the book help improve your skills and future in detection engineering.

We hope you enjoyed this book and wish you all the luck on your detection engineering journey!

Index

A

B

C

F

G

H

I

K

L

Packtpub.com

Subscribe to our online digital library for full access to over 7,000 books and videos, as well as industry leading tools to help you plan your personal development and advance your career. For more information, please visit our website.

Why subscribe?

- Spend less time learning and more time coding with practical eBooks and Videos from over 4,000 industry professionals

- Improve your learning with Skill Plans built especially for you

- Get a free eBook or video every month

- Fully searchable for easy access to vital information

- Copy and paste, print, and bookmark content

Did you know that Packt offers eBook versions of every book published, with PDF and ePub files available? You can upgrade to the eBook version at packtpub.com and as a print book customer, you are entitled to a discount on the eBook copy. Get in touch with us at customercare@packtpub.com for more details.

At www.packtpub.com, you can also read a collection of free technical articles, sign up for a range of free newsletters, and receive exclusive discounts and offers on Packt books and eBooks.

Other Books You May Enjoy

If you enjoyed this book, you may be interested in these other books by Packt:

Incident Response Techniques for Ransomware Attacks

Oleg Skulkin

ISBN: 9781803240442

- Understand the modern ransomware threat landscape
- Explore the incident response process in the context of ransomware
- Discover how to collect and produce ransomware-related cyber threat intelligence
- Use forensic methods to collect relevant artifacts during incident response
- Interpret collected data to understand threat actor tactics, techniques, and procedures
- Understand how to reconstruct the ransomware attack kill chain

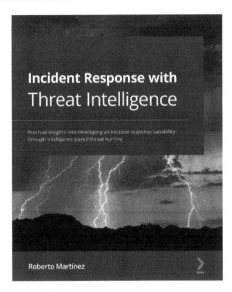

Incident Response with Threat Intelligence

Roberto Martinez

ISBN: 9781801072953

- Explore the fundamentals of incident response and incident management
- Find out how to develop incident response capabilities
- Understand the development of incident response plans and playbooks
- Align incident response procedures with business continuity
- Identify incident response requirements and orchestrate people, processes, and technologies
- Discover methodologies and tools to integrate cyber threat intelligence and threat hunting into incident response

Packt is searching for authors like you

If you're interested in becoming an author for Packt, please visit authors.packtpub.com and apply today. We have worked with thousands of developers and tech professionals, just like you, to help them share their insight with the global tech community. You can make a general application, apply for a specific hot topic that we are recruiting an author for, or submit your own idea.

Share Your Thoughts

Now you've finished *Practical Threat Detection Engineering*, we'd love to hear your thoughts! Scan the QR code below to go straight to the Amazon review page for this book and share your feedback or leave a review on the site that you purchased it from.

https://packt.link/r/1801076715

Your review is important to us and the tech community and will help us make sure we're delivering excellent quality content.

Download a free PDF copy of this book

Thanks for purchasing this book!

Do you like to read on the go but are unable to carry your print books everywhere?

Is your eBook purchase not compatible with the device of your choice?

Don't worry, now with every Packt book you get a DRM-free PDF version of that book at no cost.

Read anywhere, any place, on any device. Search, copy, and paste code from your favorite technical books directly into your application.

The perks don't stop there, you can get exclusive access to discounts, newsletters, and great free content in your inbox daily

Follow these simple steps to get the benefits:

1. Scan the QR code or visit the link below

https://packt.link/free-ebook/9781801076715

2. Submit your proof of purchase

3. That's it! We'll send your free PDF and other benefits to your email directly

Made in the USA
Middletown, DE
21 July 2023

35551559R00183